A Transdisciplir. to International Teaching Assistants

Full details of all our publications can be found on http://www.multilingual-matters.com, or by writing to Multilingual Matters, St Nicholas House, 31-34 High Street, Bristol BS1 2AW, UK.

A Transdisciplinary Approach to International Teaching Assistants

Perspectives from Applied Linguistics

Edited by
Stephen Daniel Looney and Shereen Bhalla

MULTILINGUAL MATTERS
Bristol • Blue Ridge Summit

DOI https://doi.org/10.21832/LOONEY5549

Library of Congress Cataloging in Publication Data

A catalog record for this book is available from the Library of Congress.

Names: Looney, Stephen Daniel, 1982- editor. | Bhalla, Shereen, 1980- editor.

Title: A Transdisciplinary Approach to International Teaching Assistants: Perspectives from Applied Linguistics/Edited by Stephen Looney, Shereen Bhalla.

Description: Bristol; Blue Ridge Summit: Multilingual Matters, 2019. | Includes bibliographical references and index. | Summary: "The chapters in this volume offer state-of-the-art research into international teaching assistants in North American universities using a variety of methods and approaches, and as such constitute a transdisciplinary perspective which argues for the importance of dialogue between research and practice"—Provided by publisher.

Identifiers: LCCN 2019018872 (print) | LCCN 2019980836 (ebook) | ISBN 9781788925549 (hardback) | ISBN 9781788925532 (paperback) | ISBN 9781788925556 (pdf) | ISBN 9781788925563 (epub) | ISBN 9781788925570 (kindle edition)

Subjects: LCSH: Graduate teaching assistants—Training of—United States. | College teaching—United States. | English language—Study and teaching (Higher)—Foreign speakers. | English language—Study and teaching (Higher)—United States.

Classification: LCC LB2335.4 T73 2019 (print) | LCC LB2335.4 (ebook) | DDC 378.1/25—dc23

LC record available at https://lccn.loc.gov/2019018872

LC ebook record available at https://lccn.loc.gov/2019980836

British Library Cataloguing in Publication Data

A catalogue entry for this book is available from the British Library.

ISBN-13: 978-1-78892-554-9 (hbk)
ISBN-13: 978-1-78892-553-2 (pbk)

Multilingual Matters

UK: St Nicholas House, 31–34 High Street, Bristol BS1 2AW, UK.
USA: NBN, Blue Ridge Summit, PA, USA.

Website: www.multilingual-matters.com
Twitter: Multi_Ling_Mat
Facebook: https://www.facebook.com/multilingualmatters
Blog: www.channelviewpublications.wordpress.com

The policy of Multilingual Matters/Channel View Publications is to use papers that are natural, renewable and recyclable products, made from wood grown in sustainable forests. In the manufacturing process of our books, and to further support our policy, preference is given to printers that have FSC and PEFC Chain of Custody certification. The FSC and/or PEFC logos will appear on those books where full certification has been granted to the printer concerned.

Typeset by Nova Techset Private Limited, Bengaluru and Chennai, India.
Printed and bound in the UK by the CPI Books Group Ltd.
Printed and bound in the US by NBN.

Contents

Stephen: for Jialing and Addison
Shereen: To my Mom

Contributors

Shereen Bhalla is the Director of Education for the Hindu American Foundation based in Washington, DC. Prior to joining HAF, she was at the Center for Applied Linguistics for over four years as the Online Manager, the Language and Policy Research (LPReN) Manager and the Research Associate for projects funded by the Gates Foundation and The Department of Education. An advocate for culturally and linguistically diverse students, Dr Bhalla has over 10 years of experience teaching both English learners as well as pre-and in-service educators on how to best meet the needs of their students. Dr Bhalla has taught for UTSA, George Washington University, the Inter-Development Bank and Johns Hopkins University.

Shiao-Yun Chiang (PhD University at Albany) is a full professor of Communication Studies at the State University of New York at Oneonta and he is the current Chair of the Department of Communication and Media at the university. His primary research interests include language pragmatics, intercultural education and communication. He has published in numerous academic journals including *Journal of Pragmatics*, *Intercultural Pragmatics*, *Discourse & Society*, *Discourse & Communication*, *Journal of Multilingual & Multicultural Development*, *Language & Education*, *English Today*, *Journal of Language, Identity, and Education*, and so forth.

James Coda is a doctoral student in TESOL and World Language Education in the Language and Literacy Department (LLED) at the University of Georgia. His research interests include identities in the class-room and gender and sexuality in language education.

Greta Gorsuch has been an ESL/EFL educator for over 30 years. She specializes in second language testing, course evaluation, second language reading and pronunciation learning. She has published many articles on these topics in journals such as *System*, *Language Teaching*, *Language Teaching Research*, *TESL-EJ* and *English for Specific Purposes*. She is co-author of *Second Language Course Evaluation* and *Second Language Testing for Student Evaluation and Classroom Research*, both with Dale T. Griffee, both with Information Age Publishing, Inc.

Linda Harklau is a Professor of TESOL and World Language Education at the University of Georgia (USA) and coordinator of ITA courses. Her research examines sociocultural and policy contexts for educating multilingual youth and the high school to college transition.

Okim Kang is an Associate Professor in the Applied Linguistics Program at Northern Arizona University, Flagstaff, AZ, USA. Her research interests are speech production and perception, L2 pronunciation and intelligibility, L2 oral assessment and testing, automated scoring and speech recognition, World Englishes and language attitudes.

Stephen Daniel Looney is an Associate Teaching Professor in Applied Linguistics and Director of the International Teaching Assistant (ITA) Program in the Department of Applied Linguistics at the Pennsylvania State University. His research takes a Conversation Analysis approach to analyzing teacher–student interaction in university STEM classrooms. Specifically, he is interested in the management of epistemics, deontics and affect in classroom interaction. He is an associate editor for the *International Journal of Teaching and Learning in Higher Education* and his work has appeared in *Journal of Pragmatics* and *Linguistics and Education*.

Lucy Pickering is Professor of Applied linguistics and Director of the Applied Linguistics Laboratory at Texas A&M-Commerce. She directs the MA/MS Program in TESOL and Applied Linguistics. Her research program is focused on aspects of spoken discourse including prosodic development in L2 learners including ITAs, intonation in classroom discourse and humor in discourse.

Jing Wei, PhD, is a former senior research associate at the Center for Applied Linguistics, Washington, DC. Her work focuses on scoring rubric development and validation, program evaluation and assessment of World Englishes. Her work has been published in *Language Assessment Quarterly*.

Meghan Moran is an Instructor in the Applied Linguistics Program at Northern Arizona University, Flagstaff, AZ, USA. Her research interests include speech production and perception, L2 pronunciation and intelligibility, language planning and policy, language education policy and linguistic discrimination.

1 A Transdisciplinary Approach to ITA

Stephen Daniel Looney and Shereen Bhalla

Introduction

North American universities depend on international teaching assistants (ITAs) as a substantial part of the teaching labor force, particularly in the fields of science, technology, engineering and mathematics (STEM). This reality has led scholars from diverse disciplines to investigate the impact of American undergraduates being taught by ITAs and has even drawn attention from non-academic, mainstream media outlets (Clayton, 2000; Finder, 2005). International graduate students teaching courses in large part populated by monolingual US and Canadian students has led to the antiquated coining of the term 'the ITA Problem' (Williams, 1992). This 'problem' has often been framed as a divergence between ITAs' linguistic competence and undergraduates' and their parents' expectations for what ITAs' speech should sound like. This outdated positioning of ITAs as deficient in their effectiveness as university instructors has diminished the invaluable role they play within the academy and the many contributions they make to the university.

Deficiency models of ITA are something we, and many of our colleagues involved in ITA research and preparation, refute and what this volume works against. Instead, we propose an approach to ITA that recognizes them as multilingual, skilled, migrant professionals who participate in and are discursively constructed through various participant frameworks, modalities and activities. We do not deny that ITAs can benefit from further English language instruction and teaching preparation but, in fact, seek to improve the institutional support that ITAs receive before and while they teach and work at US universities. We recognize that undergraduates, faculty and administrators all play an active role in what has been inaccurately deemed a problem, and what in actuality is a stated goal in many institutions' own mission statements, i.e. internationalization of the university.

The real problem from our perspective is a lack of cohesiveness in ITA practice, research and policy. This incoherence is the result of several factors including the education, academic home and institutional role of many ITA professionals, where research is published, and institutional support for ITA programs. Many ITA practitioners are trained English as a Second Language (ESL) teachers and hold graduate degrees in TESOL, Education and related fields. ITA Programs are situated in a plethora of units across universities including Intensive English Programs (IEP), centers for teaching and learning excellence, graduate schools and academic departments to mention. Across these units, ITA practitioners do their job in various ways: running seminars, teaching semester-long courses and assessing ITAs' English proficiency.

As most ITA practitioners are teachers by both training and trade, research on ITAs often goes unnoticed or is thought to be irrelevant. Nonetheless, there has been a steady stream of ITA research over the past 30 years. While seemingly disjointed, this body of literature has produced a wealth of findings that will be reviewed later in this chapter. Another challenge for practitioners and researchers trying to get their arms around ITA, is the diversity of epistemological and methodological perspectives underlying studies. We argue that a recent group of scholars in the field of Second Language Acquisition (SLA) have provided an adaptable framework for conceptualizing ITA coherently as a subdiscipline of Applied Linguistics and TESOL – transdisciplinarity (Douglas Fir Group [DFG], 2016). In the remainder of this chapter, we ask what a transdisciplinary approach to ITA looks like. We begin with an introduction to recent conceptualizations of SLA as transdisciplinary and then outline the history of ITA research and make the argument that, though it has not been explicitly stated, ITA research and practice has always been transdisciplinary. Finally, our own transdisciplinary approach to ITA research is outlined and each chapter is briefly summarized.

Transdisciplinarity and SLA

For nearly a decade, a sizeable group of scholars in SLA have been proposing transdisciplinary approaches to SLA (Atkinson, 2011; DFG, 2016; Duff & Byrnes, 2019; Hall, 2019a). The group is composed of scholars representing 'alternative' approaches to SLA (Atkinson, 2011) including but not limited to Conversation Analysis, Dynamic Systems Theory, Language Socialization, Post-structural Feminism, Socio-Cognitive Theory, Sociocultural Theory and Systemic Functional Linguistics. DFG argues for a transdisciplinary approach to SLA that views language learning as a complex 'ongoing process [...] that assumes the embedding, at all levels, of social, sociocultural, sociocognitive, sociomaterial, ecosocial, ideological, and emotional dimensions' (DFG, 2016: 24). Therefore, SLA is more than an individual acquiring input, and involves multiple actors interacting in situated contexts for various reasons over space and time.

From this perspective, SLA is a social and biological phenomenon that operates on various scales and is influenced by a plethora of factors existing on three levels: micro, meso and macro. The micro level involves 'multilingual contexts of action and interaction contributing to multilingual repertoires' (DFG, 2016: 25; Hall, 2019b; Kasper & Wagner, 2011). Multilingual repertoires are collections of semiotic resources and practices that speakers draw upon in interaction and include linguistic, prosodic and non-verbal resources. SLA's meso level is composed of sociocultural institutions and communities. These institutions and communities include schools, work places and social organizations. Research concerned with the meso level of SLA often investigates communities of practice, social identities, investment, agency and power (Darvin & Norton, 2015; Duff, 2019; Duff & Talmy, 2011; Lave & Wenger, 1991; Norton & McKinney, 2011). The macro level of SLA involves ideological structures such as cultural, political and economic values (Ortega, 2019) From a transdisciplinary perspective, the three levels of SLA are not distinct entities but holistically interact with one another in reciprocal fashions.

In addition to rethinking the scope and scale of what SLA is, a transdisciplinary approach makes us rethink L2 speakers all together. Language learners are multilinguals whose identity as a language novice is complex, dynamic and perhaps not always relevant to the here and now (Firth & Wagner, 1997). Multilingual identities exist in harmony and conflict with professional, personal and political identities. These identities are dynamic in that they evolve over time and are affected both by the individual and the communities of practice (Lave & Wenger, 1991) in which the individual participates. For instance, a multilingual at a US university might be the language novice in their Biology lab group but a stand out and leader in their English as a Second Language (ESL) writing course. In these different contexts, a multilingual speaker's access to speaking rights are constrained and enabled in different ways.

The transdisciplinary framework is not only a lens through which to view research though. It also has two stated practical imperatives. The first is to expand researchers' and teachers' view of 'learners' diverse multilingual repertoires [...] and identities so as to enable their participation in a wide range of social, cognitive, and emotional activities, networks, and forms of communication and learning' (DFG, 2016). The second goal is to develop learners' 'awareness not only of the cultural, historical, and institutional meanings that their language-mediated social actions have [and] of the dynamic and evolving role their actions play in the shaping of their own and others' worlds' (DFG, 2016: 25). To accomplish these goals, language teachers and researchers must collaborate with one another as well as making their research and practice comprehensible and relevant for parties outside their own disciplines. The most important of these parties are policymakers who can affect the kind of institutional change that could enable improved understanding of and support for ITAs.

Framing ITA as Transdisciplinary

Divided into three subsections, this section will give a brief history of ITA research and argue that the field of ITA has always been transdisciplinary in that it emerges from a variety of fields and focuses on various topics. The first subsection, the micro, covers ITA research on language and social interaction. The second reviews research on ITA and undergraduate identity, experience and biases. The third subsection lays out why implicit transdisciplinarity is not a sufficient model to sustain ITA as a field.

The micro: Language and social interaction

The micro level of a transdisciplinary SLA involves the biological and cognitive mechanisms of language learning as well as the semiotic systems participants use and the interactions in which learners participate (DFG, 2016). While we know of no research on the biological and cognitive mechanisms of ITA development, language and social interaction has been the one theme extending from beginning to the end of ITA research (Gorsuch, 2015; Madden & Myers, 1994; Young, 1989). The implementation of laws mandating certification of English fluency for ITAs in and of itself created a focus for ITA research and practice: locate and resolve the discrepancies between ITA spoken-English and so-called Standard American English (SAE).

ITA talk: Grammar and lexis

Throughout the 1990s and the 21st century, communicative competence (Canale & Swain, 1980) has remained the dominant paradigm in ITA research on language and social interaction (Madden & Myers, 1994; Oreto, 2018). Understanding how ITAs and their L1 English-speaking counterparts use specific grammatical and lexical constructions such as modal verbs, interrogatives and discourse markers to guide student action and thought has been the key concern. The underlying assumption is that more indirect forms, e.g. modal verb constructions, are preferred to more direct constructions such as imperatives (Myers, 1994; Reinhardt, 2010; Tapper, 1994). Findings show that ITAs use fewer questions (Myers, 1994) and modal constructions (Reinhardt, 2010; Tapper, 1994) than TAs do in interactions with students. It has been argued that an overreliance on forms with more direct illocutionary force has a negative impact on interactions with students because actions such a telling are more face-threatening and less intellectually engaging than are questions.

Like the use of modal verbs and questions in lab settings, when lecturing, ITAs often utilized fewer discourse markers and in more limited contexts than TAs (Liao, 2009; Tyler, 1992). Using fewer discourse markers negatively affects ratings of ITA speech and participants characterize ITA lectures as disjointed and difficult to follow (Tyler, 1992). ITAs use fewer discourse markers not only because of L2 competence but also time to plan before lecturing, self-regulation, personal attitudes and contexts of interaction (Liao, 2009; Looney, 2015; Looney *et al.*, 2017; Williams, 1992). In the context of lectures, ITAs employ more explicit discourse marking when given time to plan than if their lecture is unplanned (Williams, 1992). This demonstrates that while ITAs may be aware of discourse markers they need time to plan lectures to maximize their use. Interestingly, in actual mathematics lectures, both ITAs and TAs use the discourse marker *okay* in stretches of self-directed talk while making transitions (Looney *et al.*, 2017). These uses of *okay* not only serve interpersonal purposes, i.e. clearly marking transitions in lectures for students, but also intrapersonal purposes, i.e. mediating teachers' own thought and action. This shows that discourse markers are not only significant for improving comprehensibility but also a powerful resource for self-mediation in L1 and L2 talk.

Liao (2009) and Looney (2015) both investigate the use of discourse markers in non-lecture contexts, sociolinguistic interviews and physics laboratory classrooms respectively. In sociolinguistic interviews, ITAs use discourse markers differently than they do when lecturing, and they are also able to speak about why they do so (Liao, 2009). Again, the use of discourse markers cannot be reduced to L2 proficiency. ITAs report different perceptions about the formality and appropriateness of lexical discourse markers like *so* and *okay* for use in the classroom. Thus, personal perceptions and preferences influence the use of discourse markers. In the physics lab, both ITAs and undergraduates use the discourse collocation *okay so* to preface turns in which they demonstrate (mis)understanding of course content, lab procedures and prior utterances (Looney, 2015). These findings show that discourse marker usage is wrapped up in individual preferences and perceptions, social context and L2 proficiency.

ITA talk: Prosody

As with lexis and grammar, ITAs have been shown to lack control of the stress and intonation system of English (Hahn, 2004; Pickering, 2001, 2004). In terms of lexical stress, misplacement of primary stress in multisyllabic words hinders intelligibility (Hahn, 2004). On the phrasal, clausal and discursive levels, stress interacts with pitch to create intonation patterns that both structure content and manage social distance. Over phrases and clauses, ITAs overuse falling and level tones, thus impeding their ability to emphasize key information or to establish common ground with undergraduates (Pickering, 2001). While earlier studies stop at the lexical, phrasal, or clausal level, Pickering (2004) identifies 'intonational paragraphs' on the discursive level of academic lectures. These are stretches of intonation units that begin with a high onset and steadily fall to a low termination before starting the next intonational paragraph with a high onset. Being able to break information into coherent intonational paragraphs is a requisite skill for university lecturers. Thus, like grammar and discourse markers, prosody has multilayered functions that manage social distance and structure content. Pickering's chapter in this volume provides a more complete overview of the research on ITA intonation.

Undergraduate talk

Student talk in office hours has been of concern to a collection of ITA studies (Chiang, 2009, 2011, 2016; Chiang & Mi, 2008, 2011). As students often come to office hours with specific questions, they play a key role in driving office hour interactions. Thus, office hour interactions are distinct from teacher-fronted classroom interaction in which student questions are infrequent (Chiang, 2011). When asking questions in office hours, students use various reformulation strategies to negotiate uncertainty in their own talk and the ITAs with whom they are interacting (Chiang & Mi, 2008, 2011). Students do not only wait for uncertainty to emerge before reformulating utterances, but also undertake preventative procedures to avoid uncertainty (Chiang, 2009). The work that students and ITAs do in interaction is not only about negotiating content knowledge though. Chiang (2016) argues that one strategy students use, i.e. sentence completions, undermines ITAs' identity as instructors by positioning them as novice language users. By looking at identity in language use, Chiang (2016) is beginning to bridge the micro and meso levels of ITA.

Work on the micro level of ITA shows us that the semiotic systems and interactional repertoires that ITAs need are more complex than traditionally conceived grammar and pronunciation. ITAs need to be able to use specific lexico-grammatical and prosodic resources to structure information and manage social distance. Additionally, students play a part in interaction and are as significant to the construction of ITAs' identity in situ as are the ITAs themselves. While work on the micro level of ITA has a long history, its findings are just beginning to scrape the surface. This work has been limited by its logocentric focus. By a logocentric focus, we mean that research on interaction between ITAs and undergraduates has focused almost exclusively on language in terms of lexis and grammar while ignoring the non-verbal resources used in interaction such as but not limited to gesture, gaze and objects in the classroom (see Looney *et al.*, 2017 and Pickering, 2004 for exceptions). This has left analysts with an incomplete picture of interaction and has led to characterizations of interaction as disorganized (Myers, 1994).

The meso and macro: Identity, attitudes and biases

Much like language and social interaction between ITAs and undergraduates, the identities of ITAs and undergraduates' attitudes toward ITAs are much more nuanced than they appear on the surface. This section reviews research on the meso and macro levels of ITA which involves ITA and undergraduate attitudes, experiences and identity. While most ITA studies on identity and attitudes do not engage directly with transdisciplinary work in SLA, there are overlapping findings and conceptual similarities.

ITA identity and attitudes

ITA identity has long been understood to be complex and dynamic, involving numerous factors such as multilingual, teacher, student and counselor (Ashavskaya, 2015; LoCastro & Tapper, 2006). This is concurrent with the translingual SLA conceptualization of identity as complex, changing across time and space, and reproduced in social interaction (Darvin & Norton, 2015: 37). Not surprisingly, L2 speaker is a primary facet of ITA identity in multiple studies. As already mentioned, when undergraduates, academics and journalists speak and write about ITAs, their status as a L2 speaker of English is at the forefront and is cast in a negative light (Borjas, 2000; Clayton, 2000; Finder, 2005; Fitch & Morgan, 2003). Additionally, ITAs cite English language proficiency as a source of anxiety or trouble (Ashavskaya, 2015; LoCastro & Tapper, 2006). It is not only that they have trouble producing speech, but ITAs also have trouble understanding students. While the focus in prior ITA research has remained deficit-oriented, a translingual approach to ITA sees multilingualism as an asset and not liability.

In addition to being multilinguals, ITAs are migrant professionals working in a new cultural context (Canagarajah, 2013, 2018a, 2018b; LoCastro & Tapper, 2006). ITAs' perspectives of how students and teachers should behave are largely shaped by their own educational experiences as students in classrooms, institutions and societies (Holliday, 1994: 16; Pialorsi, 1984). According to the 2018 Open Doors Report (2018) (Institute of International Education, 2018), 56% of international students at US universities hail from China, India and South Korea. In East and South Asia, the teacher–student relationship is more hierarchical (Twale *et al.*, 1997), and students prefer to ask questions after class (Jin & Cortazzi, 2002). Conflicts can arise when US undergraduates expect ITAs to behave in a manner that is in alignment with the seemingly more egalitarian North American classroom norms, but ITAs adhere to the more hierarchical norms of their home countries (Althen, 1991; Davies & Tyler, 2005; Sarkasian, 1990). They may exhibit passive and distant expert roles, which connote lacking leadership and authority, and may lack the experience to negotiate effectively with students simply because in their home cultures 'behavior is much more restricted' (Shaw & Bailey, 1990: 318).

ITAs are, or become, aware of cultural differences and pedagogical styles between home cultures and the US which can be a source of anxiety (Ashavskaya, 2015; Gokcora, 1989). It is important for ITAs to learn how to negotiate different types of behaviors that are appropriate in academic contexts, and consequently, to negotiate instructor–student roles relevant to specific activities in the classroom (Shaw & Bailey, 1990; Pialoris, 1984). In some cases, ITAs even perceived themselves to be at a disadvantage in the overall university context. This is because most newly arrived ITAs are less familiar with the interactional norms of US classroom culture that are necessary for gaining power in undergraduate class settings, thus often viewing themselves as incompetent.

As well as being novice teachers adjusting to US academic culture, ITAs themselves are students, an identity which they share with their own students (LoCastro & Tapper, 2006). As a result of the shared position, the status difference between the two groups is reduced, which may lead to greater degree of freedom for negotiation of the behavior patterns between ITAs and their students. Paradoxically, ITAs are expected to help undergraduates adjust to a culture which they themselves are experiencing for the for the first time. Interestingly, when asked about the classroom management issues they face, ITAs and TAs report many of the same challenges (Luo et al., 2000). While emphasis has been placed on the adjustment of college freshmen to the university setting, the guidance for ITAs is not as abundant. As is the case outside the university as well, it is often the responsibility of the individual to become familiar with the host country (Black & Mendenhall, 1990).

In sum, the ITA identity is much more complex than just being a multilingual speaker. ITAs are migrant professionals, novice teachers, students and counselors to their students. These components of identity are overlapping and in constant flux. While research has painted a complex picture of ITA identity, the body of literature is scarce and increasingly dated. Most studies also lack the theoretical underpinnings that frameworks such as Communities of Practice (CoP) (Lave & Wenger, 1991), Language Socialization (Duff, 2019) and Post-structural SLA (Darvin & Norton, 2015; Norton & McKinney, 2011) can provide.

Undergraduate attitudes and biases

A second pair of themes operating on the meso and macro levels of ITA are undergraduate students' attitudes and biases. Perhaps no two studies paint a richer picture of the relationship between ITA and US undergraduates than the those whose titles aptly contain the verbiage 'Not a lick of English' (Fitch & Morgan, 2003) and 'She does have an accent but…' (Subtirelu, 2015). In both studies, students frame ITAs as deficient English speakers whose lacking L2 proficiency is a detriment to learning and return on investment. In posts on a well-known online public forum, students make more statements such as 'best teacher ever' about teachers with US names than those with Chinese and Korean names. Likewise, teachers with Chinese and Korean names are more likely to receive comments like 'worst teacher ever' than are those with frequent non-Latino US surnames (Subtirelu, 2015). One does not have to read between the lines to see the tension and discord between students and ITAs as well as students' preference for teachers who are speakers of so-called standard English.

The picture undergraduates paint of ITAs and their experiences with them is not as black and white as 'their (ITAs) English is bad!' In fact, undergraduates recognize that ITAs are academically gifted and are conscious of the part they play in interaction and their own shortcomings (Fitch & Morgan, 2003; Plakans, 1997). On the aforementioned online forum, students frequently use frames such as 'hard to understand at first' and 'she has an accent but' to preface statements of praise (Subtirelu, 2015). Fitch and Morgan (2003: 305) present similar examples of what they call 'the culturally uncommon tale.' For instance, one participant said, 'I know this is hard to believe, but I had a good experience with my ITA.' Subtirelu (2015) argues that such constructions and utterances mildly resist the dominant monolingual ideologies that pervade other more negative and monolingual-centric comments.

In the early 1990s, Don Rubin and his associates began to investigate how biases and experience influence listener perceptions. Rubin (1992), Rubin and Smith (1990) and Kang and Rubin (2009) have shown that ratings of speech samples are impacted by the assumed ethnicity of the speaker, lecture topics and listener expectations. This seminal work empirically demonstrates that it is not only the segmental or suprasegmental pronunciation of the speaker that influences listeners' perceptions but also latent biases and life experiences that impact how they hear. In a logical extension and application of this work, studies have looked at how US undergraduate attitudes about ITAs through short-term, low-stakes, structured interactions (Kang et al., 2015; Yook & Albert, 1999). Kang and Moran synthesize three such studies in their contribution to this volume.

The problem: Implicit transdisciplinarity

ITA research has enriched our understanding of the complexity and nuance of the ITA experience. It has shown us that ITAs' identities are multilayered and dynamic as are the embodied and multilingual resources ITAs use to teach and interact in the university. It has also illuminated the role that students play in interaction and how biases and experiences affect students' perception of ITAs. Thus, the idea that the ITA experience is multifaceted is not novel. One might even argue, as we have here, that ITA has been transdisciplinary for quite some time. What has been lacking is a coherent framing of ITA as a distinct subdiscipline of Applied Linguistics and TESOL. Without this framing, we are left with a body of literature that is unwieldy to most ITA practitioners.

Thus, we want to draw attention to a real challenge for ITA policymakers, practitioners and researchers. This has little to do with ITAs themselves and everything to do with ITA research, practice and policy. This problem is two-pronged:

(1) ITA research and practice are not in dialogue.
(2) Policy drives ITA practice but is not informed by research.

By addressing the first issue, this volume hopes to affect the second. While a significant array of scholarship has focused on ITA issues from a variety of perspectives, these perspectives seldom are in dialog with each other. This has resulted in a fragmented body of work that is often disconnected from and inaccessible to those tasked with making and carrying out ITA assessment and instructional policies at universities. While research on language in use has informed a small number of ITA pedagogical materials (Gorsuch *et al.*, 2012; Smith *et al.*, 1992), it has been sorely lacking in ITA assessment which has largely focused on validating TOEFL iBT scores as a form of ITA assessment (Farnsworth, 2013). In this volume, we call for more coherent, unified, national research-based policies on ITAs' testing and instruction.

The diversity of approaches taken to the ITA experience make one theoretically-grounded approach untenable. The questions asked about ITAs are too varied to be accommodated by one theory or research methodology. Transdisciplinarity provides an approach in which researchers and pedagogues can think about their research and practice in relation to others and as part of a large community looking at the same issue from multiple perspective. It also provides the aforementioned imperatives for transformation of the way that we teach and create opportunities for learners to use and reflect upon language use. These imperatives create a condition in which researchers and practitioners must collaborate to tackle questions and challenges in practical and transformative ways. To clarify, by practical, we mean that research should be able to inform practice in a meaningful way. In using transformative, we mean that research and practice are aimed at affecting positive change in the institutional support ITAs receive and how ITAs are framed in academic and public discourse.

A Transdisciplinary Approach to ITA

This section outlines what a transdisciplinary conceptualization of ITA is first by illustrating the tri-layered nature of ITA as a subfield of Applied Linguistics and TESOL and then by laying out five tenets for a transdisciplinary ITA. Figure 1.1 is a visual depiction of the micro, meso and macro levels of ITA.

In Figure 1.1, the innermost circle is divided into eighths, representing the multiple stakeholders involved in a transdisciplinary approach to ITA: ITAs, undergraduates, faculty, practitioners, researchers, university

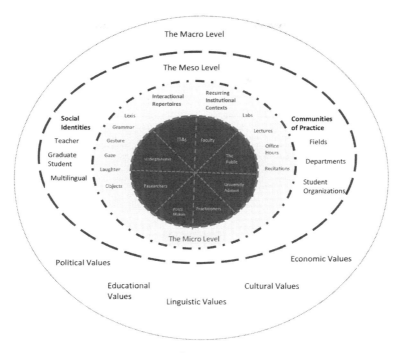

The Macro Level

The Meso Level

Interactional Repertoires

Recurring Institutional Contexts

Social Identities

Lexis

Labs

Communities of Practice

Teacher

Grammar

Lectures

Fields

Graduate Student

Gesture

Gaze

ITAs

Faculty

Office Hours

Departments

Multilingual

Laughter

Undergraduates

The Public

Recitations

Objects

Researchers

University Admin

Student Organizations

Policy Makers

Practitioners

The Micro Level

Political Values

Economic Values

Educational Values

Cultural Values

Linguistic Values

Figure 1.1 The multifaceted nature of ITA

administrators, policymakers and the public. The next circle moving outward contains the interactional repertoires and recurring institutional contexts. The third circle (or oval) represents the meso level of a transdisciplinary ITA. This level is composed of ITAs' social identities and the communities of practice in which they participate. The fourth circle contains the political values, economic values, cultural values, educational values and linguistic values involved in ITA. Each circle is composed of a dotted line to signify that the levels are not separately contained wholes but interact with one another.

A transdisciplinary approach to ITA recognizes the common values and similarities between paradigms while also respecting boundaries and divergences. While the chapters in this volume come to ITA from diverse paradigms and perspectives, there are a few basic points of agreement that bear stating. This section outlines five tenets of a transdisciplinary approach to ITA. A transdisciplinary approach to ITA is outlined below.

1. ITAs are multilingual, skilled (and perhaps novice) professionals and historical bodies who participate in various communities of practice inside and outside the university

A transdisciplinary approach to ITA forces us to reimagine who ITAs are. ITAs, for the most part, are intermediate to advanced-level speakers of English. Many of them have been educated in English-medium schools and some have attended tertiary institutions in the US Almost all of them have received formal English language instruction since elementary school. While some potential ITAs need instruction addressing the rudimentary aspects of developing lexis, grammar and segmental and suprasegmental pronunciation, what they generally require is instruction aimed at developing high-level professional competencies. The competencies that ITAs need to develop include the mastery of their own professional discourse, the ability to share their knowledge with students in an effective manner, and the ability to empathize with undergraduates.

From this perspective, ITAs are not a homogenous group but instead a diverse collection of multilinguals who participate in different social contexts and have a variety of needs. ITAs are not only L2 users but are also graduate students, teachers in training and highly skilled immigrants who bring with themselves cultural practices and experiences. They are global citizens in universities in which they come in contact with people from around the world and, in the cases of students from China and India, are often surrounded by people from their own country. Even within ethnic or linguistic groups there is much diversity in terms of academic disciplines, career aspirations, religion and sexuality. ITAs have a life history that they carry within themselves. This reality creates dynamic experiences in which ITAs arrive at the university in different professional and academic places, metaphorically speaking and take different developmental trajectories.

2. The interactional repertoires ITAs must develop are embodied, complex, dynamic, situated and holistic

A transdisciplinary ITA views language use and culture as inextricable. ITAs are not just learning English. They are learning the discourse of their discipline and of the US university and are becoming socialized to the culture and norms of this space. Our stance on language recognizes that grammar alone is not sufficient to account for the interactional work required of ITAs. Interactional competence (Hall *et al.*, 2011; Kramsch, 1986; Sert *et al.*, 2018) for ITAs involves undertaking actions such as asking questions, directing attention, managing social distance and correcting misunderstanding using linguistic and non-linguistic resources including lexis, grammar, prosody, gesture, gaze and objects. Developing interactional competence for ITAs thus involves the cultivation of sophisticated professional repertoires for engaging in classroom and one-on-one interactions with undergraduate students as well as supervisors, professors and colleagues.

Interactional repertoires for university teaching are embodied. In other words, language does not act alone but is part of a constellation of resources including gaze, gesture, objects, facial expressions and laughter. These are all resources in teachers' and students' interactional repertoires and are crucial to the management of epistemics, alignment and affiliation

(Hall & Looney, 2019; Looney & Kim, 2018). Non-verbal resources do not merely compensate for lacking English proficiency, as has been suggested elsewhere (Canagarajah, 2018a, 2018b), but are essential components to teacher and student talk. A transdisciplinary approach to ITA must continue to account for the interactional repertoires of ITAs both in research and pedagogy.

As well as being embodied, the interactional repertoires for ITAs are distributed, sequential and situated. They are not the possession of individuals but are observable to and constructed by two or more participants in context. In fact, the ability to interpret and manipulate past utterances and actions are key skills in developing professional vision in university STEM interactions (Goodwin, 2013, 2018). Teachers do not produce questions in isolation nor do students produce responses without prompting. They do so as responses to contingencies in the environmental situation. To adjust to these contingencies, teachers must be attuned to the prosodic and visual cues students provide as well as the lexical and grammatical.

3. ITA development is identity work

ITA development is identity work and like the interactional repertoires they must develop, they also must cultivate complex identities as multilinguals, migrant professionals, teachers, students and experts in their respective fields. These identities are tied up in investment and do not develop in isolation. ITA work has shown that ITAs are aware of and reflect upon the multiple hats they wear within and outside the university (Ashavskaya, 2015; LoCastro & Tapper, 2006). Social identities influence 'learners' motivation, investment in and access to learning opportunities in L2 contexts of interaction in particular social institutions, and ultimately, the substance of their multilingual repertoires, are their social identities' (Block, 2014; DFG, 2016: 31; Kramsch, 2009; Norton, 2013). Identities are also not the individual's own.

ITA identities are tied directly to the Communities of Practice (CoPs) in which they interact. Identities and development are tied to and constrained (or enabled) by the communities to which ITAs have access. As transnational professionals, ITAs must quickly adapt to new cultural norms while also learning to teach and maintaining existing relationships back home. These cultural norms are not static nationwide norms as each university has its own culture. Even within the same university, department norms are localized and the pedagogical culture shifts depending on the school and college, i.e. social sciences vs STEM programs. When international students 'join an American institution [...] they not only have to adjust to the American way of life but also to the more specific and localized values and norms of the organization that they enter' (Ross & Krider, 1992: 279). Those values and norms vary based on geographic location as well as first hand experiences as students in their home country. In the transdisciplinary spirit, Gorsuch (2003) suggests that ITAs should be encouraged to recognize that their own experiences as individuals and as learners should help guide their experiences as ITAs. Thus, encouraging ITAs to use their own experiences as students to guide their work as TAs.

4. ITA development is not a linear process and requires sustained institutional support

To thrive in the US university, ITAs must have a clear understanding of norms related to interactive teaching styles, appropriate student–teaching relationships and knowledge of departmental and colleges rules and standards (Fox *et al.*, 1994; Trebing, 2007). In addition to understanding ITAs' identities and CoPs as complex, dynamic and existing on multiple scales, we must have a similar view of their development as multilinguals and professionals. However, developing interactional competence for the university classroom does not happen overnight. Thus, sustained support through course work, workshops and other professional development is essential.

While it is clear that ITAs may need assistance adjusting to life the US, it is unclear as to *where* they might receive this guidance as the training created for ITAs is often limited and the focus solely or mostly on language proficiency (Chalupa & Lair, 2000; Olaniran, 1996). Apart from the general training for TAs, the assimilation process should be facilitated through more extensive ITA training (Chalupa & Lair, 2000; Gorsuch, 2003; Luo *et al.*, 2000; Twale *et al.*, 1997). Gokcora (1989) found that many of the ITAs who had attended TA training were able to understand desirable norms and typical classroom behaviors in undergraduate classes. In addition to further cultural training for ITAs, it could be determined that many American undergraduates need cultural sensitivity training.

5. Ideologies permeate all levels of ITA. Thus, researchers and practitioners must work as agents of change

Language ideologies permeate all levels of ITA. The formulation of the so-called 'ITA Problem' encapsulates at least two prevalent ideologies in US culture: monolingual ideologies and the commodification of education. Monolingual ideologies are not only reflected in research on ITAs but also in the slashing of foreign language departments in higher education, the underfunding of ESL programs, and the broader public discourse around English. Monolingual ideologies position normative varieties of English at the center of assessment and instruction. They also value normative models of English.

The second major ideology at work in ITA is the commodification of education. This ideology is reflected in the words of interviewees repeatedly. As mentioned earlier, students speak of being shortchanged by the university because their instructors are ITAs (Fitch & Morgan, 2003). Such language has been echoed by at least one state congressperson who also introduced legislation that would force universities to refund tuition for courses in which a student could not understand the instructor (Finder, 2005). Such ideologies frame education as service and ITAs as inadequate service providers. While reversing the commodification of education is unlikely, ITA practitioners and university administrators could actively work to frame multilingual interactions as an invaluable part of a world-class education in the 21st century.

A transdisciplinary ITA approach recognizes that policy, practice and research must share a reciprocal relationship. Others have made similar calls but little has been done to advance an agenda as a field (Gorsuch, 2016; Tapper & Kidder, 2006). These oversights must be revisited as we move deeper into the 21st century. If we are going to provide the support ITAs need, researchers, practitioners and departmental faculty must coordinate their efforts. In addition, these stakeholders must be in dialogue with policymakers at the university, state and national level.

Chapter Summaries

The chapters investigating the micro in this volume (Pickering, Looney, Chiang) are interested in language and social interaction in three academic contexts: the lecture, the STEM lab and office hours. In Chapter 2, Lucy Pickering synthesizes her body of work on Discourse Intonation (DI) and ITAs. Her work shows that prosody functions from the lexical, phrasal and clausal level all the way to the discursive level to manage the delivery of instruction and the management of social distance. Pickering concludes her chapter by proposing a model of conversational involvement for ITAs based on research and learning principles. Looney's chapter (Chapter 3) looks at interaction between a TA and three undergraduates in a university physics lab. Using Conversation Analysis (CA) and Chuck Goodwin's (2018) concept of co-operative action, the chapter shows how a TA draws on language and non-verbal resources, e.g. gesture, from prior student turns to set up questions and explanations. Looney's analysis suggests that CA is a powerful tool for understanding the repertoires ITAs need to interact competently in the classroom and for developing materials and assessments for ITA.

Chiang's chapter studies recordings of interactions between ITAs and undergraduates during office hours meetings. The analysis focuses on how an ITA manages his instructional authority during negotiations with students about graded assignments. The chapter also proposes specific communicative acts that can trigger negotiations, the dimensions of instructional authority which may become negotiable, and the discourse domains in which instructional authority may be susceptible to negotiation. Chiang's chapter, like Looney's, shows that ITAs must manage difficult to plan for contingencies that might involve correcting misunderstanding and negotiating institutional identities. By providing rich descriptions of academic interactions, the chapters on the micro-level of ITA provide practitioners with empirical evidence of what ITAs need to do with English in the classroom. This evidence should inform both materials and assessment development.

The meso level of SLA is composed of social identities and the immediate social contexts in which language is used, and the macro-level is made up of the language ideologies and policies operating within contexts. The chapters investigating the meso level of ITA (Bhalla, Kang and Moran, Wei) involve examining how ITAs construct their identities in relation to English, how undergraduates' attitudes can be improved, and what a World Englishes approach to assessment means for ITA. These chapters demonstrate that the ITA situation extends beyond and interacts with language and the ITA.

Kang's and Moran's chapter delves into US undergraduate student's attitudes towards ITAs through three structure inter-group contact studies: (1) a single one-hour culture-sensitization activity; (2) three sessions of structured activities embedded in an intercultural communication course; and (3) a semester-long (one hour per week) informal language/cultural partner program. The goals of these activities are to reduce prejudice towards ITAs and Kang and Moran make a strong call for future applications of contact activities. They show that institutional support is crucial for the success of inter-group contact studies, highlighting the need for an interface between ITA research and policy.

Continuing the examining of mutual engagement, Bhalla's chapter examines how the CoP framework is a means of support for ITAs as they navigate their experiences as experts in the course content and the challenges they face when with being foreigners to the country in which they are instructing. In particular, this chapter focused on the South Asian ITA perspective and the complexities of Indian English and the linguistic and cultural issues which arise in both the university and classroom setting. The professional socialization process for South Asian ITAs as they develop their professional and social identities in a new country is explored in Bhalla's chapter.

Wei's chapter also examines the Outer and Expanding Circle English varieties but from the perspective of standardized international language tests among Indian English and Chinese English speaking ITAs. Wei examines how a special training package targeting these two varieties of English affects raters' scores and scoring criteria by using a mixed method design. Findings from this study revealed that a possible lack of consistency in scores could be attributed to the awareness of these linguistic features and possible attitudes towards standard English. Therefore, because training raises raters' awareness of the linguistic aspects of varieties of English it does not mean the training will also overcome language attitudes and ideologies. Such findings have significant implications for assessment design not only for ITA but for ESL/EFL assessments worldwide.

The macro chapters discuss the long-standing international recruitment practices at US universities (Harklau and Coda) and how program administrators can evaluate and explain their curriculum to vested stakeholders (Gorsuch). Harklau's and Coda's chapter is the first chapter that we know of to look at the ITA experience in light of international student recruitment policies and migration patterns. The chapter traces how, since before and especially after World War II, US universities have actively pursued international students first at the graduate level and progressively more and more at the undergraduate level. The driving forces behind this recruitment have been both political and economic. In political terms, education has been viewed as a powerful form of soft power that not only improves the US's standing in the minds of international citizens but also enriches the places where those citizens live. In economic terms, international students have provided both a cheap and skilled labor force for universities as well as pumping billions of dollars into the national and local economies. Harklau and Coda conclude by warning that national policies, increased efforts by universities and governments in other countries, and perceived return on investment may all be deleterious to the sustained success of US universities in attracting international students.

Lastly, Gorsuch focuses on the course logic for ITA trainers and the essential role it plays in evaluation research as it is need to play the evaluation and explanation of the course to others, particularly non-ITA instructional personnel. This chapter provides an account of the 'big picture' of instructional planning with the goal of becoming a resource for ITA educators as they seek out the best outcomes for ITAs and their own programs. Gorsuch makes recommendations for instructors, administrators and other stakeholders who are invested in enhancing ITA programs and instructional practices.

Conclusion

While the chapters in this volume do not promise to provide solutions to all the challenges faced by ITAs, they do all contribute to an understanding of the obstacles that ITAs face as well as a deeper view into their experience. Applying a transdisciplinary approach to ITA research allows us to consider these evolving issues in light of globalization and transnationalism. The macro, meso and micro dimensions of the language and culture socialization process for ITAs align with our call for research that provides a holistic view of the ITA experience. Central to this volume, is the recognition of the rich linguistic and cultural traditions that the ITAs bring with them which contribute to a global climate for which many universities strive. An examination of the ITA trajectory from the classroom/academic experience they bring with them as students and potentially instructors, to the policies that dictate their institutional roles and responsibilities, to the community they create with colleagues, the student interactions, the assessments they must pass to become ITAs, to the logic that dictates their course work, is provided in this volume.

References

Althen, G. (1991) Teaching 'culture' to international teaching assistants. In J. Nyquist, R. Abbott, D. Wulff and J. Sprague (eds) *Preparing the Professoriate of Tomorrow to Teach* (pp. 350–355). Dubuque, IA: Kendall Hunt.

Ashavskaya, E. (2015) International teaching assistants' experiences in the U.S. classrooms: Implications for practice. *Journal of the Scholarship of Teaching and Learning* 15 (2), 56–69.

Atkinson, D. (ed.) (2011) *Alternative Approaches to Second Language Acquisition*. New York: Routledge.

Block, D. (2014) *Second Language Identities* (2nd edn). London: Bloomsbury.

Black, J.S. and Mendenhall, M. (1990) Cross-cultural training effectiveness: A review and a theoretical framework for future research. *Academy of Management Review* 15, 113–136.

Borjas, G.J. (2000) Foreign-born teaching assistants and the academic performance of undergraduates. *American Economic Review* 90, 355–359.

Canagarajah, S. (2013) *Translingual Practice: Global Englishes and Cosmopolitan Relations*. New York: Routledge.

Canagarajah, S. (2018a) Materializing 'competence': Perspective from international STEM scholars. *The Modern Language Journal* 102 (2), 1–24.

Canagarajah, S. (2018b) Translingual practice as spatial repertoires: Expanding the paradigm beyond structuralist orientations. *Applied Linguistics* 39 (1), 31–54.

Canale, M. and Swain, M. (1980) Theoretical bases of communicative approaches to second language teaching and testing. *Applied Linguistics* 1, 1–47.

Chalupa, C. and Lair, A. (2000) Meeting the needs of international TAs in the foreign language classroom: A model for extended training. *Mentoring Foreign Language Teaching Assistants, Lecturers, and Adjunct Faculty. Issues in Language Program Direction: A Series in Annual Volumes.*

Chiang, S.-Y. (2016) 'Is this what you're talking about?': Identity negotiation in international teaching assistants' instructional interactions with U.S. college students. *Journal of Language, Identity & Education* 15 (2), 114–128.

Chiang, S.-Y. (2009) Dealing with communication problems in the instructional interactions between international teaching assistants and American college students. *Language and Education* 23 (5), 461–478.

Chiang, S.-Y. (2011) Pursuing a response in office hour interactions between international teaching assistants and US college students. *Journal of Pragmatics* 43 (14), 3316–3330.

Chiang, S.-Y. and Mi, H.-F. (2011) Reformulation: A verbal display of interlanguage awareness in instructional interactions. *Language Awareness* 20 (2), 135–149.

Chiang, S.-Y. and Mi, H.-F. (2008) Reformulation as a strategy for managing 'understanding uncertainty' in office hour interactions between international teaching assistants and American college students. *Intercultural Education* 19 (3), 269–281.

Clayton, M. (2000) Foreign teaching assistants' first test: The accent. *The Christian Science Monitor.* https://www.csmonitor.com/2000/0905/p14s1.html

Darvin, R. and Norton, B. (2015) Identity and a model of investment in applied linguistics. *Annual Review of Applied Linguistics* 35, 36–56.

Davies, C.E. and Tyler, A. (2005) Discourse strategies in the context of crosscultural institutional talk: Uncovering interlanguage pragmatics in the university classroom. In K. Bardovi-Harlig and B.S. Hartford (eds) *Interlanguage Pragmatics* (pp. 133–156). Mahwah, NJ: Lawrence Erlbaum Associates.

Douglas Fir Group (2016) A transdisciplinary framework for SLA in a multilingual world. *The Modern Language Journal* 100 (Supplement 2016), 19–47.

Duff, P.A. (2019) Social dimensions and processes in second language acquisition: Multilingual socialization in transnational contexts. *The Modern Language Journal* 103 (Supplement 2019), 6–22.

Duff, P.A. and Byrnes, H. (2019) SLA across disciplinary borders: Introduction to the special issue. *The Modern Language Journal* 103 (Supplement 2019), 3–5.

Duff, P.A. and Talmy, S. (2011) Language socialization approaches to second language acquisition: Social, cultural, and linguistic development in additional languages. In D. Atkinson (ed.) *Alternative Approaches to Second Language Acquisition* (pp. 95–116). New York: Routledge.

Finder, A. (2005) Unclear on American campus: What the foreign teacher said. *The New York Times*.

Firth, A. and Wagner, J. (1997) On discourse, communication, and (some) fundamental concepts in SLA research. *The Modern Language Journal* 81 (3), 285–300.

Fitch, F. and Morgan, S. (2003) 'Not a lick of English': Constructing the ITA identity through student narratives. *Communication Education* 52 (3/4), 297–310.

Fox, W. S. and Gay, G. (1994) Functions and effects of international teaching assistants. *Review of Higher Education* 18 (1), 1–24.

Gokcora, D. (1989, November) A descriptive study of communication and teaching strategies used by two types of international teaching assistants at the University of Minnesota, and their cultural perceptions of teaching and teachers. Paper presented at the meeting of the National Conference on Training and Employment of Teaching Assistants, Seattle, WA. (ERIC Document Reproduction Service No. ED351730).

Goodwin, C. (2013) The co-operative, transformative organization of human action and knowledge. *Journal of Pragmatics* 46, 8–23.

Goodwin, C. (2018) *Co-Operative Action*. New York: Cambridge University Press.

Gorsuch, G.J. (2003) The educational cultures of international teaching assistants and U.S. universities. *Teaching English as a Second or Foreign Language (TESL-EJ)* 7 (3).

Gorsuch, G. (ed.) (2012) *Working Theories for Teaching Assistant Development: Time-Tested and Robust Theories, Frameworks, and Models for TA and ITA Learning*. Stillwater, OK: New Forums Press.

Gorsuch, G. (ed.) (2015) *Talking Matters: Research on Talk and Communication of International Teaching Assistants*. Stillwater, OK: New Forums Press.

Gorsuch, G. (2016) International teaching assistants at universities: A research agenda. *Language Teaching* 49 (2), 275–290.

Gorsuch, G., Meyers, C.M., Pickering, L. and Griffee, D.T. (2012) *English Communication for International Teaching Assistants*. Long Grove, IL: Waveland Press, Inc.

Hahn, L. (2004) Primary stress and intelligibility: Research to motivate the teaching of suprasegmentals. *TESOL Quarterly* 38 (2), 201–223.

Hall, J.K. (2019a) *Essentials of SLA for L2 Teachers: A Transdisciplinary Framework*. New York: Routledge.

Hall, J.K. (2019b) The contributions of conversation analysis and interactional linguistics to a usage-based understanding of language: Expanding the transdisciplinary framework. *The Modern Language Journal* 103 (Supplement 2019), 80–94.

Hall, J.K. and Looney, S.D. (2019) Introduction: The embodied work of teaching. In J.K. Hall and S.D. Looney (eds) *The Embodied Work of Teaching*. Bristol: Multilingual Matters.

Hall, J.K., Hellermann, J. and Pekarek Doehler, S. (eds) (2011) *L2 Interactional Competence and Development*. Bristol: Multilingual Matters.

Holliday, A. (1994) *Appropriate Methodology and Social Context*. Cambridge: Cambridge University Press.

Institute of International Education (IIE) (2018) Open Doors Report (2018, November), https://www.iie.org/Research-and-Insights/Open-Doors

Jin, L. and Cortazzi, M. (2002) Cultures of learning, the social construction of educational identities. In D.C.S. Li (ed.) *Discourses in Search of Members: In Honor of Ron Scollon* (pp. 49–77). University Press of America.

Kang, O. and Rubin, D.L. (2009) Reverse linguistic stereotyping: Measuring the effect of listener expectations on speech evaluation. *Journal of Language and Social Psychology* 28 (4), 441–456.

Kang, O., Rubin, D.L. and Lindemann, S. (2015) Mitigating U.S. undergraduates' attitudes toward international teaching assistants. *TESOL Quarterly* 49 (4), 681–706.

Kasper, G. and Wagner, J. (2011) A conversation-analytic approach to second language acquisition. In D. Atkinson (ed.) *Alternative Approaches to Second Language Acquisition* (pp. 117–142). New York: Routledge.

Kramsch, C. (1986) From language proficiency to interactional competence. *The Modern Language Journal* 70 (4), 366–372.

Kramsch, C. (2009) *The Multilingual Subject: What Foreign Language Learners Say about their Experience and Why it Matters*. Oxford: Oxford University Press.

Lave, J. and Wenger, E. (1991) *Situated Learning: Legitimate Peripheral Participation*. Cambridge: Cambridge University Press.

Liao, S. (2009) Variation in the use of discourse markers by Chinese teaching assistants in the US. *Journal of Pragmatics* 41, 1313–1328.

LoCastro, V. and Tapper, G. (2006) International teaching assistants and teacher identity. *Journal of Applied Linguistics* 3 (2), 185–218.

Looney, S.D. (2015) Interaction and discourse markers in the ITA-led physics laboratory. In G. Gorsuch (ed.) *Talking Matters* (pp. 77–111). Stillwater, OK: New Forums Press.

Looney, S.D., Jia, D. and Kimura, D. (2017) Self-directed *okay* in mathematics lectures. *Journal of Pragmatics* 107, 46–59.

Looney, S.D. and Kim, J. (2018) Humor, uncertainty, and affiliation: Cooperative and co-operative action in the university science lab. *Linguistics and Education* 46, 56–69.

Luo, J., Bellows, L. and Grady, M. (2000) Classroom management issues for teaching assistants. *Research in Higher Education* 41 (3), 353–383.

Madden, C.G. and Myers, C.L. (eds) (1994) *Discourse and Performance of International Teaching Assistants*. Alexandria, VA: Teachers of English to Speakers of Other Languages, Inc.

Myers, C. (1994) Question-based discourse in science labs: Issues for ITAs. In C.G. Madden and C.L. Myers (eds) *Discourse and Performance of International Teaching Assistants* (pp. 83–102). Alexandria, VA: Teachers of English to Speakers of Other Languages, Inc.

Norton, B. (2013) *Identity and Language Learning: Extending the Conversation* (2nd edn). Bristol: Multilingual Matters.

Norton, B. and McKinney, C. (2011) An identity approach to second language acquisition. In D. Atkinson (ed.) *Alternative Approaches to Second Language Acquisition* (pp. 73–94). New York: Routledge.

Olaniran, B.A. (1996) Social skills acquisition: A closer look at foreign students on college campuses and factors influencing their level of social difficulty in social situations. *Communication Studies* 22, 72–88.

Oreto, R. (2018) Building buy-in: Your website says it all [Keynote]. *International Teaching Assistant Professionals Symposium*. University of Pittsburgh. Pittsburgh, PA.

Ortega, L. (2019) SLA and the study of equitable multilingualism. *The Modern Language Journal* 103 (Supplement 2019), 23–38.

Pialorsi, F. (1984) Toward an anthropology of the classroom: An essay on foreign teaching assistants and U.S. students. In K. Bailey, F. Pialorsi and J. Faust-Zukowski (eds) *Foreign Teaching Assistants in U.S. Universities*. Washington: NAFSA.

Pickering, L. (2001) The role of tone choice in improving ITA communication in the classroom. *TESOL Quarterly* 35 (2), 233–255.

Pickering, L. (2004) The structure and function of intonational paragraphs in native and nonnative speaker instructional discourse. *English for Specific Purposes* 23, 19–43.

Plakans, B. (1997) Undergraduates' experiences with and attitudes toward international teaching assistants. *TESOL Quarterly* 31 (1), 95–119.

Reinhardt, J. (2010) Directives in office hour consultations: A corpus-informed investigation of learner and expert usage. *English for Specific Purposes* 29, 94–107.

Ross, P. and Krider, D. (1992) Off the plane and into the classroom: A phenomenological explication of international teaching assistants' experiences in the American classroom. *International Journal of Intercultural Relations* 16, 277–293.

Rubin, D. (1992) Nonlanguage factors affecting undergraduates' judgements of nonnative English-speaking teaching assistants. *Research in Higher Education* 33 (4), 511–531.

Rubin, D. and Smith, K. (1990) Effects of accent, ethnicity, and lecture topic on undergraduates' perceptions of nonnative English-speaking teaching assistants. *International Journal of Intercultural Relations* 14, 337–353.

Sarkasian, E. (1990) *Teaching American Students: A Guide for International Faculty and Teaching Assistants in Colleges and Universities*. Cambridge, MA: Derek Bok Center for Teaching and Learning.

Sert, O., Kunitz, S. and Markee, N. (2018) Editorial. *Classroom Discourse* 9 (1), 1–2.

Shaw, P.A. and Bailey, K.M. (1990) Cultural differences in academic settings. In R.C. Scarcela, E.S. Andersen and S.D. Krashen (eds) *Developing Communicative Competence in a Second Language*, (pp. 317–328). New York: Newbury House

Smith, J.A., Meyers, C.M. and Burkhalter, A.J. (1992) *Communicate: Strategies for International Teaching Assistants*. Long Grove, IL: Waveland Press.

Subtirelu, N. (2015) 'She does have an accent but…': Race and language ideology in students' evaluations of mathematics instructors on RateMyProfessor.com. *Language in Society* 44, 35–62.

Tapper, G. and Kidder, K. (2006) A research-informed approach to international teaching assistant preparation. In D. Kaufman and B. Brownworth (eds) *Professional Development of International Teaching Assistants* (pp. 17–33). Alexandria, VA: Teachers of English to Speakers of Other Languages, Inc.

Tapper, J. (1994) Directives used in college laboratory oral discourse. *English for Specific Purposes* 13 (3), 205–222.

Trebing, D. (2007) International teaching assistants' attitudes toward teaching and understanding of U.S. American undergraduate students (Unpublished doctoral dissertation). Southern Illinois University, Carbondale.

Twale, D.J., Shannon, D.M. and Moore, M.S. (1997) NGTA and IGTA training and experience: Comparisons between self-ratings and undergraduate student evaluation. *Innovative Higher Education* 22 (1), 16.

Tyler, A. (1992) Discourse structure and the perception of incoherence in international teaching assistants' spoken discourse. *TESOL Quarterly* 26 (4), 693–711.

Williams, J. (1992) Planning, discourse marking, and the comprehensibility of international teaching assistants. *TESOL Quarterly* 26 (4), 693–711.

Young, R. (1989) Introduction. *English for Specific Purposes* 8 (2, Special Issue), 101–107.

Yook, E. and Albert, R. (1999) Perceptions of international teaching assistants: The interrelatedness of intercultural training, cognition, and emotion. *Communication Education* 48, 1–17.

2 The Role of Intonation in the Production and Perception of ITA Discourse

Lucy Pickering

The 1980s witnessed growing legal and scholarly concerns regarding what was then called the 'Foreign TA Problem.' The issue was taken up by state governments and university systems, which often resulted in the establishment of mandatory training programs. One such program was developed at the University of Florida by Andrea Tyler and her colleagues (Tapper *et al.*, 2018). It addressed the underlying causes of perceived unintelligibility in international teaching assistants (ITA) discourse by undergraduates (UGs) and promoted an approach based on multilayered discourse analysis that was designed to uncover areas important for cross-cultural miscommunication. Specifically, it focused on the achievement of comprehensible discourse through the production and interpretation of multiple cues or signals present at all levels of the discourse, i.e. lexical, syntactic, prosodic and non-verbal. At that time, very little had been reported in terms of the role of prosody in classroom discourse particularly as it pertained to cross-cultural communication. This chapter traces the history of the work in this area and the discourse-pragmatic approach to intonation structure that has been used to elucidate its importance. Finally, a model of conversational involvement is proposed which contextualizes ITA preparation within a transdisciplinary framework.

Introduction

US universities have a long history of maintaining an open-door policy with regard to international graduate students, particularly in disciplines now referred to as science, technology, engineering and mathematics (STEM) fields. However, by the 1980s, there were growing legal and scholarly concerns regarding what was then termed the 'Foreign TA Problem' (Bailey, 1983). By 1992, 14 states had passed legislation requiring some kind of mandatory training program to be instituted at state universities (Smith, 1992). In response, institutions quickly put into place program resources to address the perceived needs of these nonnative English-speaking instructors. These early ITA programs were essentially triage operations that employed some variation of an English for Specific Purposes (ESP) approach. Course designs often reflected specific disciplines or contexts, and classroom activities comprised pedagogical tasks designed to mirror the real-world tasks in which the ITAs were about to engage (Byrd & Constantinides, 1992; Jacobson, 1986; Myers, 1994).

An early consensus was reached that in addition to language intervention, ITAs lacked an understanding of the cultural and pedagogical norms of US college classrooms. Perceived language difficulties were most often generalized as 'a pronunciation issue' and addressed using traditional, piecemeal approaches focusing primarily on phonemic accent reduction. Stevens (1989: 183), however, proposed that these three areas should be seen as different aspects of the same issue:

> We need to ask ourselves just where does the linguistic aspect of the ITA problem end and the cultural part begin? Obviously there is no clear boundary. Speech is understood in terms of a cultural context. Intelligibility is the problem, yet we cannot dissect it in terms of discrete elements of pedagogy, culture, and language to be addressed individually.

Stevens (1989: 183) recognized that what was being described as problematic was something more akin to 'oral intelligibility,' and that this comprised multiple aspects of presentation including the role of prosodic features such as rhythm and intonation. He noted that when students were asked to be more specific about where the problems lay with their ITA instructors, they would 'often point to the nonstandard production of intonation, stress (on the word and sentence level), linking, rhythm and fluency, and projection – though they seldom use these terms in their comments' (Stevens, 1989: 182).

Other early studies reached similar conclusions. Undergraduate complaints mentioned the 'boring, monotonous quality of the ITAs explanations' (Smith, 1992: 73), and Hinofotis and Bailey (1980) linked these comments to the monotonic intonation patterns that they noted characterized many ITA presentations. Anderson-Hsieh (1990: 200) suggested that 'American undergraduates seem to be bothered more by suprasegmental deviance than segmental deviance in the speech of ITAs' and called explicitly for a focus on suprasegmentals in language training.

The most extensive contribution to the understanding of intonation in non-native speaker (NNS) discourse at this time was made by Ann Wennerstrom (1991, 1994, 1997, 1998), who was the first to apply a fully developed intonation framework (Pierrehumbert & Hirschberg, 1990) to NNS spoken production. Wennerstrom focused on the role of intonation as it contributed to the perception of the overall coherence of the discourse. In 1998, for example, she conducted a study of 18 Chinese graduate students who were preparing to be ITAs and demonstrated that the prosodic features of the ITA discourse differed significantly from that of their native speaker (NS) TA colleagues. Among other issues, in the NNS presentations, identification of new information by hearers was compromised by multiple syllable prominences and the use of final, falling intonation contours at phrase medial boundaries rather than rising or level contours.

Wennerstrom's work represented a critical step forward in demonstrating that patterns of intonation usage could be systematically identified and described in NNS discourse. They were also shown to be qualitatively different from those of native speakers resulting in obfuscation of the information structure of the discourse for the NS hearer. However, it did not directly confirm Stevens' observation that prosodic features cross the boundary between the linguistic and the sociolinguistic or pragmatic and are thus at the heart of the 'ITA problem.'

The remainder of the chapter outlines the development of a program of research that directly addresses this question. It begins with an early program designed at the University of Florida in which ITA–student interaction was viewed within the broader lens of cross-cultural communication. Using a multilayered discourse analysis of classroom interaction, which included intonational features, sources of miscommunication between ITAs and students were made explicit and could be examined. Although Tyler and her colleagues were the first to focus on the importance of intonation structure in contributing to relational work in the ITA classroom, they lacked a comprehensive model of prosody that would allow them to systematically reconstruct how students and teachers produce and interpret intonation cues to mark both relationship-building and information-structuring in classroom discourse. This was achieved with the addition of Brazil's (1985/1997) model of discourse intonation in the late 1990s. Sections three and four of this chapter describe Brazil's framework and the insights that it made possible regarding the role of intonation in the ITA context. The final part of the chapter presents a model of conversational involvement (Pickering, 2014) which fully integrates prosodic features into a model that contextualizes the ITA experience within a transdisciplinary context as one example of a group of multilingual transnational workers who can usefully deploy the multiple 'semiotic resources' that they have at their disposal (Douglas Fir Group, 2016).

The University of Florida ITA Program

This program, developed by Andrea Tyler and her colleagues in the 1980s and early 1990s (Tapper *et al.*, 2018), espoused an interactional sociolinguistic perspective (Gumperz, 1982) that prioritized the established sociocultural use of the linguistic code. Gumperz's framework proposes that spoken discourse is comprised of multiple 'contextualization cues' or signals present at all levels of the discourse, i.e. lexical, syntactic, prosodic and non-verbal. For production and interpretation of these devices, speaker-hearers use institutionalized linguistic and cultural knowledge and moment–by-moment inferences regarding the speaker's intent based on the immediate context of the interaction. Over time, within speech communities, these cues become tacit, conventionalized choices that interlocutors rely on for successful interaction. They do not necessarily span speech communities however, and prosodic cues are particularly vulnerable to misinterpretation in cross-cultural interaction. Unlike errors in syntax or morphology that are clearly perceived by native speaker interlocutors as typical learner errors, prosodic miscues are often not perceived as linguistic choices at all, but as expressions of a speaker's attitude or personality:

> A speaker is said to be unfriendly, impertinent or rude, uncooperative or fail to understand…miscommunication of this type in other words is regarded as a social faux pas and leads to misjudgments of the speaker's intent…it is not likely to be identified as mere linguistic error. (Gumperz, 1982: 139)

Within the framework of conversational inference, Tyler and her colleagues looked at the role of prosodic cues as part of the system of contextualization cues in both information structuring and relationship building between ITAs and their students. Tyler *et al.* (1988: 101) conducted an analysis of teaching demonstrations given by 18 Korean and Chinese ITAs in which they report that the instructors 'construct an undifferentiated, flat discourse structure within which the native-speaker listener is unable to perceive the intended relationships among the ideas presented.' They further note that prosodic signals frequently did not align with other discourse cues in the syntactic, lexical and non-verbal systems, thus many of the cues that listeners usually rely on to create a coherent representation of the text were either violated or absent. Tyler (1992: 723) described a similar pattern in a Chinese ITA presentation that resulted in the perception of the discourse as 'rambling and scrambling.' With regard to the relational aspect of intonation cues, Tyler *et al.* (1988: 105) state that a persistent use of falling intonation contours by the ITAs made them sound 'abrupt, cold, impatient, angry and/or confrontive' to their North American student hearers. Overall, they concluded that these miscues can negatively shape students' perceptions of an ITA's personality, competence and interest in their students' well-being.

The addition of Brazil's model of discourse intonation in the 1990s made it possible to systematically map the intonation structure of both teacher and student contributions to the discourse and further interrogate the role of this linguistic feature. In agreement with Gumperz's model of conversational inference, Brazil also views choices as conventionalized by speaker-hearer(s) within speech communities and even within specific genres of discourse, based on shared sociocultural and linguistic experiences. Brazil's model conceptualizes intonation as a linguistic system that operates concurrently with other language systems present in discourse yet is independent of them. Thus, its contribution to the communicative value of the utterance is neither predetermined nor rendered redundant by simultaneous grammatical and lexical choices.

Furthermore, the model has two unique advantages that make it particularly insightful with regard to ITA discourse. First, Brazil describes intonational choices as designed to help negotiate *a state of convergence* with the listener. In other words, the speaker designs their intonation choices to link the ongoing discourse message to a context that the specific listener(s) can make sense of. Critically, this notion of convergence includes both informational *and* social confluence between participants. Thus, successful interaction is understood to be the maintenance of comfortable interactional involvement between interlocutors in both informational and relational respects. Second, Brazil developed the discourse intonation model with classroom discourse specifically in mind (see for example, Brazil *et al.*, 1980). Much of the initial work that was undertaken by him and his colleagues focused on classrooms in the UK. However, further research has shown that it has proven value in the analysis of nonnative speech in ESL/EFL contexts including studies of English language learners from Germany (Koester, 1990), Italy (Pirt, 1990), and Korea, Greece and Indonesia (Hewings, 1995). The following section briefly introduces the formal intonational choices that comprise the model before focusing on the ITA research that has derived from it.

The Discourse Intonation Model

The discourse intonation model comprises four systems under the executive control of the speaker: (1) division of the speech stream into tone units; (2) choice of prominent syllables/words within speech units; (3) choice of pitch movement on the tonic syllable; and (4) choice of pitch height on prominent syllables. All transcription conventions are given in the appendix.

Tone units are typically separated by pauses and comprise one idea or piece of information such as a clause or other language 'chunk' that makes semantic sense. Prominence, or utterance level stress, falls on the information-bearing syllables in the unit. At least one prominent syllable, termed the tonic syllable, will occur in each complete tone unit; however, multiple prominences may appear depending on the amount of information contained within the unit. A useful guide is to think of the typical structure of a tone unit in English as comprising 3–7 words and containing one or two prominences.

The third system, tone choice, describes the choice of a rising, falling or level pitch movement on the tonic syllable. Tone selection marks both the informational status of the utterance and its social significance within the context of the interaction. Falling tones (both fall [↘] and rise-fall [↗↘]) indicate the speaker's assumption that the matter of the tone unit is a new assertion for the hearer, i.e. in some way world-changing. Choice of a rising tone (both rise [↗] and fall-rise [↘↗]), on the other hand, indicates that the speaker assumes this information is part of the shared background between participants and agrees with the current worldview of the hearer. The final level tone choice (→) is marked as communicatively neutral and presents the information as a language specimen. Speakers may choose this tone for any number of reasons; for example, ritualized or routinized language such as giving directives in the classroom: //→ stop WRITing// →PUT your PENS down// (Brazil, 1997: 138).

The final system – key and termination – concerns pitch height on prominent syllables as opposed to pitch movement. It operates in conjunction with the tonal system and plays an important role in the local management of turn-taking structure, inter-speaker cooperation, and in signaling larger prosodic units. Key choice is realized on the onset syllable (the first prominent syllable in the tone unit) and termination choice on the tonic syllable. In cases where there is only one prominent syllable in the tone unit, both key and termination choice fall on the tonic syllable. Using the voice range of the speaker as a 'minimally fixed framework' (Couper-Kuhlen, 1986), the first onset key is identified as either high (⇑), mid (⇒) or low (⇓). Subsequent termination levels are identified as appreciably higher than or lower than the preceding key choice.

Similarly to tone choice, each of the pitch level choices carries a specific pragmatic value. Choice of high key/termination denotes matter as either contrastive or particularized with respect to the surrounding information. Mid key and termination choices have an additive function and invite agreement as the unmarked choice. Finally, a low key/termination choice indicates that no new information is added. For this reason, the use of a low termination indicates that an exchange or intonational paragraph is complete.

We can exemplify these choices using a typical short classroom interaction called an Initiation-Response-Feedback (IRF) exchange in which the teacher asks a question and then evaluates the student's response. Example 1 is adapted from a chemistry lab presentation given by a native English-speaking TA in which students are reviewing previously completed work. Following the orthographic transcription of the exchange (1a), I have given the prosodic transcription using the conventions of the model (1b).

Example 1 Orthographic and prosodic transcription of a teacher–student exchange

(1a)

Teacher: What does it tell us if the flame turns orange?

Student: That there's sodium

Teacher: Sodium good

(1b)

Teacher: //⇒WHAT does it tell us if the flame turns ↗ Orange//

Student: //that there's ⇒ ↗ SOdium//

Teacher: // ⇒ ↘ SOdium// ⇓↘ GOOD//

In this example, the teacher poses the question in a tone unit with a mid key and rising tone, which glosses as something like *'let's confirm that you remember what it means when the flame turns orange.'* Note that the TA could instead have used a falling tone //WHAT does it tell us if the flame turns ↘Orange//which would gloss rather as *'tell me if you know what it means when the flame turns orange.'* The student responds using a mid key and a rising tone on 'sodium.' This glosses as *'please confirm that I am correct that it is sodium'* as opposed to a falling tone which would gloss rather as *'I'm telling you it is sodium.'* Students in these exchanges frequently opt for the rising, 'making sure' tone as opposed to the 'telling' falling tone (Cheng *et al.*, 2008). The teacher responds in a mid key on 'sodium' and then closes the exchange with a low termination and falling tone on the positive evaluation 'good.' In interactions between participants of unequal status, such as between a teacher and a student, it is expected that the participant with the higher status will signal the closing of the exchange as shown in the example.

In summary, the four interlocking systems of tone unit structure, prominence, tone and key/termination form the basic components of the intonation system in English. Thus, the model provides a systematic framework within which to analyze intonation structure, which can then be compared to other levels of linguistic description. In the following section, I summarize studies that have been undertaken using this model in the analysis of ITA classroom discourse. Overall, these show that intonation choices made by ITAs can hamper the success of their interaction with their students by disrupting both informational and social convergence between the participants.

ITA Studies

Establishing rapport: Projecting and negotiating common ground

Tertiary level classroom discourse in the US is typically thought of as a more interactive register in comparison to classroom discourse that involves children. Both verbal and non-verbal teacher immediacy behaviors have been consistently shown to play an important role in students' perceptions of their instructors' interest in them and willingness to help (Myers *et al.*, 1998). College students respond well to an interactive and engaging style that downplays status differences and emphasizes the role of the teacher as a co-participant rather than as an authority figure. Within early examples of ITA research, NNSs were encouraged to use strategies such as inclusive rather than exclusive pronouns (Rounds, 1987) and interactional strategies (Douglas & Myers, 1989). However, the role of intonation choices in communicating this 'positive affect' (Bailey, 1984) remained opaque.

In order to investigate this, Pickering (2001) examined the tonal composition of 12 parallel teaching presentations in STEM labs taught by six Chinese ITAs and six North American male teaching assistants. As noted above, tone choice summarizes the common ground between speakers at any given moment in the interaction. Falling tones reflect the speaker's assumption that the information in the tone unit is new or in some way world-changing for the hearer. Rising tones, on the other hand, indicate that the speaker assumes the information is part of the background, shared knowledge between speaker and hearer(s).

In the six presentations given by the North American teaching assistants (TA), the majority of the tone choices used, between 60–75%, were falling tones. This is expected in a discourse event largely involved with the communication of new information from one interlocutor to another. The percentage of rising tones used varied between 15–30% and was greatest in those lab presentations in which the TA reviewed material or procedures that the students were already familiar with. Example 2 is a typical illustration of this usage. It is taken from a US. TA chemistry laboratory presentation in which the TA reminds the students of what they have already covered prior to being given the task of analyzing an unknown sample.

Example 2 Rising tone choices to project common ground
(Pickering, 2001: 242)

> //now of course you remember that potassium was ⏶PURple// gave a purple or a ⏶VIolet flame// you MIGHT see that as ⏶WELL// . . .// and the THIRD possibility is that there be no color at ⏶ALL//

Throughout this presentation, the US TA selected tone choices that built on the prior common ground between himself and his students and that aligned with his lexical choice of 'now of course you remember.' Although the use of falling tones in this example would also have been grammatical and appropriate (e.g. //now of course you remember that potassium was ⏷PURple//gave a purple or a ⏷VIolet flame//), they would not have communicated the inclusive stance that the TA wished to project.

North American TAs also frequently used rising tones on comprehension markers such as //↗RIGHT// and //↗oK// regardless of whether there was any expectation of an overt student response as in most cases there was no time given for the students to respond. In this sense, they were 'solidarity markers' rather than comprehension markers as they implicitly acknowledged a negotiation between the TA and the students and again, projected a mutual understanding. In fact, throughout the analyses, NS TAs were shown to be exploiting the tonal system to promote a sense of community and shared space in the classroom.

Conversely, analysis of the equivalent ITA presentations revealed an average of 8% use of rising tones. The difference between the two groups was particularly noticeable in those presentations in which ITAs reviewed previously covered material. Example 3 shows the parallel presentation given by the ITA to that shown in Example 2. In his presentation, the ITA used almost exclusively falling tones that failed to capitalize on the students' previous experience in the class.

Example 3 Falling tone choices on negotiated common ground (Pickering, 2001: 248)

> //the FIRST ↘STEP// you do is FLAME ↘TEST// for ↘SOdium ion//if YOU have ↘SOdium ion// you will get BIG yellow ↘Orange//

An examination of the context in which rising tones did appear in this group of presentations showed that ITAs marked common ground infrequently and only as it applied to the immediate physical context. This is illustrated in Example 4 in which the Chinese ITA uses rising tones as he points to a bottle and glass plate that he is holding up for the students:

Example 4 Rising tone choices to mark immediate physical context (Pickering, 2001: 248)

> //you put Into the ↗JAR// this is ↗BOTtle// THIS your ↘PLATE// HERE your STARTing ↗LINE//

In addition to very little recognition of actual common ground with their students, the ITAs also did not use the intonation system to *project* a common understanding. For example, there were only eight solidarity or interactive markers found the ITA presentations as compared to 26 across the NS TA presentations.

Clarifying information structure: The role of intonational cues in boundary recognition

The speech stream is divided into a series of utterances that form tone units and these, in turn, form part of larger phonological units or intonational paragraphs that are analogous to written paragraph structures. Both Coulthard and Montgomery (1981) and Shaw (1994) describe sections of teaching discourse that include verbal and non-verbal boundary markers that mark the opening and closing of the unit; for example, lexical phrases such as 'for the first part', micro makers such as 'ok', and topic length pauses; however, the possible role of intonational cues had not been consistently applied in these analyses.

Brazil's model allows for this investigation and phonological paragraphs, or paratones, are termed pitch sequences (PSs) within this framework. Prominent phonetic boundary cues for pitch sequences, include a high key onset with increased volume and rate, and a low termination close often accompanied by a drop in volume and narrowing of the pitch range. In addition to the boundary criteria, there is typically a gradual descent in pitch across the unit.

Pickering (1999, 2004), examined the role of phonological paragraphing in NS TA and ITA discourse. The analytical approach begins with Gumperz's contention that intonation structure will be systematically connected to other layers of the discourse structure in order to create informational transparency. In other words, when multiple discourse cues are co-extensive, this is seen as evidence of the speaker's intention to organize the discourse for the benefit of the hearer by providing a constellation of cues at the different levels of discourse structure. In an analysis of six NS TA lab presentations in chemistry, physics and mathematics (Pickering, 2004), pitch sequence structure was readily identifiable, and an example is shown in Example 5.

Example 5 Phonological paragraphing in a chemistry lab presentation by a NS TA

> ///⇑Ok for TLC you're gonna need →SEveral// ⇒pieces of ↘eQUIPment// ⇑ok ↘FIRST OFF// ⇒you're gonna →need one of your two hundred and fifty milliliter →beakers// ⇒and one of your ↘WATCH GLASSES// ⇒ok this is gonna be your developing →chamber for the// ⇒ ↘ TLC// ⇓you're gonna make you OWN little developing ↘CHAMbers/// [1.14 second pause]

This extract opens with a high key on 'TLC' (thin layer chromatography) and closes with a low termination and falling tone on 'chambers.' Throughout the unit, the pitch height (shown in key and termination choices) steadily drops from high to mid, and finally, low. These intonation cues coincide with an initial lexical boundary marker 'ok,' a final topic length pause of over one second, and a unified topic, i.e. the creation of a developing chamber.

A second example is shown in Table 2.1. In this case, the PS boundaries align with visual cues. As the NS TA speaks, at each major topic juncture he adds real-time board-work. Each time he begins a new topic and turns to the board to write these notes, he simultaneously marks these junctures as new intonational paragraphs. Thus, he uses the interaction between sequence chain (SC) boundaries, topic-based units and real-time board work to multiply mark these informational chunks.

Table 2.1 Visual cues corresponding with SC structure in a NS TA presentation (adapted from Pickering, 2004: 29)

Opening tone unit of SC	Boardwork
//// ⇑But FOR our unKNOWN we HAVE SEven ions we have to TEST for//...	Na+ , K+ , Nh4+ , OH-, NO3-, Cl-, HsO4-
////⇑One of the FIRST things that we did was a FLAME test//...	1. Flame test
////⇑the SEcond set of TESTS we did was//that cobaltiNItrate TEST//...	2. Colbaltnitrate test

Turning to the ITA presentations, although it was possible to identify some phonological paragraphing, boundaries marked by intonational cues frequently did not coincide with cues at co-occurring levels of the discourse structure, and internal disruption to these units due to pauses and unexpected prominences, rendered them far less effective. Following Brown *et al.* (1980: 56), pauses in the discourse of 0.8 seconds or longer were identified as topic pauses that 'clearly coincide with major semantic breaks.' These only occurred at PS boundaries in the NS TA presentations; however, in the ITA presentations, possible PS structures were consistently disrupted by these long, erratic pauses. An example of unit disruption is given below from an ITA physics presentation:

Example 6 Unit disruption in an ITA physics presentation

> //// ⇑one <u>CASE</u> is that YOU ARE// **[1.0]** //⇑BAsically you ALways have the <u>CEN</u>ter// **[0.82]** //⇒ME ter stick <u>CEN</u>ter// **[0.92]** //⇓to BE <u>THE</u>// **[0.2]**// ⇓ to BE <u>THE</u>// **[0.53]** //the// **[0.53]** ⇒the pivot <u>POINT</u> but er//...

Topic length pauses are marked in bold and clearly do not indicate major structural or semantic breaks. This finding is consistent with previous research in NNS discourse production, and in ITA discourse specifically, Rounds (1987: 653) notes that these empty silences during mathematics classroom presentations indicated a 'dysfunction in the machinery' on which students commented unfavorably:

> You can tell that he's having trouble communicating with the class, you know, he has to pause and get his thoughts together in the middle of his sentence and a lot of times (.) I don't know (.) it just doesn't, he just doesn't hold your attention like I think a good TA should or a good teacher or a professor or anything.

The transcription in Example 6 also shows truncated tone units with multiple prominences (e.g. //⇓ to BE <u>THE</u>// [0.2]// ⇓ to BE <u>THE</u>//). This further obscures the information structure as it makes it difficult for the hearer(s) to focus on the linguistically significant prominences, i.e. the onset and tonic syllable. This pattern of multiple prominences in shortened units is even more striking in an analysis of laboratory presentations in engineering given by Indian English (IE) speaking ITAs (Pickering, 1999). As shown in Example 7, in addition to these issues, IE speakers often 'jumped' between pitch levels within the space of one or two syllables:

Example 7 Orthographic and Prosodic transcription of IE speaker

   (a) **ITA:**   //and the angle is// ten point// five
   (b) **ITA:**   //⇨ and the ⇩ANgle ⇧<u>IS</u> // ⇩TEN ⇧ <u>POINT</u>// ⇩ <u>FIVE</u> //

These pitch leaps across a given speaker's range interfered with the analysis of all phonological units including tone units and pitch sequences. In tone units specifically, the low-high pitch pattern also occurred within words comprised of two or more syllables, which often also made tonal value (i.e. identification of linguistically significant falls or rises) difficult to assess. Unlike American English, in which prominence is typically indicated by an increase in pitch and volume on the stressed syllable, IE speakers frequently realized stressed syllables with a dip in pitch and no reliable increase in amplitude (Pickering & Wiltshire, 2000). The low-high pattern is not easily interpreted by North American hearers, and their perception of which syllable receives lexical stress often shifts as shown in Table 2.2 below:

Table 2.2 Examples of North American hearings of IE word stress (Pickering & Wiltshire, 2000: 181)

Example word	Indian English speaker says...	North American NS hears...
defense	DEfense	difference
rendered	renDERED	endured
impedance	IMpedance	impudence

Taken as a whole, this research shows that prosodic cues play a critical role in reinforcing boundary marking in spoken classroom discourse. In conjunction with lexico-grammatical and non-verbal cues, they are used by the speaker to organize the discourse into a series of structural units that clarify information structure for the hearer. Thus, they affect the hearers' perceptions of both the internal cohesion and overall coherence of the discourse structure.

Of course, intonation is only one of the ways in which teachers use linguistic cues to routinely perform informational functions in discourse, and it is important to recognize that comprehensibility for the hearer lies in the redundancy that such a multiple cueing system allows (Wright *et al.*, 1997). If cues are consistently either absent or in conflict with other cues in the system, this will violate listener expectation and require them to make continual adjustments to their understanding of the text and their predictions as to what will follow which can result in 'listener irritation' (Eisenstein, 1983), a dual response to NNS discourse consisting of a negative cognitive reaction to reduced comprehensibility, and a negative emotional reaction due to annoyance and distraction.

It is argued here that prosodic features of discourse contribute to the perception of a speaker's discourse as both informationally relevant and positively oriented toward the hearer in equal measure with other linguistic and non-linguistic resources. In the following section, they are fully integrated into a model that brings together both the insights from the work discussed in earlier sections and current understandings of L2 learning within a transdisciplinary framework.

The Frontier

Over the past 30 years, we have moved away from the discipline-specific ESP frameworks that characterized many early ITA training programs, and we have eschewed oversimplified models that appear to suggest that ITAs should be 'pale imitations' of their NS TA colleagues. In this regard, the Florida program was prescient. The focus was not on transforming ITAs into native speakers, but on using pragmatic feedback at multiple levels of the discourse to understand how language behaviors were being interpreted by both ITAs and undergraduate students in this specific cross-cultural context. As such, this work is consistent with the most recent approaches in the field of SLA in which L2 learning is conceived of as multilayered and taking 'all available semiotic resources' including 'linguistic, prosodic, interactional, nonverbal, graphic, pictorial, auditory and artifactual resources' (Douglas Fir Group, 2016: 24).

In this spirit, Pickering (2013/2014) proposed a model of conversational involvement as a theoretical foundation for how we might continue to redefine our approach to the ITA context. The initial framework outlined here prioritizes features used by interlocutors to collaborate in everyday interaction and proposes that classroom discourse can be fundamentally reconfigured as a form of conversation. This acknowledges its essence as a co-operative achievement between at least two participants that involves language in communication, and the relationship between linguistic features and situational context (Tsui, 1994). Accordingly, the basic principles of interaction underlying conversational discourse can be brought to the forefront of our practice in ITA preparation.

The current iteration of the model, shown in Figure 2.1, comprises three discourse principles and two learning principles that describe the ways in which classroom discourse can be seen to reflect real-world interaction and how that can be transmitted. As the skills that would be developed are non-domain- and register-specific, they could be applied in whatever workplace environment second language speakers may find themselves.

The first assumption is that the three-part exchange, ubiquitous in the classroom, should be considered the 'natural basic unit of conversation' as opposed to two part adjacency pairs (Tsui, 1994). Tsui (1994: 42) argues that the third follow-up move is always used in communication to signal

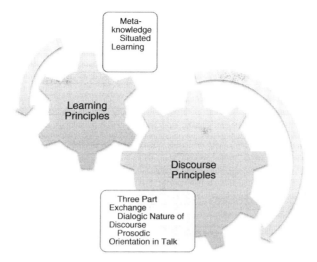

Figure 2.1 Model of conversational involvement (Pickering, 2014)

some kind of verbal or non-verbal acknowledgment and is a crucial part of the perceived success of an interaction:

> It may be too strong a statement to say that when the follow-up more does not occur, its non-occurrence is noticeable and noticed in the way the absence of a second pair part is, but it is certainly true that when it does not occur, it is often perceived by participants to be deliberately withheld for social or strategic reasons.

Of course, this does not prescribe the specific nature of an IRF exchange between a dominant (teacher) and non-dominant (student) participant. Outside of this context, feedback may fulfill a range of functions other than evaluation. The crucial point is the absence of a follow-up, be it only a nod or a smile, maybe felt as a deliberate withholding.

This conceptualization of the basic building block of successful interaction clearly aligns classroom discourse with conversational discourse and leads directly to the second assumption, which is the fundamentally dialogic nature of classroom discourse. A distinction is often made between classroom and conversational discourse with regard to their goals as primarily transactional (information-giving) in the case of classroom discourse and primarily interactional (rapport-building) in conversational discourse. This dichotomy does not adequately describe what happens in the moment-by-moment interaction that typifies the classroom context; rather, close inspection of this language event supports a view of classroom discourse as an ongoing negotiation between teachers and their students regardless of whether the hearer(s) verbally respond to the message or not. Thus, teaching discourse becomes a systematic variant of more overtly dialogic discourse events and restructures the role of the teacher as a co-participant.

The third assumption draws from a focus on prosodic orientation in talk. As we demonstrated in previous sections, prosodic features are used consistently in successful interaction to minimize the gap between conversational interlocutors both with regard to information and rapport-building. Szczepek Reed (2006) describes this usage as 'prosodic matching' – a process in which participants match their prosodic immediacy behaviors such as pitch register, speech rate, rhythm or volume to those of their interlocutors in order to signal their positive orientation. This is uniquely important in face-to-face interaction as it establishes shared participation; conversely, a lack of orientation or 'prosodic mismatching' can signal dissonance or the perceived absence of shared understanding.

The inclusion of the first learning principle, metaknowledge, derives from the nature of prosodic marking. Prosodic features are largely tacit and as a rule, participants are unaware of the crucial role that they play in interaction. This is particularly true for ITAs, who have come from outside the particular sociocultural community of the institution within which they find themselves (Douglas Fir Group, 2016). By metaknowledge, I mean 'knowing something about what you already know or are learning.' For example, ITAs will not be unaware of the importance of the creation of a positive effect in the classroom. They have had years of experience in that environment. However, they do not necessarily know what their students expect in a US STEM laboratory presentation as opposed to a lecture class, and even if they do, they do not necessarily know how to meet that expectation linguistically. For example, they may misunderstand how a more informal pedagogical setting is created. In the case of laboratory work, they may view this kind of teaching activity as requiring less preparation time than they would give to a lecture class. In fact, these presentations, often comprising a great deal of content in a limited amount of time, can be quite complex. In addition, they may be the students' only source of that particular set of information thus they are high stakes interactions between ITAs and their students.

Finally, we consider the method of transmission. ITAs are both teachers and students in their workplace; as such, they are in a unique position to observe the multiple roles that they and those around them take on within the institution. This opens up the opportunity for informal or situated learning as opposed to traditional models of formal, highly structured classroom-based learning. Situated learning emphasizes the dynamics of everyday interaction, focuses on the interactive relationship between co-workers and prioritizes social practices of the workplace (Lave & Wenger, 1991). As a learning mode, it fits together particularly well with the discourse principles that we have outlined above. In order to become present to situated learning, learners are encouraged to observe and challenge their experiences in the workplace and then reflect upon them. Crucially, the approach is self-directed and occurs when learners 'continually scan their environment' in order to reflect on their actions (Marsick & Volpe, 1999: 1). Perhaps most importantly, it recognizes ITAs as stakeholders in their own experience as language learners in the workplace and allows them greater scope for agency.

Conclusion

This chapter has taken a primarily chronological approach to an overview of how intonation has been addressed in ITA practice over the past thirty years. From an early focus on intonation as one pronunciation feature to be addressed as part of a basic linguistic competence, it has been re-examined most recently as one of an assemblage of interactional resources (Looney, 2015) that ITAs can develop as part of what Canagarajah (2013: 12) has referred to as 'competence for translingual communication.' It is important, however, to strike one note of caution. ITAs are in a unique position as compared to other skilled transnational workers as they do not typically carry the prestige or 'social capital' of these professionals. In Canaragarajah's (2013: 7) study of skilled migrants, one physician from Zimbabwe states:

> I think because it is such a professional job, people are prepared to overlook the language issue…I think medicine and other technically demanding fields don't really need someone to be fluent in English, as long as they can make a diagnosis that is all that matters. It's more like football, Ronaldo didn't speak a word of English, neither does Messi, but they are technically very good at it.

ITAs may not have this advantage. They typically fall along a continuum in terms of experience with teaching and expertise, thus some will be neither qualified teachers nor, as yet, experts in their fields. Because of this, it is important that we do not expect either them or their students to comfortably overcome the many barriers that this particular high-stakes environment brings with it by 'learning in the wild.'[1] However, it is possible to reimagine a pedagogical approach that both moves beyond native speaker competence and invests more heavily in an individual's translingual resources.

Note

(1) Cited in Canagarajah (2013) from 2010. Learning in the wild. *Nature*, 813–814. http://www.nature.com/nature.

References

Anderson-Hsieh, J. (1990) Teaching suprasegmentals to international teaching assistants using field-specific materials. *English for Specific Purposes* 9, 195–214.
Bailey, K.M. (1983) Foreign teaching assistants at U.S. universities: Problems in interaction and communication. *TESOL Quarterly* 17 (2), 308–310.

Bailey, K.M. (1984) The 'foreign TA problem.' In K.M. Bailey, F. Pialorsi and J. Zukowski-Faust (eds) *Foreign Teaching Assistants in U.S. Universities* (pp. 3–15). Washington D.C.: National Association for Foreign Student Affairs.

Brazil, D. (1985) *The Communicative Value of Intonation in English.* Birmingham UK: University of Birmingham, English Language Research.

Brazil, D. (1997) *The Communicative Value of Intonation in English.* Cambridge: Cambridge University Press.

Brazil, D., Coulthard, M. and Johns, C. (1980) *Discourse Intonation and Language Teaching.* London: Longman.

Brown, G., Currie, K. and Kenworthy, J. (1980) *Questions of Intonation.* London: Croom-Helm.

Byrd, P. and Constantinides, J.C. (1992) The language of teaching mathematics: Implications for training ITAs. *TESOL Quarterly* 26 (1), 163–167.

Canagarajah, S. (2103) Skilled migration and development: Portable communicative resources for transnational work. *Multilingual Education* 3, 8. http://www.multilingualeducation.com/content/3/1/8

Cheng, W., Greaves, C. and Warren, M. (2008) *A Corpus-driven Study of Discourse Intonation The Hong Kong Corpus of Spoken English (prosodic).* Amsterdam: John Benjamins.

Coulthard, M. and Montgomery, M. (eds) (1981) *Studies in Discourse Analysis.* London: Thomas Litho Press.

Couper-Kuhlen, E. (1986) *An Introduction to English Prosody.* Tubingen: Max Niemeyer-Verlag.

Douglas, D. and Myers, C. (1989) TAs on TV: Demonstrating communication strategies for international teaching assistants. *English for Specific Purposes* 8, 169–179.

Douglas Fir Group (2016) A transdisiciplinary framework for SLA in a multilingual world. *The Modern Language Journal* 100, 19–47.

Eisenstein, M. (1983) Native reactions to nonnative speech: A review of empirical research. *Studies in Second Language Acquisition* 5, 160–176.

Gumperz, J.J. (1982) *Discourse Strategies.* Cambridge University Press.

Hewings, M. (1995) Tone choice in the English intonation of nonnative speakers. *International Review of Applied Linguistics* 33, 251–265.

Hinofotis, F. and Bailey, K. (1980) American undergraduates' reactions to the communication skills of foreign teaching assistants. In J. Fisher, M. Clarke and J. Schachter (eds) *On TESOL '80: Building Bridges* (pp. 120–136). Washington, DC: TESOL.

Jacobson, W. (1986) An assessment of the communicative needs of nonnative speakers of English in an undergraduate physics lab. *English for Specific Purposes* 5, 173–187.

Koester, A. (1990) The intonation of agreeing and disagreeing in English and German. In M. Hewings (ed.) *Papers in Discourse Intonation* (pp. 83–101). Birmingham: University of Birmingham: English language research.

Lave, J. and Wenger, E. (1991) *Situated Learning: Legitimate Peripheral Participation.* Cambridge University Press.

Looney, S.D. (2015) Interaction and discourse markers in the ITA-led physics laboratory. In G. Gorsuch (ed.) *Talking Matters: Research on Talk and Communication of International Teaching Assistants* (pp. 75–104). Oklahoma: New Forums Press.

Marsick, V.J. and Volpe. M. (1999) The nature and need for informal learning. *Advances in Developing Human Resources* 1, 1–9.

Myers, C.L. (1994) Question-based discourse in science labs: Issues for ITAs. In C. Madden and C.L. Myers (eds) *Discourse and Performance of International Teaching Assistants* (pp. 83–103). Alexandria, VA: TESOL Inc.

Myers, S., Zhong, M. and Guan, S. (1998) Instructor immediacy in the Chinese college classroom. *Communication Studies* 49 (3), 240–254.

Pandey, P.K. (1994) On a description of the phonology of Indian English. In R.K. Agnihotri and A.L. Khanna (eds) *Second Language Acquisition: Socio-cultural and Linguistic Aspects of English in India: Research in Applied Linguistics* (pp. 198–207). Delhi: Sage.

Pickering, L. (2014) Revisiting practice: A model of conversational involvement for the ITA context. *ITA/AL Interest Section Newsletter* 16–19.

Pickering, L. (2013) Revisiting practice: A model of conversational involvement for the ITA context. Invited paper for the ITA Academic Session at the TESOL 2013 Annual Convention, March 21, Dallas TX.

Pickering, L. (2001) The role of tone choice in improving ITA communication in the classroom. *TESOL Quarterly* 35, 233–255.

Pickering, L. (2004) The structure and function of intonational paragraphs in native and nonnative instructional discourse. *English for Specific Purposes* 23, 19–43.

Pickering, L. (1999) An analysis of prosodic systems in the classroom discourse of native speaker and nonnative speaker teaching assistants. Unpublished Dissertation. University of Florida, Gainesville, FL.

Pickering, L. and Wiltshire, C. (2000) Pitch accent in Indian English TAs' teaching discourse. *World Englishes* 19, 173–183.

Pierrehumbert, J. and Hirschberg, J. (1990) The meaning of intonational contours in English. In P. Cohen, J. Morgan and M. Pollack (eds) *Intentions in Communication* (pp. 271–311). Cambridge, MA: MIT Press.

Pirt, G. (1990) Discourse intonation problems for nonnative speakers. In M. Hewings (ed.) *Papers in Discourse Intonation* (pp. 145–155). Birmingham, England: University of Birmingham, English Language Research.

Rounds, P.L. (1987) Multifunctional personal pronoun use in an educational setting. *English for Specific Purposes* 6 (1), 13–29.

Shaw, P.A. (1994) Discourse competence in a framework for ITA training. In C. Madden and C. Myers (eds) *Discourse and Performance of International Teaching Assistants* (pp. 27–51). Alexandria, VA: TESOL.

Smith, R. (1992) Crossing pedagogical oceans: International teaching assistants in U.S. undergraduate education. *ASHE-ERIC Higher Education Report, No. 8.* Washington D.C. Association for the study of higher education.

Stevens, S. (1989) A 'dramatic' approach to improving the intelligibility of ITAs. *English for Specific Purposes* 8, 181–194.

Szczepek Reed, B. (2006) *Prosodic Orientation in English Conversation.* New York: Palgrave Macmillan.

Tapper, G., Drzazga, G., Mendoza, M. and Grill, J. (2018) Discourse management strategies revisited: Building on Tyler's early insights regarding international teaching assistant comprehensibility. In L. Pickering and V. Evans (eds) *Language Learning, Discourse and Cognition: Studies in the Tradition of Andrea Tyler* (pp. 45–73). John Benjamins.

Tsui, A.B.M. (1994) *English Conversation.* Oxford University Press.

Tyler, A. (1992) Discourse structure and the perception of incoherence in international teaching assistants' spoken discourse. *TESOL Quarterly* 26 (4), 713–729.

Tyler, A.E., Jefferies, A.A. and Davies, C.E. (1988) The effect of discourse structuring devices on listener perceptions of coherence in non-native university teacher's spoken discourse. *World Englishes* 7 (2), 101–110.

Wennerstrom, A. (1991) *Techniques for Teachers: A Guide for Nonnative Speakers of English.* Ann Arbor, MI: University of Michigan Press.

Wennerstrom, A. (1994) Intonational meaning in English discourse. *Applied Linguistics* 15, 399–421.

Wennerstrom, A. (1997) Discourse intonation and second language acquisition: Three genre based studies. Unpublished doctoral dissertation, University of Washington, Seattle.

Wennerstrom, A. (1998) Intonation as cohesion in academic discourse: A study of Chinese speakers of English. *Studies in Second Language Acquisition* 20, 1–25.

Wright, R., Frisch, S. and Pisoni, D. (1997) *Research on Spoken Language Processing* (Progress Report No. 21). Bloomington: Indiana University, Speech Research Laboratory.

Appendix: Transcription symbols

/// ///	Paratone boundaries
// //	Tone Unit boundaries
CAPS	Prominence
UNDERLINE	Tonic syllable
[ ]	Pause lengths in ms

High key	⇑
Mid key	⇒
Low key	⇓
Rising tones	↗ (r+); ↘↗ (r)
Falling tones	↘ (p); ↗↘ (p+)
Level tone	→ (o)

3 Co-operative Action – Addressing Misunderstanding and Displaying Uncertainty in a University Physics Lab

Stephen Daniel Looney

This chapter contributes to our understanding of international teaching assistant (ITA)–undergraduate interaction by looking in micro-analytic detail at recurrent sequences of embodied actions and practices in a university physics lab. The analysis will unpack sequences of co-operative actions (Goodwin, 2013) through which participants demonstrate and address misunderstanding. The analysis shows how sequences of teaching and learning are built by participants who decompose, reuse and transform resources such as lexis or gesture from prior turns as they negotiate understanding of the lab. The findings demonstrate the necessity for studies of micro-level interactions in various settings and collaboration between language experts, content experts and students in ITA pedagogy.

Introduction

Skillful teaching in the university demands that instructors have control of complex interactional repertoires (Hall, 2018; Rymes, 2014) composed of resources such as but not limited to lexis, morphosyntax, prosody, gesture and objects. It is not enough for university-level instructors, including ITAs, to have comprehensible pronunciation. They must also be able to use linguistic and non-linguistic resources to structure their talk and guide the instructional project. While prior ITA research has shown us the significance of ITA talk, the focus has been almost exclusively on the lexical, syntactic and prosodic forms of utterances, while ignoring the non-verbal and sequential aspects of turns at talk. Oftentimes, the focus has been on creating counts of linguistic features and taxonomies that provide a bird's eye view of language use but miss the finer details of how participants accomplish their everyday worlds.

This chapter contributes to our understanding of ITA–undergraduate interaction by looking in micro-analytic detail at recurrent sequences of embodied actions and practices in a university physics lab. The analysis will unpack sequences of co-operative actions (Goodwin, 2013) through which participants demonstrate and address misunderstanding. The analysis shows how sequences of teaching and learning are built by participants who decompose, reuse and transform resources such as lexis or gesture from prior turns as they negotiate understanding of the lab. The findings demonstrate the necessity for studies of micro-level interactions in various settings and collaboration between language experts, content experts and students in ITA pedagogy.

Science Lab Interaction

While leading science, technology, engineering and mathematics (STEM) labs is one of the most common assignments for ITAs, studies on laboratory contexts are sparse (Looney, 2015; Myers, 1994; Singer *et al.*, 2012; Tapper, 1994). Like other ITA research on language use and social interaction, the main concerns of research on lab settings has been the management of information and affect. The science lab has been noted to be a unique classroom context in that, as opposed to lecture and recitations in which the teacher leads the discourse and student contributions are rare, science lab discourse is question-based (Myers, 1994). In other words, student questions drive most lab interactions. Student questions are imprecise and difficult for ITAs to address because of the problem-solving nature of lab discourse and an incorrect perception of shared context. Students initiate interactions with ITAs because they have some sort of misunderstanding. Student questions typically deal with 'the mechanics of the lab' and not '*why* the experiment is set up the way it is, *how* the experiment validates their theoretical knowledge of the discipline, or *what* the process of the experiment will teach them' (Myers, 1994: 91). At the same time, student questions are composed of imprecise language, e.g. pronouns with no clear antecedent. These features create ambiguous conditions that could be challenging for ITAs to navigate (Myers, 1994).

In addition to the challenges involved in deciphering student questions, ITAs must be able to deliver information and guide interaction in a manner that meets US undergraduate expectations. The underlying assumption is that US undergraduates prefer instruction in which illocutionary force is excerpted less directly, for example through questions instead of imperatives (Myers, 1994; Tapper, 1994). Questions are seen as particularly important in both the management of information, i.e. course content, and affect in the university classroom. ITA questions can improve classroom rapport by guiding student action and thinking instead of using imperatives which seem hierarchical and face threatening (Tapper, 1994). Teacher questions in science labs are of two types Myers (1994): echoic and epistemic (Kearsley, 1976; Long & Sato, 1983). Echoic questions are clarification requests, comprehension checks and confirmation checks. This type of question helps teachers negotiate meaning or understanding and help teachers 'communicate more effectively with students' (Myers, 1994: 97). Epistemic questions are questions that check students' comprehension and probe their thinking (Myers, 1994: 97). Evaluative questions, one type of epistemic question, have been widely covered in the classroom Conversation Analysis (CA) and discourse studies under the moniker 'display questions' (Lee, 2006; Long & Sato, 1983). In display questions, teachers ask questions to which they know the answers. Most ITAs use few to no display questions (Myers, 1994) or questions as directives (Tapper, 1994). This variation exists not only between ITAs and TAs but also among ITAs (Myers, 1994).

Questions are not the only linguistic resources that teachers and students use to structure information during classroom interactions. Discourse markers, a feature widely associated with lecturing (Liao, 2009; Looney et al., 2017; Tyler, 1992; Williams, 1992), have been the focus of one laboratory study. Looney (2015) analyzes how undergraduates and an ITA use the lexical discourse markers okay and so as transitions and as prefaces to turns in which they display and demonstrate understanding. Okay is used by students to display understanding, but when okay is followed by so, the collocation precedes a demonstration of understanding. When a speaker displays understanding, he or she merely confirms understanding with a lexical item such as 'okay' or 'yes,' but a demonstration of understanding typically involves the use of phrasal and/or clausal constructions in which speakers make statements about what they know or think. Being able to recognize such constructions and what they are doing is important for lab instructors who must monitor and adjust to students' sense-making practices in situ.

While findings have advanced our understanding of ITA and student language use in the university science lab, two critiques must be levied. First, ITA studies of pedagogical interaction have maintained a logocentric approach to language use and social interaction. With the exception of Pickering (2001, 2004) and Tyler (1992), who analyze prosodic patterns, and Pickering (2004), who analyzes ITAs writing on the chalkboard, only lexis and grammar are taken into consideration. This chapter suggests that non-verbal, or embodied, resources have been ignored at our peril and that in fact separating the linguistic from the non-linguistic is a counterproductive bifurcation. Considering only lexis and grammar leaves us with an incomplete view of classroom interaction.

Additionally, studies have ignored sequences of interaction and instead analyzed lectures or individual turns at talk. While lecturing is undoubtedly a common teaching task, it is not the only, or even the primary, task of many ITAs who lead labs or office hours. In labs and office hours, the interactional repertoires (Hall, 2018; Rymes, 2014) for managing turns and in the moment contingencies that come from interacting with students in pairs or small groups are potentially different than those for giving a lecture. At the same time, analyzing individual turns at talk only gives us a partial view of the interactional work ITAs and undergraduates do much like analyzing only language and not also non-verbal resources. The following section begins rectifying these two oversights by presenting a conversation analytic approach to ITA research in the physics lab.

Classroom CA and Co-operative Action

Conversation Analysis (CA) views teaching (and learning) as specialized and co-constructed interactional work that involves the sequential use of linguistic and non-linguistic resources such as facial expression, gaze, gesture and laughter. Teachers and students draw on various embodied resources (Goodwin, 2000) such as gaze to manage turn taking and allocation (Mortensen, 2008, 2009; Mortensen & Hazel, 2011), specific lexical and syntactic turn designs to initiate initiation-response-follow up (IRF) sequences (Koshik, 2002; Lee, 2006; see Pickering, this volume for a definition of IRF) and prosody as part of evaluations of student responses (Hellermann, 2003). These resources do not act alone but as part of constellations of resources that make up the actions and practices of everyday classroom life. For instance, when a teacher allocates a turn, he or she not only calls a student's name but also establishes mutual gaze with the student before saying anything and gestures toward the student (Mortensen, 2008; Sert, 2019). This suggests that in fact visual, not vocal, resources do the work of initiating turn allocation sequences. It also helps us see the cooperative nature of classroom interaction: teachers choose willing participants, i.e. those who establish mutual gaze with the teacher.

In addition to being embodied and cooperative, the actions that make up classroom interaction are co-operative. Co-operative actions are 'built by performing systematic operations on a substrate' (Goodwin, 2013: 8). In simplistic terms, yet terms that are adequate for our purposes, the substrate is composed of the embodied resources that made up prior turns. Thus, the substrate is 'an immediately present semiotic landscape with quite diverse resources that has been given its current shape through the transformative sequences of action that culminate, at this moment, in the current action' (Goodwin, 2013: 11). From this perspective, 'language structure and social interaction are deeply intertwined' (Goodwin, 2018: 9). Co-operative action is integral to the development of professional vision and the creation of skilled and competent members of communities, i.e. teaching and learning (Goodwin, 2018). It is by building on the utterances of each other that teachers and students do teaching and learning by presenting and recalibrating their understanding or misunderstanding. Co-operative actions are built in part through the decomposition and reuse of materials with transformation (Goodwin, 2013, 2018).

The decomposition and reuse of materials with transformation involves the use of resources that have been used in a prior turn. In the IRF below, we see that the teacher, Carlos (CAR), poses a close-ended either/ or question and that the student reuses one of the choices Carlos presented.

Excerpt 1 Uh less relaxed

```
45.      CAR:   so it will be more relaxed?
46.             or less relaxed.
47.  →   LIN:   u:::::h less relaxed
48.      CAR:   huh?
```

In lines 45–46, Carlos poses a close-ended question. In line 47, Lindsey reuses one of the options Carlos provided but prefaced it with an extended *uh* displaying uncertainty. By reusing the lexis provided by Carlos, Lindsey provides a response that aligns (Stivers, 2008; Stivers *et al.*, 2011a) with the action projected by Carlos' question but the transformation she makes, i.e. adding an extended *uh*, displays her uncertainty about the accuracy of her response. This is a quite basic example of co-operative action, but this chapter's analysis will show in greater complexity how a teacher and three students co-operatively build an extended sequence of action in which they negotiate a common misunderstanding in the physics lab. This chapter argues that co-operative action is an essential practice for negotiating misunderstanding in the university physics lab.

Data and Methods

The data presented in this chapter are part of the Corpus of English for Academic and Professional Purposes (CEAPP, 2014). The extended sequence of interaction comes from a 200-level university physics lab specifically for non-physics majors led by a multilingual from Puerto Rico. The participants are Carlos (the TA) and three undergraduate students (Alison, Tracy and Lindsey). The lab they are completing investigates the optics of the human eye. In the lab, students shine a light into an apparatus that serves as a model of a human eye. Using different lenses and a diaphragm which simulates a contracted pupil, students make observations about how the different conditions, e.g. lens thickness, lens curvature and pupil size, affect a pattern of light that is projected on the rear of the experimental apparatus which simulates the retina. One of the questions in the lab manual is a challenge for several lab groups across two lab sections. The question is presented in Frame 1.

Frame 1 Question eight

> **Q8.** Given that your eyes experience less strain when the ciliary muscles
> are relaxed, would it be better for your eyes to read in a brightly lit room
> or in a dimly lit room? Explain your answer in terms of what you learned
> while answering the previous questions.

The answer to question eight is that reading in a brightly lit room is better
for your eyes because in bright conditions the pupil contracts and does
some of the work focusing images thus allowing the lens to remain in a
relaxed position.

This chapter's analysis was conducted in two phases. First, the video was
transcribed according to CA conventions (Jefferson, 2004; Kunitz, 2018, see
Appendix). Secondly, the transcript and video were subjected to iterative
line-by-line analyses of sequence and turn design. The micro-analysis of science lab interaction presented here adds to the ITA discussion by providing
a methodology intent on providing an *emic* perspective of how ITAs and
undergraduates use conversational, linguistic and non-linguistic, resources
to construct meaning in the science lab classroom. In other words, the analysis will focus on what participants do and orient to instead of what participants should theoretically do. The analysis will demonstrate that teaching,
learning and interaction are socially distributed and inextricable from one
another. It is through 'inhabit[ing] each other's actions' (Goodwin, 2013: 15)
that teaching and learning are accomplished, and one way that teachers and
students inhabit each other's actions is through co-operative action.

Analysis

This chapter's analysis is broken into two sections. The first focuses
on the embodied nature of co-operative classroom action, and the second
unpacks the co-operative accomplishment of displaying uncertainty and
addressing misunderstanding. The data will be presented in excerpts and
figures. There are seven excerpts, each presented in conventional CA fash-
ion with arrows in the second column indicating turns of interest. All of
the excerpts come from the same short interaction and are presented in
temporally sequential order. In addition to the excerpts, there are seven
figures. The figures break down specific parts of excerpts that illuminate
co-operative action. The figures with white backgrounds focus on lexico-
syntactic features in co-operative action. The figures with black backgrounds focus on the co-operative use of gesture in actions aimed at
addressing misunderstanding.

The embodied nature of co-operative classroom action

In the following excerpts, the students, Alison (ALI), Tracy (TRA)
and Lindsey (LIN), are struggling with a question asking whether there is

more or less strain on the eye when reading in a brightly lit room. The turns Alison produces are characteristic of other student-initiated interactions throughout the data set.

Excerpt 2 Seven is the more relaxed one

```
1.        ALI:    okay. we have a question about number eight.
2.        CAR:    number eight.
3.        ALI:    yeah. we just need you to like help us.
4.        CAR:    °there's more paper towels now there,°
5.                [°I opened that thing up,°
6.        TRA:    [$oh? okay.$
7.                (1.0)
8.   →    CAR:    +◉yeah.◉ so what,
```

```
9.   →    ALI:    +so we know that like seven. is the more
```

```
10.  →    ALI:    {relaxed one. but is [blurry
11.       CAR:                          [okay.
```

Excerpt 2 is preceded by a summons-answer sequence, i.e. Alison raising her hand and Carlos approaching the table (Schegloff, 2007). Perhaps no two turns in this analysis show so clearly the embodied nature of interaction. Alison raises her hand and turns her gaze to Carlos. Carlos sees Alison's hand raised and walks toward the table. As Carlos is still approaching the lab station, Alison uses the transitional discourse marker *okay* and states that she and her lab partners need help (lines 1–3). Her utterance identifies the part of the lab that the students are struggling with, 'number eight,' (line 3) and Carlos' verbatim repetition in line 2 displays understanding. Setting the initial parameters of the interaction by specifying the part of the lab worksheet with which the students are struggling is a common action in the data set. While Alison and Carlos are talking, the teacher and students begin arranging themselves physically around a work station.

After a side sequence in which Carlos directs the students' attention elsewhere (lines 4–6), Carlos says, 'yeah, so what' while leaning forward and resting his left forearm and right elbow on the lab station (line 8). The students are also positioned toward and gazing at the lab apparatus. This 'ecological huddle' (Goffman, 1964: 64) created by the participants

'publicly demonstrates through visible embodied practice that the participants are mutually oriented toward each other and frequently toward particular places, objects, and events in the surrounding environment'
(Streeck *et al.*, 2011: 2, citing Heath *et al.*, 2002). At this moment, all
participants are oriented to the lab station and Alison states what she and
her partners 'know' while pointing toward the front of the lab apparatus
(lines 9–10). The embodied features of Alison's turn are again ubiquitous
features found at the onset of student-initiated lab interactions. Student
regularly state what they know or have done and gesture and/or gaze
toward lab worksheets or the lab apparatus. In overlap with Alison's turn,
Carlos produces the continuer *okay* (line 11).

Excerpt 3 follows directly after Excerpt 2. In lines 12–13, Alison
states, 'when you make seven dimmer it's less blurry.' This statement
stands in contrast to the statement that she made in her prior turn, i.e.
seven is more relaxed but blurrier. Alison's demonstration of misunderstanding in line 12 leads to a repair sequence which significantly alters the
trajectory of the interaction.

Excerpt 3 When you make seven dimmer, it's less blurry

```
12.  →  ALI:   but then when you make seven dimmer. it's less
13.  →         blurry.
14.      CAR:   s- what do you mean. dimmer,
15.             (.)
16.  →         [like the. +this is dimmer,
```

```
17.      ALI:   [like with the
18.  →  TRA:   +(no like the)
```

```
19.  →  LIN:   it's darker
20.             (3.0)
21.  →  ALI:   like with the diaphragm th[ing.
22.      CAR:                            [uhuh.
```

The end of Alison's turn (lines 12–13) demonstrates misunderstanding
by contrasting what the speaker 'knows' with what she has observed. In
line 14, Carlos initiates repair (Schegloff *et al.*, 1977) and produces a candidate understanding while pointing with his right index finger toward the
rear of the experimental apparatus (line 16). In this case, the trouble
source is Alison's use of the word 'dimmer' (line 12). Carlos's repair and
candidate understanding reuse lexis and deictic gesture with transformation
from the trouble source, i.e. Alison's immediately prior utterance. Figure 3.1

is a graphic display of how Carlos builds his repair co-operatively using lexis from Alison's demonstration of misunderstanding.

In terms of lexis, Carlos's repair initiation (line 14) takes 'dimmer' from the prior turn and incorporates it into a wh- interrogative. The subsequent clause serves as a candidate repair and is spoken while pointing at the lab apparatus (line 16). Like the lexis Carlos reuses, he also transforms Alison's earlier gesture. His deictic gesture is much closer to the apparatus (line 16) than was hers (Excerpt 2, line 9) and is clearly pointing to the back of the apparatus while Alison's seems aimed at the front. In lines 18–21, Alison, Tracy and Lindsey collaboratively repair Carlos' candidate understanding. During the collaborative repair, Tracy says 'no' while pointing to the front of the apparatus (line 18), reusing a gesture with transformation from Carlos's prior turn (line 16). As Carlos's pointing was more precise than Alison's, Tracy's is even more precise than Carlos's. Figure 3.2 visually breaks down how Tracy reuses deictic gesture from Carlos's prior turn to do correction.

In addition to Tracy's contribution to the collaborative correction, Lindsey and Alison piece together the clause 'it's darker like with the diaphragm thing' (lines 19–21). In line 22, Carlos closes the repair sequence with a display of understanding, 'uhuh.' Interestingly, all the students self-select and act in overlap with each other and Carlos after his initiation of repair. Thus, we see that the understanding Alison demonstrated in her earlier turns was not hers alone but had been arrived at in concert with her lab partners. This excerpt clearly demonstrates the distributed and co-constructed nature of classroom interaction and cognition (Schegloff, 1991).

Carlos's other-initiated repair is an almost unnoticeable yet powerful action, shifting the polarity of the interaction. The extended sequence began with Alison producing the first pair parts. In contrast, Carlos steers the remaining interaction. It is also crucial to note that Carlos' other-initiated repair and the collaborative correction by the students were co-operative. In these two excerpts, we have seen the embodied

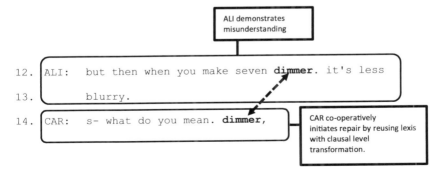

Figure 3.1 Co-operatively initiating repair

```
16.  CAR:    ⌈like the. +this is dimmer,
```
CAR's candidate repair includes deictic gesture.

```
17.  ALI:    ⌊like with the
18.  TRA:    +(no like the)
```
TRA uses deictic gesture with transformation to correct CAR's candidate repair.

```
19.  LIN:    it's darker
```

Figure 3.2 Co-operative correction: Reusing gesture with transformation

interactional work that Carlos, Alison, Tracy and Lindsey do to demonstrate and negotiate misunderstanding. This involves a number of pervasive embodied actions and sequences in the opening phases of physics lab interactions like the summons-answer sequence, explicit statements about what part of the lab students need help with, and gesture.

Co-operative turn design for displaying uncertainty and addressing misunderstanding

This section analyzes how Carlos addresses the misunderstanding he noticed and negotiated with the students in the first two excerpts. Excerpt 4 is the first of two attempts by Carlos to use IRFs to guide student thought. Each IRF is preceded by a tag question that establishes shared knowledge by reusing lexis from prior student turns before posing a question that initiates the IRF.

Excerpt 4 So it's less blurry right

```
23.  CAR:    so it's less blurry right?
24.  ALI:    yeah.
25.  CAR:    so it will be more relaxed?
26.          or less relaxed.
27.  LIN:    u:::::h less relaxed
28.  CAR:    huh?
29.  LIN:    °less relaxed°
```

In line 23, Carlos poses a tag question that recycles 'it's less blurry' from Alison's turn in Excerpt 3 (lines 12–13). The juxtaposition between

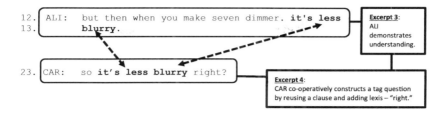

Figure 3.3 Co-operatively constructing a tag question

the language reused from student talk in the repair initiation (Excerpt 3) and that in the tag question (Excerpt 4) is striking. Unlike 'dimmer,' a trouble source in line 12, we will see that Alison's observation 'it's less blurry' is relevant to resolving the students' misunderstanding. The tag question Carlos asks in line 23 draws on Alison's prior turn design to establish shared knowledge before launching the IRF, and she provides the preferred affirmative continuer in line 24. Figure 3.3 is a visual depiction of how in Excerpt 4 (line 23) Carlos reuses a clause with transformation from Alison's turn in Excerpt 3 (lines 12–13), a move that incorporates relevant and accurate observations from Alison's demonstration of misunderstanding.

Carlos then launches an IRF. In lines 25, he gives the first option in a close ended question and in line 26 he gives the second option. While Carlos is speaking, his gaze is directed to his right, away from Lindsey who produces the response. Her response co-operatively displays uncertainty, reusing one of the options provided by Carlos and prefacing it with an extended 'uh' (line 27). In line 28, Carlos turns his gaze toward Lindsey and says 'huh' with rising intonation. She repeats her incorrect response with lower volume, once again displaying uncertainty (line 29). Figure 3.4 shows how Carlos reuses an adjective phrase (Excerpt 4, lines 25–26) with

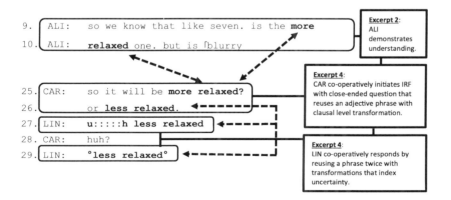

Figure 3.4 Co-operatively constructing an IRF

transformation from Alison's turn in lines 9 and 10 of Excerpt 2 to design the initiation turn of an IRF. It also depicts how in the response turn of the IRF Lindsey reuses one of the options provided in Carlos's initiation turn (lines 25–26) with modification to display uncertainty (lines 27 and 29).

In Excerpt 5, Carlos provides negative follow up (line 30) to Lindsey's response (Excerpt 4, line 29). He then formulates another tag question, again recycling both lexis and gesture from prior student turns, i.e. the collaborative repair (Excerpt 3, lines 17–21).

Excerpt 5 The diaphragm helps focusing this, right

```
30.      CAR:     we::::::::ll. >let's see< +the diaphragm f- helps focusing
```

```
31.               +this. right?
```

```
32.               (.)
33.      TRA:     yeah,
34.      CAR:     >okay so will that put< more strain in your ey::::::e, or
35.               less.
36.      ALI:     uh that puts more.
37.      CAR:     mmm.
38.      ALI:     no?
```

In line 30, Carlos provides negative feedback in the form of the discourse markers *well* with an extended vowel and falling intonation (Jucker, 1993). He then quickly utters 'let's see' and poses another tag question, which receives an affirmative response (lines 30–31). Figure 3.5 is a representation of how Carlos reuses a noun phrase from prior talk in his tag question. In Excerpt 3 (line 21), Alison says 'the diaphragm' during the collaborative repair she completes in chorus with Tracy and Lindsey.

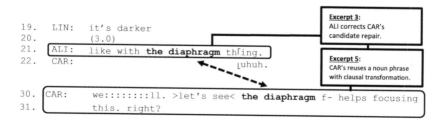

Figure 3.5 Co-operatively constructing a tag question

Then, in Excerpt 5 (line 30), Carlos incorporates the noun phrase into a tag question, again drawing attention to relevant and accurate understandings that Alison and her classmates have already demonstrated.

The co-operative work Carlos does in Excerpt 5 is not only linguistic. It also involves the reuse of deictic gesture. While saying 'diaphragm,' he points first at the front of the apparatus (line 30). As he says, 'this,' he points to the back of the apparatus (line 31). Once again, Carlos draws on a phrase and gesture from prior interaction to establish common ground. Figure 3.6 illustrates how Carlos uses deictic gestures in Excerpt 5 (lines 30–31) that resemble those he and Tracy used in Excerpt 3 (lines 16 and 18).

The IRF in Excerpt 5 transpires in lines 34–37. Carlos once again provides two choices in a close-ended question prefaced by the discourse markers *okay so* (line 34). Carlos does not present the options in the same form as he did in Excerpt 4. The initiation turn in Excerpt 4 projects a preferred response of 'more' while the 'more strain in your eye or less' construction in Excerpt 5 projects a preference for a 'less' response. A student, this time Alison, provides a response that is built co-operatively to display uncertainty (line 36). In the third turn, Carlos produces negative assessment, and Alison displays misunderstanding by uttering 'no' with rising intonation (lines 37–38).

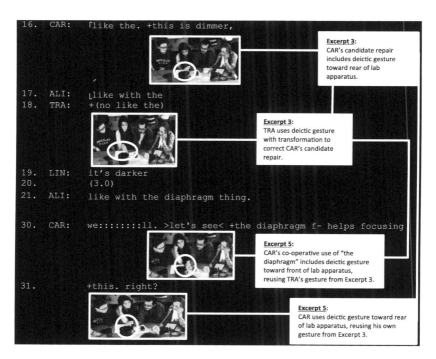

Figure 3.6 Co-operative gesture during a tag question

In Excerpts 4 and 5, Carlos uses tag questions to preface IRF sequences. The tag questions commence with discourse markers, *okay* and *so*. The tag questions and IRFs also involve the use of deictic gesture. The tag questions and IRFs that Carlos designs reuse materials from prior student turns in Excerpts 2 and 3 with transformation. In contrast to his reuse of lexis in the repair initiation in Excerpt 3, in Excerpts 4–5, Carlos reuses information that highlights students' already displayed understanding and uses it to establish shared knowledge. Student response turns are also co-operatively built. They reuse options provided by Carlos with transformation. The transformation in two cases is the discourse marker *uh* and in the other quieter voice, both displays of uncertainty. Thus, we see that how students display uncertainty and how Carlos addresses misunderstanding are co-operative actions.

Excerpt 6 occurred immediately after the IRF in Excerpt 5. Here Carlos abandons his use of IRFs and does a telling. Nonetheless, his telling is preceded by two tag questions. The tag questions in Excerpt 6, like those in Excerpts 4–5, establish common ground based on past utterances and contain repetitions of a phrase and gestures from prior turns.

Excerpt 6 Okay so there's the diaphragm

```
39.      CAR:    less::: cause the diaphr- okay. +so there's the diaphragm.
```

```
40.              and then there's the +lens. right, the cornea. whatever.
```

```
41.              (0.8)
42.      CAR:    so the diaphragm is doing some of the focusing now. right?
43.      ALI:    yeah
44.      CAR:    so now the ↑lens. doesn't have to +scrunch up as much.
```

```
45.              (0.9)
46.      CAR:    okay? so ⌈it'd it'll be more relaxed.
47.      ALI:           ⌊so
48.              (0.9)
49.      ALI:    okay,
50.      CAR:    okay?
```

Excerpt 6 opens with Carlos explicitly correcting the students' response from Excerpt 5 (line 39). He launches another *so* + tag question construction with deictic gesture (line 39). This utterance reuses both lexis and gesture from Excerpts 3 and 5. In this first tag question, Carlos is referring back to Alison's turns and the repair sequence in Excerpts 2 and 3. He reuses 'the diaphragm' coupled with deictic gesture that is similar to Tracy's in Excerpt 3 and his in Excerpt 5. When he speaks of the lens and the cornea (line 40), he is referring to is what Alison called 'seven' in Excerpts 2–3. While saying 'the lens' and 'the cornea,' Carlos draws his right hand near his right eye, roughly parallel with the palm open toward his face in an iconic gesture (line 40). Following a noticeable pause, Carlos begins another *so* + tag question construction that once again uses the noun phrase 'the diaphragm' and emphasizing that it helps focus the image (line 42). Figure 3.7 visually unpacks how Carlos reuses 'the diaphragm,' a phrase initially used by Alison (Excerpt 3, line 21), with transformation three times in tag questions (Excerpt 5, line 30 and Excerpt 6, lines 39 and 42).

Alison displays understanding in line 43. Carlos next produces a *so* + declarative clause construction (line 44) which does a telling that is expanded through line 46. He places exaggeratedly high pitch on lens and clenches his fist when he says scrunch up (line 44). Following a pause, Carlos does the second part of his explanation when he again uses the collocation *okay so* before reusing the phrase 'more relaxed' (line 46) The telling sequence closes with Alison displaying understanding, and Carlos saying okay with rising intonation (lines 49–50). Even though the interactional trajectory of Excerpt 6 differs from those of Excerpts 4 and 5, i.e. a telling instead of IRFs, there are three similarities of note. First, both the IRFs in Excerpts 4 and 5 and the telling in Excerpt 6 are preceded by tag

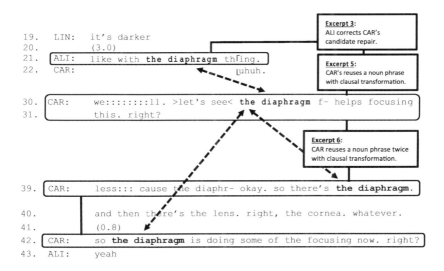

Figure 3.7 Co-operatively constructing two tag questions

questions that reuse embodied resources, specifically phrases, clauses and gesture. Secondly, both the telling and IRFs themselves are composed of reused and modified embodied resources. Third, the resources that speakers reuse are not only used from the immediately prior turn but also from actions that occurred many turns ago.

Excerpt 7 follows Excerpt 6 and is another example of an IRF. Unlike the earlier IRF sequences, this one contains an accurate response from the students and minimal explicit positive evaluation from Carlos (Waring, 2008).

Excerpt 7

```
51.    CAR:    now they're questioning when does that happen.
52.            when does your pupil clos::::e down.
53.            (0.6)
54.    TRA:    when the
55.    ALI:    when the light is on.
56.    CAR:    yeah.
57.    ALI:    when there's more light.
58.    CAR:    yep?
```

As with the other sequence initiating turns, the one in Excerpt 7 starts with a discourse marker. In contrast to the earlier excerpts though, the discourse marker is *now* instead of *okay* and *so*. Here too, Carlos does not re-establish common knowledge about the lab equipment or procedure but instead about the question the students had in Excerpt 2 about 'number eight.' In line 51, Carlos states 'they're questioning when that happens.' The 'they're' in line 51 indexes the authors of the question in the student's lab manual. In line 52, Carlos asks 'when does your pupil close down?' Tracy and Alison collaboratively respond (lines 54–57) and Carlos provides explicit positive evaluation.

So, to summarize, sequences in which students and teachers negotiate misunderstanding are co-operatively built. Co-operative actions are embodied and thus composed of, but not limited to, resources such as language, lab apparatuses, lab manuals and gesture. This analysis has shown us in empirical terms that interaction is situated, sequential and embodied. The situated, sequential and embodied characteristics of interaction help form the substrate. Therefore, interaction can be analyzed and decomposed into teachable parts.

CA and Transdisciplinarity in ITA

As this chapter has shown, CA is a powerful lens through which to describe the situated, sequential and embodied unfolding of ITA-undergraduate interaction. Above, we saw that in a science lab, a context that has been characterized as messy (Myers, 1994), participants systematically build sequences of co-operative action (Goodwin, 2018) that simultaneously draw on past actions and point to upcoming actions. It is through these co-operative actions that misunderstanding is located and corrected. There are three main findings in the analysis:

(1) Sequences in which students and a teacher negotiate misunderstanding are built co-operatively through the decomposition and reuse of materials with transformation.
(2) Tag questions are co-operatively designed and serve to establish shared understanding before IRFs and telling sequences.
(3) Initiation and response turns in IRFs are co-operatively designed by Carlos to elicit demonstrations of understanding and by the students to display uncertainty.

Co-operative action, in the form of the decomposition and reuse of materials with transformation is essential to locating and resolving misunderstanding. By reusing lexis and gesture in combination with other resources, e.g. interrogative syntax, Carlos and the students collaboratively locate and resolve misunderstanding in Excerpts 2 and 3 (Schegloff *et al.*, 1977). The lexis and gesture Carlos reuses in his initiation of repair draw attention to a peripherally relevant observation by the student. In subsequent sequences, Carlos and the students again decompose and reuse words and gestures from prior turns. The linguistic units that Carlos reuses in tag questions before IRFs and a telling (Excerpts 4–6) draw attention to information that was accurate and relevant in prior student turns. Specifically, the image students observe is more in focus when the diaphragm is in place with the seven-diopter lens; the intensity of the light forming the image is irrelevant. The lexis the students reuse in Excerpts 4 and 5 form aligning (Stivers, 2008; Stivers *et al.*, 2011a) responses that advance the instructional project but do so in a way that demonstrates uncertainty. Non-verbal resources, primarily gesture and objects, are as integral to co-operative action as are lexis and grammar. In fact, we see gesture recycled by users in sequences just like we do linguistic units.

In the end, we see that the work a lab instructor must do is much more nuanced than just speaking in an intelligible manner. ITAs working in labs must be able to interpret student demonstrations of misunderstanding and displays of uncertainty. And more than interpret, they must be able to co-operatively operate on the resources provided to them on the substrate of interaction. As we see in Alison's first few turns at talk in Excerpts 2 and 3, the demonstration of misunderstanding contains accurate and relevant information. Carlos is able to identify that information in the linguistic constructions and gesture provided by Alison, Tracy and Lindsey. He then reuses that content throughout the rest of the sequence to guide student thought.

This chapter's findings demonstrate the need for scholars to apply and develop methodologies for describing the embodied nature of classroom interaction in the university and also to document how ITAs' and undergraduates' language use varies from context to context. Past research on ITA talk has overwhelmingly focused on data from lectures (Liao, 2009; Pickering, 2001, 2004; Tyler, 1992; Williams, 1992), and specific lexical and grammatical forms such as discourse markers (Liao, 2009; Looney, 2015), questions (Myers, 1994; Rounds, 1994) and modal verbs (Reinhardt, 2010; Tapper, 1994). While lexis and grammar are without a doubt significant, they are only parts of a broader interactional machine that includes but is not limited to sequence, non-verbal action and objects. Additionally, the contexts in which ITAs interact with undergraduates are not only lectures. If we are to better understand interaction between ITAs and undergraduates, we must better understand how they accomplish the various academic tasks in which the participate. Future studies should involve analyses of actions and practices across various teaching contexts. By identifying and describing the actions and practices of various settings, CA researchers can pinpoint specific recurrent sequences of action, and their component resources, through which ITAs and undergraduates make sense of the lab. Such findings could empirically illuminate the language and interactional repertoires needed for specific contexts in the university and thus inform assessment and instructional materials for ITA.

A key point for the transdisciplinarity of this chapter is that CA research can and should inform ITA preparation. It has long been recognized '[t]he discourse used in different pedagogical settings presents different challenges for an ITA' (Myers, 1994: 83). The different academic discourses also present challenges for teachers of ITA preparation courses. We as ESL teachers have been armed with the tools of structural grammar but that is not necessarily the grammar we see in the contexts where ITAs teach. A transdisciplinary approach to ITA requires that we design and implement curricula that address the nuanced needs of ITAs also requires that ITA researchers and practitioners collaborate, or at least coordinate, efforts with the departments in which ITAs will teach.

If we have real data, engaging ITAs in analysis of classroom interaction from a CA perspective can provide them with the opportunity to begin noticing and developing their own interactional competencies and strategies. As Wong and Waring (2010: 251) write, 'CA not only enriches our knowledge of what to teach, it also sharpens our understanding of how to teach.' In addition, they can familiarize themselves with recurrent questions students ask and common problems they encounter. ITAs can also engage with the realia that they will be using in their teaching assignments. Such engagement allows ITAs to familiarize themselves with the vocabulary they will need to use to socialize students into the discourse of their field as well as the processes they will need to explain.

Microanalytic approaches to classroom interaction are not only excellent starting points for the development of classroom materials to teach potential ITAs but also for developing and validating ITA assessments. A group of scholars have recently been using CA as a component in the validation process of assessments that use role plays (Al-Gahtani & Roever, 2012, 2013; Roever & Kasper, 2018; Youn, 2015). Al-Gahtani and Roever (2012, 2013) and Youn (2015) have demonstrated that lower-proficiency English language learners do not use pre-sequences in the same manner that higher-proficiency learners do as part of requests in academic role plays. For instance, a high-proficiency English speaker would acknowledge the burden that requesting a letter of recommendation puts on a professor before making the request. The speaker might say something like 'I know you are busy but' and then make the request. In contrast, a low-proficiency speaker would make the request with no preceding acknowledgement of the potential inconvenience it causes for the professor. CA provides an empirically informed metalanguage for describing how the work of the classroom is accomplished and that metalanguage and conceptualization of interaction can be put to work to develop observable and assessible tasks and rating criteria for ecologically valid ITA assessments.

To conclude, ITA practitioners must develop 'practical and sustainable solutions for L2 pedagogy that are responsive to the challenges of contemporary life' (Hall, 2018: 15). Without understanding those challenges in terms of the embodied actions and practices through which classroom action is accomplished, ITA practitioners can be of only limited assistance to their students. Studies like this one begin to shed light on classroom interaction and the specialized nature of teaching. While the chapter by no means addressed teaching in all its complexity, it did outline how a teacher and group of students co-operatively built sequences of action in which they displayed misunderstanding, located misunderstanding and corrected misunderstanding. Future studies should continue unpacking the intricacies of co-operative action in university classrooms. It is only by better understanding exactly what it is ITAs do, and are expected to do, that we can provide the tailored support they need to cultivate the interactional repertoires for teaching in their fields.

References

Al-Gahtani, S. and Roever, C. (2012) Role-playing L2 requests: Head acts and sequential organization. *Applied Linguistics* 33 (1), 42–65.

Al-Gahtani, S. and Roever, C. (2013) 'Hi doctor, give me handouts': Low-proficiency speakers and requests. *ELT Journal* 67 (4), 413–424.

Corpus of English for Academic and Professional Purposes (2014) Corpus of videos and accompanying transcripts from educational contexts. Unpublished raw data.

Douglas Fir Group (2016) A transdisciplinary framework for SLA in a multilingual world. *The Modern Language Journal* 100 (Supplement 2016), 19–47.

Goffman, E. (1964) The neglected situation. *American Anthropologist* 66 (6), 133–136.

Goodwin, C. (2000) Action and embodiment within situated human interaction. *Journal of Pragmatics* 32, 1489–1522.

Goodwin, C. (2013) The co-operative, transformative organization of human action and knowledge. *Journal of Pragmatics* 46, 8–23.

Goodwin, C. (2018) *Co-Operative Action*. New York: Cambridge University Press.

Hall, J.K. (2018) From L2 interactional competence to L2 interactional repertoires: Reconceptualising the objects of L2 learning. *Classroom Discourse* 9 (1), 25–39.

Hellermann, J. (2003) The interactive work of prosody in the IRF exchange: Teacher repetition in feedback moves. *Language in Society* 32 (1), 79–104.

Heath, C., Luff, P., vom Lehn, D., Hindmarsh, J. and Cloeverly, J. (2002) Crafting participation: Designing ecologies, configuring experience. *Visual Communication* 1, 9–33.

Jefferson, G. (2004) Glossary of transcript symbols with an introduction. In G.H. Lerner (ed.) *Conversation Analysis: Studies from the First Generation* (pp. 13–31). Philadelphia, PA: John Benjamins.

Jucker, A.H. (1993) The discourse marker well: A relevance-theoretical account. *Journal of Pragmatics* 19 (5), 435–452.

Kearsley, G. (1976) Questions and question asking in verbal discourse: A cross-disciplinary review. *Journal of Psycholinguistic Research* 5 (4), 355–375.

Koshik, I. (2002) Designedly incomplete utterances: A pedagogical practice for eliciting knowledge displays in error correction sequences. *Research on Language and Social Interaction* 35 (3), 277–309.

Kunitz, S. (2018) Collaborative attention work on gender agreement in Italian as a foreign language. *The Modern Language Journal* 102 (Supplement 2018), 64–81.

Lee, Y.A. (2006) Respecifying display questions: Interactional resources for language teaching. *TESOL Quarterly* 40 (4), 691–713.

Lee, Y.A. (2007) Third turn position and teacher talk: Contingency and the work of teaching. *Journal of Pragmatics* 39, 180–206.

Liao, S. (2009) Variation in the use of discourse markers by Chinese teaching assistants in the US. *Journal of Pragmatics* 41, 1313–1328.

Long, M. and Sato, C. (1983) Classroom foreigner talk discourse: Forms and functions of teachers' questions. In H. Seliger and M. Long (eds) *Classroom-Oriented Research in Second Language Acquisition* (pp. 268–286). Rowley, MA: Newsbury House.

Looney, S.D. (2015) Interaction and discourse markers in the ITA-led physics laboratory. In G. Gorsuch (ed.) *Talking Matters* (pp. 77–111). Stillwater, OK: New Forums Press.

Looney, S.D., Jia, D. and Kimura, D. (2017) Self-directed okay in mathematics lectures. *Journal of Pragmatics* 107, 46–59.

Margutti, P. and Drew, P. (2014) Positive evaluation of student answers in classroom instruction. *Language and Education* 28 (5), 436–458.

Mehan, H. (1979) *Learning Lessons*. Cambridge, MA: Harvard University Press.

Mortensen, K. (2008) Selecting next speaker in the second language classroom: How to find a willing next speaker in planned activities. *Journal of Applied Linguistics* 5 (1), 55–79.

Mortensen, K. (2009) Establishing recipiency in pre-beginning position in the second language classroom. *Discourse Processes* 46 (5), 491–515.

Mortensen, K. and Hazel, S. (2011) Initiating round robins in the L2 classroom – preliminary observations. *Novitas-ROYAL (Research on Youth and Language)* 5 (1), 55–70.

Myers, C. (1994) Question-based discourse in science labs: Issues for ITAs. In C.G. Madden and C.L. Myers (eds) *Discourse and Performance of International Teaching Assistants* (pp. 83–102). Alexandria, VA: Teachers of English to Speakers of Other Languages, Inc.

Pickering, L. (2001) The Role of tone choice in improving ITA communication in the classroom. *TESOL Quarterly* 35 (2), 233–255.

Pickering, L. (2004) The structure and function of intonational paragraphs in native and nonnative speaker instructional discourse. *English for Specific Purposes* 23, 19–43.

Reinhardt, J. (2010) Directives in office hour consultations: A corpus-informed investigation of learner and expert usage. *English for Specific Purposes* 29, 94–107.

Roever, C. and Kasper, G. (2018) Speaking in turns and sequences: Interactional competence as a target in testing speaking. *Language Testing* 35 (3), 331–355.

Rounds, P. (1994) Student questions: When, where, why, and how many. In C. G. Madden and C.L. Myers (eds) *Discourse and Performance of International Teaching Assistants* (pp. 103–115). Alexandria, VA: Teachers of English to Speakers of Other Languages, Inc.

Rymes, B. (2014) *Communicating Beyond Language*. New York: Routledge.

Schegloff, E. (1991) Conversation analysis and socially shared cognition. In L.B. Resnick, J.M. Levine and S.D. Teasley (eds) *Perspectives on Socially Shared Cognition* (pp. 150–171). Washington DC: American Psychological Association.

Schegloff, E. (2007) *Sequence Organization in Interaction: Volume 1: A Primer in Conversation*. New York: Cambridge University Press.

Schegloff, E., Sacks, H. and Jefferson, G. (1977) The preference for self-correction in the organization of repair in conversation. *Language* 53 (2), 361–382.

Sert, O. (2019) Mutual gaze, embodied go-aheads, and their interactional consequences in L2 classrooms. In J.K. Hall and S.D. Looney (eds) *The Embodied Work of Teaching*. Bristol: Multilingual Matters.

Singer, S.R., Nielsen, N.R. and Schweingruber, H.A. (eds) (2012) *Discipline-Based Education Research: Understanding and Improving Learning in Undergraduate Science and Engineering*. Washington, D.C.: National Academies Press.

Stivers, T. (2008) Stance, alignment, and affiliation during storytelling: When nodding is a token of affiliation. *Research on Language and Social Interaction* 41 (1), 31–57.

Stivers, T., Mondada, L. and Steensig, J. (2011a) Knowledge, morality and affiliation in social interaction. In T. Stivers, L. Mondada and J. Steensig (eds) *The Morality of Knowledge in Conversation* (pp. 3–24). New York: Cambridge University Press.

Stivers, T., Mondada, L. and Steensig, J. (eds) (2011b) *The Morality of Knowledge in Conversation*. New York: Cambridge University Press.

Streeck, J., Goodwin, C. and LeBaron, C. (eds) (2011) *Embodied Interaction: Language and Body in the Material World*. New York: Cambridge University Press.

Tapper, J. (1994) Directives used in college laboratory oral discourse. *English for Specific Purposes* 13 (3), 205–222.

Tyler, A. (1992) Discourse structure and the perception of incoherence in international teaching assistants' spoken discourse. *TESOL Quarterly* 26 (4), 693–711.

Waring, H.Z. (2008) Using explicit positive assessment in the language classroom: Three turn sequence, feedback, and learning opportunities. *The Modern Language Journal* 92 (4), 577–594.

Williams, J. (1992) Planning, discourse marking, and the comprehensibility of international teaching assistants. *TESOL Quarterly* 26 (4), 693–711.

Wong, J. and Waring, H.Z. (2010) *Conversation and Second Language Pedagogy: A Guide for ESL/EFL Teachers*. New York: Routledge.

Youn, S.J. (2015) Validity argument for assessing L2 pragmatics in interaction using mixed methods. *Language Testing* 32 (2), 199–225.

Appendix: Transcription conventions (adapted from Jefferson, 2004; Kunitz, 2018)

```
[ ]          overlapping utterances or nonverbal
             conduct
{ }          nonverbals and speech, pause or gap
             co-occurrences
=            contiguous utterances (latching)
(( ))        nonverbal behaviors
```

(.)	micro-pause; a number inside the parentheses represents the length of the pause
:	elongation (more colons demonstrate longer stretch)
.	fall in intonation at the end of an utterance
,	slight rise in intonation at the end of an utterance
?	rising in intonation at the end of an utterance
-	an abrupt stop in articulation
↑ in speech	marked upstep in pitch
↓ in speech	marked downstep in pitch
hhh	outbreath
.hhh	in-breath
@haha, @hhh	marks laughter
wo(h)rd	marks aspiration within a word
CAPS	loud speech
°word°	soft speech
word	stress/accentuation
<	hurried start of the turn
>word<	surrounds talk that is spoken faster
>word<	surrounds talk that is spoken more slowly
word	description of nonverbal conduct
(word)	uncertain utterances; surrounds the transcriber's best guess
(xxxx)	unintelligible syllables; the number of Xs represents the number of syllables
$word$	smiley, laughing voice
#word#	creaky voice
+	marks location of still frame in talk

4 Instructional Authority and Instructional Discourse

Shiao-Yun Chiang

This chapter examines the discursive procedures in which the interpretive authority of international teaching assistants (ITAs) is negotiated or challenged in their instructional interactions with US college students. The matter of analytic interest is the interactional moments wherein US students initiate and carry out their disputes and the specific ways in which ITAs make responses so as to enact their instructional authority. Drawing upon the framework of interactional sociolinguistics, this study aims to show that ITAs' instruction is largely contingent on their performance of instructional discourse. In contrast to some existing studies that attribute the success or failure of ITAs' instruction to the US college student's cooperation or resistance, this chapter demonstrates the constitutive function of discourse when communication becomes difficult due to linguistic and sociocultural differences between international teaching assistants and US college students.

Introduction

An increasing number of studies have shown that instructional authority is not always taken for granted but negotiated and even challenged by students (cf. Cothran & Ennis, 1997; Graham, 1999; He, 2004; Mayes, 2010). The negotiation of instructional authority often takes place in classrooms that involve non-native speaker (NNS) teachers of English and native speaker (NS) students (see Amin, 1997; Duff & Uchida, 1997). This is particularly true in US research universities where a large number of undergraduate instructors are foreign graduates whose native language is not English (see Gravois' report in *The Chronicle of Higher Education* on 8 April 2005). They are often referred to as international teaching assistants (ITAs) in existing studies.

There exists a large body of studies on the instructional performance of ITAs (for a most recent review, see Chiang, 2011; Gorsuch, 2016). ITAs are often negatively perceived by US college students (Fitch & Morgan, 2003; Plakans, 1997; Rubin, 2002) owing to linguistic and cultural differences. While performing the role of content expert, ITAs are mostly viewed as language novices, which often renders their instructions vulnerable for negotiation by US college students (cf. Chiang, 2013). In particular, Asian TAs from China, Korea and Japan are often considered as incapable of dealing with US college students' attempts to negotiate their instructional authority and expertise due to their culturally conditioned mode of instruction (see Tyler, 1995).

In contrast to most existing studies on ITA's instructional performance (cf. Rubin, 1993), the present study provides an analysis of the specific discourse domains in which an ITA deals with a US student's repeated attempts to negotiate his authority in office hours. The matter of analytic interest is the interactional moments wherein the US student disputes the ITA's expertise and the specific way in which the ITA makes an effort to enact his instructional authority. In other words, the analyses here will reveal (1) what communicative acts may trigger negotiations and help enact instructional authority, (2) what dimensions of instructional authority may become negotiable and (3) in what discourse domains instructional authority may be vulnerable for negotiation and likely invoked or exercised. This study contributes to a transdisciplinary framework for ITAs by looking at how institutional roles and responsibilities are negotiated between students and ITAs.

Instructional Authority

The modern conceptualization of authority is often associated with Max Weber. Weber (1968: 53) defined authority as the legitimate form of power – 'the probability that one actor within a social relationship will be in a position to carry out his own will despite resistance.' Authority is established on charisma, tradition and legality. Of the three types of authority, Weber endorsed the legal one that defines roles and positions in social relationships. Individuals choose to follow other people because they believe that it is right (or socially desirable) to do so. In Weber's view, authority is essentially a form of influence that is embedded in the structure of social relationships and it provides an explanation for the organization of social actions.

Studies on authority and all its related concepts such as power, status, or role may be roughly classified into two groups. One maintains that authority exists in social relations and it defines or accounts for the uses of language (for a review see Spence-Oatey, 1996). For example, Brown and Levinson (1987) consider power as a constant parameter in their politeness theory. The other contends that social reality (including all social relationships) is constituted in/through the use of language (cf. Searle, 1997). For example, Sanders (1995, 2007, 2012) looks into the dynamics of social discourses and explicates the specific ways in which authority is formed and performed in and through speech acts (see also Chiang, 2009; Cooren & Matte, 2010).

Instructional authority is traditionally considered as a constant in education for two reasons. First, the educational institution grants the instructor the legitimate status for instruction. Second, the instructor possesses the expertise to teach a subject matter in a discipline. In other words, the instructor is *in* authority and *an* authority (see Peters, 1966). The former refers to the instructor's status as an institutional representative to direct or regulate actions in an educational context, and the latter to the instructor's competence to impart legitimated forms of knowledge. Thus, the two conditions, status and expertise, allow the instructor to receive 'automatic respect from students' (Cothran & Ennis, 1997: 541).

Two positions on the role of authority in education may be identified. One position maintains that education must be authoritarian as its aim is to serve the state. This view may be traced back to ancient Chinese and Greek philosophies (see Spring, 1999). From the Confucian perspective, a society would be ideal with rulers governing the state by virtue and everyone assuming a proper role. The aim of education is to teach virtue and provide guidance. From the Socratic perspective, the primary goal of education is to sustain a moral state with rulers propagating the idea of social positions for different people in different abilities. The authoritarian view remained dominant in both the eastern and western educations for centuries.

In contrast, the other position argues that the authoritarian view does not fit with the process of democracy (Spring, 1999). In a democratic state, elected rulers may use education systems to influence the knowledge of students and thus control the decisions of future citizens. The public concern about the source and role of authority in education finds a clear expression in the works of John Dewey. Education from the democratic view should be related broadly to the communal lives of society (Dewey, 1902). Democracy means freeing human minds and intelligence through intellectual instructions (Dewey, 1903). The source of authority lies not in the external means of coercion, but intelligence gained from the application of scientific inquiry (Dewey, 1936).

Instructional Discourse

Instructional authority constitutes an integral part of teachers' identity which is contingent on the practice of professional discourse. The type of professional discourse for instructors is termed as instructional discourse and regulative discourse by Basil Bernstein (1990). The former refers to the discourse for transmitting knowledge that students are expected to acquire while the latter refers to the discourse for transmitting values that legitimizes relations and social order. The two types of discourses correspond respectively to the teachers' competencies to be *an* authority and places to be *in* authority. Instructional authority is mostly related to instructional discourse that informs the teachers' expertise in the discipline and their abilities to exercise that expertise.

Instructional authority is not necessarily taken for granted, but is often contested and negotiated in educational contexts. For example, He (2004) displays how the expert–novice relationship between teachers and students is contested in the give and take of directives in Chinese heritage language classes. Waring (2005) finds out a number of verbal tactics that a tutee may use to resist a tutor's expertise in tutoring interactions. Elliott (2009) demonstrates that even pupils can challenge their teachers' authority by asking questions, making unnecessary requests, ignoring instructions and delaying responses to the teacher. Authority relations between teachers and students are found to be generally unstable in existing studies (see also Pace & Hemmings, 2007).

Instructional authority is thus considered as discursively formed in educational contexts. For example, Buzzelli and Johnston (2001) look into the verbal details of a classroom interaction and display the specific ways in which a school teacher acts out her status in the regulative discourse and exercises her expertise in the instructional discourse. Chiang (2009) provides an analysis of two dissertation supervisors' advising sessions with a doctoral student and reveals how the two professors' formulations of instructional acts index their respective preferences for appealing to expertise or status. Authority, whether in the form of expertise or status, is shown as a discursive construction in existing studies (see also Mayes, 2010).

The negotiation of instructional authority often takes place when the instructor is an NNS English speaker. NNS English language teachers are often negatively perceived (Butler, 2007), and their instructional authority may be questioned and challenged (Tang, 1997) as native speakers (NS) are awarded the authenticity in the use of English language (Amin, 1997). Hence, multilingual English instructors must make an effort to establish their instructional authority (Subtirelu, 2011) and maintain their teacher identity (Reis, 2011). While the definition of NNS is debatable (Davies, 2003), NNS English instructors' identity has remained a significant question in applied linguistics (see Chiang, 2016; Kramsch, 1999; Pavlenko, 2003).

The challenge to instructional authority is not limited to NNS English language teachers but extended to NNS instructors in all disciplines, particularly in the areas of science and technology (Finder, 2005). While NNS teachers possess expertise in their academic areas, they may not enjoy the same level of English proficiency as NS students. In US research universities, multilingual teachers' instruction is often perceived as problematic (Pickering, 2004), and their instructional authority is often contested by US college students (Rubin, 2002; Tyler, 1995). For example, Chiang (2013) shows the interactional procedure by which a US college student probed an NNS teacher's expertise by challenging the validity of an exam question.

Aims of the Present Study

This study aims to demonstrate that instructional authority is not necessarily a presupposed entity which routinely grants an individual instructor with a constant privilege, but contingent practice of professional discourses. Every profession requires its members to practice a type of discourse that informs the specialized area of knowledge and legitimizes its application within an institution (Sarangi & Roberts, 1999). In a sense, to be an instructor is to practice the type of instructional discourse that is appropriate for a particular educational context (cf. Axelson & Madden, 1994) and instructional authority is thus accomplished in instructional discourse.

Existing studies on the construction of authority and all its related concepts are mostly one-sided. That is, the focus is placed upon one participant in context. Although these studies are mostly informative with regard to the composition and presentation of one or two speech acts (e.g. Benoit-Barne & Cooren, 2009; Mayes, 2010), they do not address fully the complexity of interaction. In this regard, Sanders' work is an exception. Sanders (1995, 2012) compares the cases in which one's self presentation is successful or unsuccessful in terms of exercising power/authority, and he shows that the exercise of power/authority is embedded in the complexity of interaction, although situational nuances and participants' different characters also might account for the successful or unsuccessful exercise of power/authority.

The case of ITAs provides a unique context in which we can observe how instructional authority is negotiated, invoked or enacted as an ongoing development of performing communicative acts. ITAs may possess the special knowledge (hence expertise) in an academic area, but they are often perceived as incapable of using English language adequately. Juxtaposed between content expert and language novice, ITAs are often involved in power/status negotiations initiated by US college students (cf. Tyler, 1995). In a sense, the ITAs' instructional performance should be most informative about the relations between instructional authority and instructional discourse. The questions here are:

(1) How does a student contest instructional authority during an office hour interaction?
(2) How does an ITA demonstrate/enact instructional authority during an office hour interaction?

(3) How do participants talk about their own ideas and experiences regarding instructional authority?

Data and method

The discourse under study here is an office hour interaction between Liu (an ITA from China) and Eric (a native-born US college student). Liu agreed to inform the researcher and have his interaction with students audio recorded when they came to office hours. Liu had been a doctoral candidate in Economics for four years at a research university in the northeastern US. As a part of the PhD requirement Liu was teaching an undergraduate course for two years and his teaching evaluations were consistently above the departmental average. In this interaction, Eric came to ask about his test results. After he found that his score was not as good as he had expected, he asked for a review with Liu.

The conversation was audio recorded in Liu's office after they signed consent forms. The interaction lasted approximately 35 minutes. The conversation was then transcribed using Conversation Analysis conventions (see Atkinson & Heritage, 1984) which account for paralinguistic features. A week later, these two participants were interviewed separately by the researcher and they were asked to identify any trouble that had occurred in the conversation, and then comment on it while listening to the recording. The playback session was intended to find out whether there is any contextual issue not directly observable in the transcript and how the participants perceive and understand each other's conversational moves.

A close examination of the interaction reveals three specific discourse domains in which Eric initiated negotiations over Liu's instructional authority. While it is commonly expected that US students would negotiate in this type of situations (see Tyler, 1995), the procedures in which Eric and Liu went through their negotiations should be contextually informative in reference to their respective interview responses. The discourse domains wherein the negotiations occurred are related to three test questions – one on the definition of a technical term, one on the interpretation of a technical term and another on the application of an economic principle.

Definitional Question

Definitional questions are factual as they constitute the basic knowledge of a subject, and thus an instructor's expertise in an academic area. In a sense, they should be less disputable than other types of questions. In the following extract, Eric made an initial attempt to defend his answer to a definitional question which he had gotten wrong, but he withdrew immediately from his previous position as Liu started to exercise his expertise. In line 23, Eric started to tackle the issue with a discourse marker 'so.' The use of 'so' may indicate the implementation of pending interactional agendas (Bolden, 2009). As shown in the formulation of his question, Eric suggested to Liu that there could be some wiggle room for an optional definition of 'scarcity'.

Excerpt 1

23. Eric: so for number one scarcity, (0.3) could it, (0.2) could it be A? or
24. did you just want the (0.2) I guess the best (0.3) cause isn't
25. scarcity, is there is less than infinite amount of a resource?
26. Liu: no, not infinite (0.2) u::m, °there is uh (0.3) less than an infin-,
27. infinite amount of a resource or good° ((reading in a low voice))
28. um
29. Eric: isn't that scarcity? cause (0.2) isn't scarcity unlimited ↑wants
30. (0.3) for a limited resource?
31. Liu: °u::m°
32. (2.0)
33. Eric: That's what confused me. You said go for the best answer, I
34. thought maybe <u>that</u> was the best answer because it's
35. Liu: °Some people wish to have° ((reading in a low voice)) (0.3) This
36. is uh, looks (.) right, buta ((but)) (.) it's <u>not</u> as good as B and C.
37. See, B said that there is less of a good or resource available than
38. people wish to have. That's <u>just</u> the definition of (.) scarcity.
39. Eric: right
40. Liu: society cannot meet the wants of every individual,
41. Eric: right
42. Liu: that's also the [<u>exactly</u> same thing
43. Eric: [right
44. Liu: This infinite, the word infinite, this is not, not so good, not,
45. Eric: not sounds like the best answer
46. Liu: not <u>exactly</u> (.) describing the (.) definition

Eric started tentatively as he asked 'could it be A?' which may imply the possibility of being wrong (cf. Brown & Levinson, 1987), but he became argumentative when Liu did not provide a prompt explanation. In line 26

Liu pointed out the problem ('not infinite') and read the question, and then he came to a pause, to which Eric responded with an argumentative question at line 29 and in this case Eric even backed it up with a reason. Liu came to another long pause at line 31. Eric pressed forward and started to make accusations ('You said go for the best answer') at line 33, but before he went on, Liu started to respond in an assertive tone which indicates his mastery of the economic discourse. From lines 37 to 46, Liu became increasingly assertive as evidenced in his use of emphatic words ('just', 'exactly') while Eric began to retreat by offering repeated back-channels ('right').

The exchange above is noteworthy for two reasons. First, Eric's attempts for negotiation became progressively explicit where Liu paused without providing an explanation. Existing studies have shown that NS students may perceive their NNS instructors' pause as an indication of understanding trouble (e.g. Chiang & Mi, 2011) or speech production problem (e.g. Chiang, 2016). In the playback session, Eric told the researcher that Liu might be fumbling for words. Eric said that Liu's English was generally all right, although imperfect and sometimes students did offer assistance in his instructional discourse. In other words, Eric's perception of a potential for negotiation might be related to the way in which Liu was seemingly struggling to make explanations.

Second, Liu's exercise of expertise became more and more explicit in his uses of emphatic words, which actually stopped Eric from going further in his attempt for negotiation. The uses of emphatic words 'just' in line 38 and 'exactly' in lines 42 and 46 made it clear to Eric that there is no gray area or fuzzy border in the definition of 'scarcity.' In the playback session, Liu told the researcher that he was aware of Eric's attempts for negotiation, which he thought was a common practice in the US classroom from his observations. In this light, Liu's awareness of Eric's intent prompted him to exercise his expertise by using those emphatic words to bear out his mastery of the subject matter.

Interpretive Question

Interpretive questions require respondents to make reasonable inter-pretations or inference. To interpret with relevant examples is a common practice for instructors to help students understand course concepts. In any highly specialized profession, as a matter of fact, all practitioners such as lawyers and medical doctors are expected to explain their technical discourse to outsiders using a plain language and they are often awarded such an interpretive authority. In the following extract, Eric strives to negotiate over a question which involves interpreting an economic term. However, Liu's interpretive authority is not reciprocated by Eric due partly to their different sociocultural backgrounds and partly to their different ways of making interpretations.

Excerpt 2

50. Eric: So for number two (0.3) number two: Water in a city is more (0.2)
51.   [scarce than air]
52. Liu: [scarce, ye::ah] becau, you chose air?
53. Eric: I put air because air gets po::lluted
54. Liu: haha, uh, that's, um
55. Eric: so becomes scarce, I gu-, every time you breathe the air you lose.
56. Liu: I don't know you [(°thought about that°)]
57. Eric: [I see, I guess I was] thinking about the
58.   oxygen more [hehe]
59. Liu: [hehe] yes now you can say [(water in a city)]
60. Eric: [because water in] a city
61.   (1.3)
62. Liu: yes, this uh (0.3) I know this (.) is kind of confusing. Water in a
63.   city, um (.) in some cities water (0.3) are not so scarce.
64. Eric: right
65. Liu: water is not so scarce, [(that's true)]
66. Eric: [right, that's] why I didn't like that, like the
67.   first two connections, I think, throw me off, haha
68. Liu: yeah > especially that < you are (.) living in America
69. Eric: yeah
70. Liu: and living in America you (0.3) you always (.) almost always have
71.   enough (.) water, and (available) there, you justa (0.3) ((just)) turn
72.   off, turn (.) on (.) tap and get water
73. Eric: °right°
74. Liu: buta ((but)) uh (.) if you look at this (.) from the (0.3) uh the
75.   viewpoint of the whole [world] and some (0.1) in some countries
76. Eric: [°right°]
77. Liu: water in a, in a (.) city is really, really very limited, like my home
78.   country China, and clean water, water in a city, especially in a big
79.   city like Beijing
80. Eric: °right°
81. Liu: and Shanghai very (.) scarce, very uh limited, it's not (0.3) far
82.   from enough, [°water°]
83. Eric: [I, I didn't] know that, um =
84. Liu: = hahaha,
85. Eric: I didn't take, I don't know

At line 53, Eric began to explain why he chose air rather than water. Liu seemed surprised by Eric's choice and his rationale for making that choice, and yet he was professional enough to not make any negative remark on his rationale, although he laughed lightly and stopped. After a long pause, Liu started to explain this question at line 62. In the first place, Liu empathized with Eric by acknowledging that water is not scarce in America, and his empathy was reciprocated by Eric as shown in the latter's repeated backchannels 'right.' Then Liu asked Eric to look at this issue globally by using his home country China as an example, which opened the door to negotiations. At line 86, Eric claimed that he did not know about China, thus posing a challenge to the fairness or reasonableness of the question.

The specific procedures for negotiating over the reasonableness of the question are exhibited in the subsequent segment. Liu seemed to have realized the gap in their sociocultural knowledge as he made a shift from his previous angle at line 89, and asked Eric to look into the phrasing of the candidate responses to the question because there are clues. At line 92, Liu tried to show Eric that the candidate response 'air' is too broad for an answer without some restrictions. While Eric did agree with Liu at line 93, he returned to his previous position that water is not scarce in the United States by presenting his rationality as shown in his repeated uses of 'I + epistemic verbs' (i.e. 'think') in lines 99, 109 and 102.

Excerpt 3

89. Liu: but if you can compare all these <u>four</u> choices, um, I think that's
90.   (0.4) water in a city is better than others.
91. Eric: °yeah?°
92. Liu: air is too broad, it didn't mention, um, (0.4) like you said, that
93. Eric: clean air, °I guess it would be better°
94. Liu: yeah, clean air in a (.) °let's say° in a u:m hea:vy industrial,
95.   industrial area,
96. Eric: right
97. Liu: maybe that's, that's true when there's °pollution, polluted area, in
98.   an area°
99. Eric: cause I, I was thinking, > especially < like New York City
100.   Liu: um huh
101. Eric: New York City gets lot of their um (0.4) water from um (0.1)
102.   upstate, in a (.) °what's that, what's called° (0.3) like Hudson
103.   mountain in all that area, like, um (0.2) all upstate. It's like clean,
104.   they, they, they say New York city as <u>pollut</u>ed as some parts <u>are</u>,

105.   they are like their cleanest water, like their tap water is really

106.   good. Do you have ever got to the city and try the tap water there?

107. Liu: mm

108. Eric: some of the best water across the coun, like across the world they

109.   say. So I was thinking out this city- water in a city that, you know,

110.   they come from springs in upstate, and it's not that scarce, hhehe

111. Liu: °mm, yeah, sounds like that°

112. Eric: That's (.) <u>just</u> confusing, I don't think, (0.3) I didn't know that was

113.   a good example.

114. Liu: mm, (2.0) yeah, I know, (0.5) °this is kind of (.) um confusing°

From line 101, Eric used New York City as an example to explain why he thought water was not scarce. The specific procedures by which Eric presented his example posed a direct objection to Liu's explanation. Eric emphasized that New York City got its tap water from the upstate, and he also emphasized that the tap water in New York City was the cleanest across the world though some areas there were polluted. It is noteworthy that Eric made a shift from 'across the country' to 'across the world' at line 108 as Liu had suggested that they should look at the issue globally. It is also noteworthy that Liu did not counteract Eric's explanation, but provided backchannels at line 111 and even an agreement as a form of empathy ('this is kind of confusing') at line 114.

Eric pressed forward in his negotiation over the fairness of the question each time Liu offered a backchannel (i.e. 'mm', 'sounds like that', 'yeah'). He became more and more assertive, for example, in his uses of emphatic voice ('<u>just</u> confusing') and epistemic verbs (for the uses of 'I + epistemic verbs' in assertive acts see Chiang, 2009). After a long pause at line 120 Eric was almost ready to move on to another question, but he turned back and became more defensive by providing a counter example, namely, 'water in a desert' at line 123.

Excerpt 4

120.   (3.1)

121. Eric: °let's see, question number° yeah, I didn't (0.4) I thought that was,

122.   I thought that was a better example maybe (.) like water, like, if

123.   like, if you said water in a desert, (0.4) [that may be]

124. Liu: [yeah, that's] that's,

125.   that'll be very (0.4) um striking, > but you can choose it < without

126.   thinking, that's yeah, [water in a desert it's]

127. Eric: [right I guess it's a] little too easy, alright,
128.   I see
129. Liu: haha, yeah,
130. Eric: alright, I see.
131. Liu: that's an example I give in [u:m class] right?
132. Eric: [yeah yeah]
133. Liu: water in desert (0.4) so I don't know how
134. Eric: that's alright

In contrast to Excerpt 3, Liu did not go along with Eric in line 125, but he repudiated Eric's counter example (i.e. water in desert) as it was too obvious for a test question. At line 127, Eric seemed to realize that his counter example did not support his own argument adequately, and he agreed instantly that 'water in desert' would be too easy even before Liu completed his utterance. It is notable that Liu emphasized that he had talked about the example in class even though Eric said 'alright, I see' twice, which conventionally signals to terminate a conversational topic (see Bardovi-Harlig *et al.*, 1991). Aware or unaware of this convention Liu made another reference to the issue at line 133 whereas Eric said again 'that's alright' (see also Beach's (1995) discussion of 'that's okay' as a sign for understanding consequentiality).

The instance here should be informative in two dimensions. First, interpretive authority may be contingent upon the availability of communicative resources. Existing studies (e.g. Gumperz, 1992; Tyler, 1995) have demonstrated how NNSs' work competence might be misjudged due to their oral communication style. In this case, Eric took longer turns when making interpretations in his repeated attempts to negotiate Liu's interpretive authority, whereas Liu's interpretation was not as much elaborate. In the playback sessions, Eric claimed that Liu's interpretation was hard to accept, although he had a good vocabulary and usage. Liu was aware of the communicative and instructional differences as he said in the playback session:

> *They* [referring to the NS American instructors] *have a better knowledge of the English language so it is much easier for them to make their instruction more fun. But when they add too much spice, they may get students lost. I give students the big picture and outline first, and stick to it. I won't go too far from it when giving examples.*

Second, interpretative procedures may be culture specific. Existing studies have revealed that interpretation and reasoning are culturally different in academic discourse. For example, Tannen (2002) maintains that Americans tend to be argumentative, whereas the Chinese value balance or harmony. Tyler (1995) shows that Eastern Asians tend to be more inductive, whereas Americans are more likely deductive. In this case Liu became empathic (i.e. 'I don't know you thought about that', 'I know this is kind of confusing') when he became aware of Eric's cognitive difference and he did not seem confrontational when Eric made his counterargument. In the playback session, when asked to compare Liu with American instructors, Eric made these comments:

> *Comparison is odious, generalization is an insult. I've only had a few instructors so far, more foreign than U.S. I suppose it's fair to say that the big difference is the fact of their foreignness itself, their backgrounds, and their worldview. But it's a valuable part of our education to be exposed to different people from different cultures.*

Applied Question

Applied questions require students to use facts and principles to generate results. They can be designed for solving problems, demonstrating procedures and making inferences. The question that Eric had gotten wrong here involves the calculation of an economic principle on opportunity cost. In contrast to those definitional and interpretive questions, the applied question below does not require much verbal specification, but procedural demonstration, which leaves little room for negotiation. It is in this discourse domain that Liu's exercise of expertise is most apparent.

Excerpt 5

138. Eric: for here, (0.4) for number nine
139. Liu: mm
140. Eric: ask opportunity cost of one car for Japan
141. Liu: mm
142. Eric: is, so I broke it down like this, five (.) fifty the one fifty will be
143.   one unit in the three units, right?
144.   (2.3)
145. Liu: °this is uh, fifty hours to make one (.) one car.°
146. Eric: right, so I wrote one here, three here, cause they're proportional,
147.   and so
148. Liu: no, I think, no!
149. Eric: no?
150. Liu: no not that, fifty hours um to make one unit, one car, so u::m (1.6)
151.   this should be three, I, you (0.2) the same time is used for, to
152.   produce three cars and one air (.) one airplane

153. Eric: okay
154. Liu: °right°? because you produce one car, use fifty hours
155. Eric: right
156. Liu: so to produce three cars (.) means you have to use (0.5) one fifty
157.   hours
158. Eric: right
159. Liu: and this is the time used for producing one airplane. So the time
160.   used ta um produce one, uh, three cars, and produce um one
161.   airplane, use the same time, same labor hours.
162. Eric: okay
163. Liu: one hundred fifty hours, so you shouldn't put one and three there.

At line 142, Eric explained how he calculated opportunity cost in the question which he had gotten wrong and he asked Liu for confirmation ('right?'). Liu did not make a prompt response. After a lengthy pause, Liu came to realize what the calculation was about at line 145. Eric then made a specification on the procedures by which he did calculation, and yet before he went on, Liu started to disapprove his calculation in an emphatic tone at line 148. Eric seemed surprised ('no?'). It is notable that Liu did not provide any mitigation in his disapproval at line 150 as he went on to show Eric the correct calculation procedures. In contrast to his repeated attempts for rebuttals in the previous case, Eric followed well as shown in his backchannels (i.e. okay, right).

While Liu did not provide an exact answer to the question, his explanations from lines 150 to 163 seemed well received and reciprocated by Eric. However, Eric made an interpretive summary of Liu's explanations in Excerpt 6, which showed that he was still confused as his answer to that question remained the same.

Excerpt 6

167. Eric: °all right° so opportunity cost (.) what's giving up by producing
168.   [one car]
169. Liu: [one car] for Japan
170. Eric: would it be (0.5) opportunity cost of one car for Japan is, isn't
171.   three airplanes?
172. Liu: NO!
173. Eric: no?
174. Liu: one third
175. Eric: one third

176. Liu: because (.) I, I just said that, you, [you cannot put one there and]
177. Eric: [right, ahahahahahahahahahah]
178. Liu: three there, you should put three [there] and one there
179. Eric: [yeah]
180. Liu: you used (.) the same one fifty hours to produce three cars for one
181.   airplane
182. Eric: right
183. Liu: so, but three cars means one airplane, so one car means one third
184.   airplane
185. Eric: yeah, okay
186.   (6.31)
187. Eric: So that's wh-, that's what happened. I got all the opa-, I got all the
188.   opportunity cost messed, that's what killed my grade (0.2) all this
189.   is five? [(.) right] in here
190. Liu: [yeah]

It is noteworthy that Eric made a change from an affirmative sentence into a confirmation request at line 170, which shows that he was struggling with the issue. Liu's negation at line 172 seemed to surprise Eric again as shown in the latter's 'no?', and then Liu just gave Eric the correct answer (i.e. 'one third'). Liu might have expected Eric to be able to deduce the correct answer from the calculation procedure as he emphasized his response (i.e. 'NO!' and 'I just said that'). Since Eric failed to deduce the correct answer, Liu made another explanation at line 183, which was more succinct than the previous one. After a long pause, Eric came to understand how he got these questions wrong.

The instance above should be most illustrative with regard to the presentation of expertise in an instructional discourse. Existing studies (Selinker & Douglas, 1985) have demonstrated the relationship between expertise and discourse performance in the NNS-NS talk. In this case, Liu exerted a consistent control over his interaction with Eric by giving clear directions and making unmitigated corrections whereas Eric showed no attempts for negotiating over Liu's expertise. In the playback sessions, Eric said that the trouble students could experience with Liu's instruction had nothing to do with expertise or skill but language only. Liu believed that his students were mostly respectful, but he needed to readdress their questions from time to time as he said:

> What sometimes happened is that after I answered a question raised by a student, and that student still cannot get it, I then asked him or her to talk to me in private so that we could pursue the issue a little more.

Conclusion

The present study should be implicative in two dimensions, one specifically addressing some critical (but underdeveloped) issues in ITA studies and the other generally related to intercultural education. ITA studies have been developed for over three decades since Bailey (1982, 1984) did the early work on the so-called foreign TA problem, and they are predominantly concerned with the linguistic, sociocultural and instructional differences of ITAs. The author of this chapter has been advocating a social interactional approach to ITA studies (Chiang, 2011, 2013, 2016). In light of the CA-inspired analytic framework, the exchanges above should evidence the significance of interaction in creating and resolving communication difficulties as often perceived and reported by US college students.

As shown in the instances above, Liu's instruction was not taken for granted but questioned and disputed, although Eric was aware that his instructor should hold the key to all the questions. While it could be an American practice to be argumentative in academic discourse (Dewey, 1903; Tannen, 2002), the exchanges reveal the specific procedures and domains in which Eric initiated and pursued his argumentation with Liu. Evidently, the negotiation here did not arise from Liu's linguistic and sociocultural differences. Rather, Eric made his attempt for negotiation wherein he perceived a possibility for overturning his case in the ongoing communicative acts. For example, Eric's attempts for negotiation became increasingly explicit as Liu paused without a timely or an adequate response. A close examination shows that Eric's attempt for negotiation is most explicit in the interpretive question which often involves the maximum use of communicative resources.

The exchanges above also evidence a necessity of putting ITA studies in the large context of intercultural education. In any society, instructional authority constitutes an integral part of our professional identity as an instructor. While instructional authority is considered as a given social status and institutional position in many eastern Asian cultures, it is often perceived as a form of communicative achievement in the process of performing instructional acts in American society. The three instances above demonstrate that the exercise of instructional authority is discursively progressed in relation to the specific procedures for negotiation. For example, Liu became progressively assertive so as to project his authoritative role as Eric's attempts for negotiation became increasingly explicit.

References

Amin, N. (1997) Race and the identity of the nonnative ESL teacher. *TESOL Quarterly* 31 (3), 580–583.

Atkinson, M. and Heritage, J. (eds) (1984) *Structures of Social Action*. Cambridge: Cambridge University Press.

Axelson, E.R. and Madden, C. (1994) Discourse strategies for ITAs across instructional contexts. In C. Madden and C. Myers (eds) *Discourse and Performance of International Teaching Assistants* (pp. 153–187). Alexandria, VA: TESOL.

Bailey, K.M. (1982) The classroom communication problems of Asian teaching assistants. In C. Ward and D. Wren (eds) *Selected Papers in TESOL* (pp. 19–30). Monterey: Monterey Institute of International Studies.

Bailey, K.M. (1984) The "Foreign TA Problem." In K.M. Bailey, F. Pialorsi and J. Zukowskiaust (eds) *Foreign Teaching Assistants in U.S. Universities* (pp. 3–16). Washington, D.C.: National Association for Foreign Student Affairs.

Bardovi-Harlig, K., Hartford, Mahan-Taylor, B.R., Morgan, M.J. and Reynolds, D.W. (1991) Developing pragmatic awareness: Closing the conversation. *ELT Journal* 45 (1), 4–15.

Beach, W.A. (1995) Conversation analysis: 'Okay' as a clue for understanding consequentiality. In S.J. Sigman (ed.) *The Consequentiality of Communication.* Mahwah, NJ: Lawrence Erlbaum Associates, Inc.

Benoit-Barné, C. and Cooren, F. (2009) The accomplishment of authority through presentification: How authority is distributed among and negotiated by organizational members. *Management Communication Quarterly* 23 (1), 5–31.

Bernstein, B. (1990) *The Structuring of Pedagogic Discourse.* Abingdon: Routledge

Bolden, G.B. (2009) Implementing incipient actions: The discourse marker 'so' in English conversation. *Journal of Pragmatics* 41, 974–998.

Brown, P. and Levinson, S. (1987) *Politeness: Some Universals in Language Usage.* Cambridge: Cambridge University Press.

Butler, Y.G. (2007) How are nonnative-English-speaking teachers perceived by young learners? *TESOL Quarterly* 41 (4), 731–755.

Buzzelli, C. and Johnston, B. (2001) Authority, power, and morality in classroom discourse. *Teaching and Teacher Education* 17, 873–884.

Chiang, S.-Y. (2009) Personal power and positional power in a power-full 'I': A discourse analysis of doctoral dissertation supervision. *Discourse & Communication* 3 (3), 255–271.

Chiang, S.-Y. (2011) Pursuing a response in office hour interactions between U.S. college students and international teaching assistants. *Journal of Pragmatics* 43, 3316–3330.

Chiang, S.-Y. (2013) 'The word isn't there!': A Foucauldian approach to power negotiation in an instructional interaction across linguistic and cultural boundaries. *Critical Discourse Studies* 10 (3), 298–311.

Chiang, S.-Y. (2016) 'Is this what you're talking about?': Identity negotiation in international teaching assistants' instructional interactions with U.S. college students. *Journal of Language, Identity, and Education.*

Chiang, S.-Y. and Mi, H.F. (2011) Reformulation: A verbal display of interlanguage awareness in instructional interactions. *Language Awareness* 20 (2), 135–149.

Cooren, F. and Matte, F. (2010) For a constitutive pragmatics: Obama, Médecins Sans Frontières and the measuring stick. *Pragmatics and Society* 1 (1), 9–31.

Cothran, D.J. and Ennis, C.D. (1997) Students and teachers' perceptions of conflict and power. *Teaching and Teacher Education* 13, 541–553.

Davies, A. (2003) *The Native Speaker: Myth and Reality.* Clevedon: Multilingual Matters.

Dewey, J. (1902) The school as social centre. *The Elementary School Teacher* 3 (2), 73–86

Dewey, J. (1903) Democracy in education. *The Elementary School Teacher* 4 (4), 193–204

Dewey, J. (1936) Authority and freedom. *Survey Graphic* 25 (11), 603–607.

Duff, P.A. and Uchida, Y. (1997) The negotiation of teachers' sociocultural identities and practices in postsecondary EFL classrooms. *TESOL Quarterly* 31 (3), 451–486

Elliott, J.G. (2009) The nature of teacher authority and teacher expertise. *Support for Learning* 24 (4), 197–203.

Finder, A. (2005) When the teacher has mastered all but English. *New York Times*. Retrieved from http://www.nytimes.com/2005/06/24/world/americas/24iht-assistant.html

Fitch, F. and Morgan, S.E. (2003) 'Not a lick of English': Constructing the ITA identity through student narratives. *Communication Education* 52 (3), 297–310.

Gorsuch, G. (2016) International teaching assistants at universities: A research agenda. *Language Teaching* 49 (2), 275–290.

Graham, P. (1999) Powerful influences: A case of one student teacher renegotiating his perceptions of power relations. *Teaching and Teacher Education* 13, 523–540.

Gumperz, J.J. (1992) Contextualization Revisited. In P. Auer and A. Di Luzio (eds) *The Contextualization of Language* (pp. 39–55). John Benjamins.

He, W.A. (2004) Identity construction in Chinese heritage language classes. *Pragmatics* 14 (3), 199–216.

Kramsch, C. (1999) Global and local identities in the contract zone. In C. Gnutzmann (ed.) *Teaching and Learning English as a Global Language* (pp. 131–143). Tubingen: Stauffenberg-Verlag.

Mayes, P. (2010) The discursive construction of identity and power in the critical classroom: Implications for applied critical theories. *Discourse & Society* 21 (2), 189–210.

Pace, J.L. (2003) Revisiting classroom authority: Theory and ideology meet practice. *Teachers College Record* 105 (8), 1559–1585.

Pace, J.L. and Hemmings, A. (2007) Understanding authority in classrooms: A review of theory, ideology, and research. *Review of Educational Research* 77 (1), 4–27.

Pavlenko, A. (2003) 'I never knew I was a bilingual' Reimaging teacher identities in TESOL. *Journal of Language, Identity, and Education* 2 (4), 251–268.

Peters, R.S. (1966) *Ethics and Education*. London: Allen & Unwin.

Pickering, L. (2004) The structure and function of intonational paragraphs in native and nonnative speaker instructional discourse. *English for Specific Purposes* 23, 19–43.

Plakans, B.S. (1997) Undergraduates' experiences with and attitudes toward international teaching assistants. *TESOL Quarterly* 31 (1), 95–119.

Reis, D.S. (2011) Nonnative English speaking teachers (NNESTs) and professional legitimacy: A sociocultural theoretical perspective on identity transformation. *International Journal of the Sociology of Language* 208, 139–160.

Rubin, D.L. (1993) The other half of international teaching assistant training: Classroom communication workshops for international students. *Innovative Higher Education* 17, 183–193.

Rubin, D.L. (2002) Help! My professor, (or doctor or boss) doesn't talk English In J. Martin, T. Nakayama and L. Flores (eds) *Readings in Intercultural Communication: Experiences and Contexts* (pp. 127–137). Boston: McGraw Hill.

Sanders, R.E. (1995) A neo-rhetorical perspective: The enactment of role-identities as interactive and strategic. In S.J. Sigman (ed.) *The Consequentiality of Communication* (pp. 67–120). Hillsdale, NJ: Lawrence Erlbaum.

Sanders, R.E. (2007) The effect of interactional competence on group problem-solving. In F. Cooren (ed.) *Interacting and Organizing* (pp. 163–183). Mahwah, NJ: Erlbaum.

Sanders, R.E. (2012) The representation of self through the dialogic properties of talk and conduct. *Language and Dialogue* 2 (1), 28–40.

Sarangi, S. and Roberts, C. (eds) (1999) *Talk, Work, and Institutional Order*. New York: Mouton de Gruyter.

Searle, J.R. (1997) *The Construction of Social Reality*. New York: Free Press.

Selinker, L. and Douglas, D. (1985) Wrestling with 'context in interlanguage theory. *Applied Linguistics* 6, 190–207.

Spencer-Oatey, H. (1996) Reconsidering power and distance. *Journal of Pragmatics* 26, 1–24.

Spring, J. (1999) *Wheels in the Head: Educational Philosophies of Authority, Freedom, and Culture from Confucianism to Human Rights*. New York: McGraw-Hill,

Subtirelu, N. (2011) Juggling identity and authority: A case study of one nonnative instructor of English. *TESL-EJ* 15 (3).

Tang, C. (1997) On the power and status of nonnative ESL teachers. *TESOL Quarterly* 31 (3), 577–580.

Tannen, D. (2002) Agonism in academic discourse. *Journal of Pragmatics* 34 (10/11), 1651–1669.

Tyler, A. (1995) The co-construction of cross-cultural miscommunication. *Studies in Second Language Acquisition* 17, 129–152.

Waring, H.Z. (2005) Peer tutoring in a graduate writing center: Identity, expertise, and advice resisting. *Applied Linguistics* 26 (2), 141–168.

Weber, M. (1968) *Economy and Society: An Outline of Interpretive Sociology.* G. Roth and C. Wittich (eds) New York: Bedminster (Original work published 1922).

5 Enhancing Communication between ITAs and US Undergraduate Students

Okim Kang and Meghan Moran

The following chapter provides a discussion of the tensions between American undergraduate students and international teaching assistants (ITAs) as well as an overview of measures that universities have taken in an attempt to alleviate those tensions. A traditional approach has been to focus on the ITA's oral English and/or pedagogical skills; more recently, researchers have noted that prejudices on the part of undergraduates must be addressed as well. Kang and colleagues have utilized Allport's (1954) Contact Hypothesis as a framework to conduct contact activity research that has consistently resulted in improved attitudes towards ITAs. Three studies are discussed: a one-hour culture-sensitization contact activity (Kang *et al.*, 2015), institutionally supported contact activities (Staples *et al.*, 2014) and course embedded contact activities (Kang & Moran, 2015). In each, undergraduate students are paired with international students or ITAs in order to complete structured tasks in a semi-controlled environment. Students' perceptions on accented English and other indicators of possible prejudices are measured before and after the intervention activity. Findings from this transdisciplinary approach indicate that structured activities such as these have the potential to ameliorate the dynamic in ITA-led classrooms. To conclude the chapter, future applications of contact activities are explored.

Introduction

Institutions of higher education (HEIs) often flaunt the benefits of international teaching assistants (ITAs), claiming that ITAs bring a welcome diversity to the classroom and, in doing so, help prepare students for an ever-globalizing future. For example, Purdue University (2017) states that their institution 'benefits from the knowledge and talents of non-native, English-speaking graduate teaching assistants in many aspects of its instructional program. These persons bring an essential diversity of culture to the campus and thus enrich our total academic environment.' Similarly, Temple University (2018) asserts, 'The International Teaching Assistant (ITA) Program supports Temple University's commitment to excellence in teaching, and linguistic and cultural diversity.' However, HEIs are also simultaneously aware of, and highly sensitive to, the reactions that ITAs can have within the university setting (see Chapters 1 and 2 for a more in-depth discussion, this volume). Students and parents often complain about ITAs and blame them for students' non-comprehension of course material and therefore poor-quality education and/or low grades (Fitch & Morgan, 2003). Rubin and Smith (1990) found that as many as 42% of students have dis-enrolled from courses led by ITAs, and some students (as well as other educational stakeholders) even go so far as to call for a ban of ITAs (Plakans, 1997).

Recognizing the problems that can occur in ITA-led classrooms, HEIs have been working to implement measures for ITAs that will, in theory, smooth their classroom interactions. For example, in most universities, ITAs are required to pass tests of oral language proficiency (Compton, 2007; Isaacs, 2008; Monoson & Thomas, 1993; Subtirelu, 2017). Furthermore, some HEIs require instructors to also pass tests of instructional competence (Compton, 2007). ITAs who do not score sufficiently on either of these assessments are relegated to remedial classes in which pronunciation and instructional strategies are targeted (Compton, 2007; Subtirelu, 2017). Often, a great deal of resources go into better preparing ITAs for their instructional context. In contrast, the other party crucial to the success of the interaction, i.e. US undergraduate students, are given little if any preparation (Rubin, 1992). As Meyer and Mao (2014: 18) argue, 'Given that ITAs have been held to higher entrance standards and additional training, it seems reasonable to prepare students as well.'

Various suggestions have been put forth to alleviate the inherent, and usually subconscious, prejudice on the part of US undergraduates (for examples, see Altinsel & Rittenberg, 1996; Ashavskaya, 2015; Ates & Eslami, 2012; Bresnahan & Sun Kim, 1993; Fitch & Morgan, 2003; Halleck, 2008; Plakans, 1997; Subtirelu & Lindemann, 2016; Yook & Albert, 1999). Inter-group interactions based on the Contact Hypothesis (Kang & Moran, 2015; Kang et al., 2015; Staples et al., 2014), in fact, incorporate at least the tenets of many of the previous suggestions. Inter-group interventions, when administered under ideal conditions, have shown robust results with only a modicum of financial and logistical burden on universities.

Literature Review

'The ITA problem'

HEIs and researchers alike have acknowledged issues in ITA-led classrooms for decades (Fitch & Morgan, 2003). Students score ITAs lower than domestic TAs on beginning and end-of-course evaluations (Jiang, 2014;

Smith *et al.*, 2005), blame ITAs for low grades (Fitch & Morgan, 2003), and even avoid enrolling for classes in which an ITA is slated to teach (Bresnahan & Sun Kim, 1993). When asked about their reasons for this, US undergraduates frequently cite a lack of English proficiency on the part of the ITAs. However, research has shown that perceived lack of proficiency, rather than actual lack of proficiency, is often the driving force (Chiang, 2016; Rubin, 1992; Rubin & Smith, 1990). Perceptions of proficiency can be influenced as much by physical attributes as actual oral production (Rubin, 1992; Rubin & Smith, 1990). Moreover, while students often point to their international instructors' difficulty in communication, it is well accepted that intelligibility is a mutually constructed enterprise with both the speaker and the listener sharing the burden of communication. Several studies conducted by applied linguists and educational psychologists have shown that when a listener holds negative views towards a variety of speech or its speaker, their comprehension of the presented material is actually reduced (Ahn & Moore, 2011; Kang & Rubin, 2009; Mayer *et al.*, 2003; Rubin, 1992). Thus, sifting out the connection between reactions of US undergraduate students, their xenophobic attitudes and the oral and instructional proficiency of ITAs is quite complex.

When real or perceived communication difficulties in ITA/undergraduate student interaction do occur, the student employs strategies that they may not in an NES–NES exchange. When communication actually breaks down, students have been shown to adopt an avoidance orientation (Lindemann, 2002; Subtirelu, 2017), which may include going to other faculty for explanations and deciding to learn the material themselves from the textbook. These strategies, while possibly leading to short-term success (that is, comprehension of the immediate material), do little to promote the intercultural understanding necessary for future success in ITA-led classes.

Scholars have also noted that in ITA-led classrooms, students are often woefully ignorant about their instructors' personal backgrounds. In Fitch and Morgan (2003), none of the 25 students that participated in focus group discussions were aware of their ITAs' academic credentials or scholarships, and many were tentative about their ethnicities and nationalities. In this way, ITAs are packaged as an out-group with all members containing similar, and reductive, characteristics – namely, inferiority in instruction with poor English-speaking ability.

These reactions may be a byproduct of the fact that many US undergraduate students have not had much exposure to people from other cultures. In fact, a class in which students have an ITA is often their first time truly and meaningfully interacting with someone from another country (Altinsel & Rittenberg, 1996; Halleck, 2008). Studies show that this insularity impacts students' attitudes towards ITAs. For example, in her analysis of 1751 undergraduate students, Plakans (1997) found that those who had limited travel experience or had only lived in their small town or rural area had more negative opinions of ITAs than students who had more extensive travel experience or had lived in urban places or other areas of the US. Compounded with this, rather than forming their own impressions of ITAs, students often rely on the negative messages they receive from peers and family members (Bresnahan & Sun Kim, 1993); therefore, they may come to class with preconceived, negative notions about their teacher. Despite these findings, there is an implicit assumption on the part of HEIs that US undergraduate students do not need to undergo training for cross-cultural pedagogical situations and a possible disbelief that even if it should occur, such large-scale training would be logistically impossible (Kaplan, 1989).

Unfortunately, the attitudes of students who take classes with ITAs do not necessarily improve throughout their course. In fact, often the opposite is true. This is due, in part, to the lack of optimal conditions of contact (see below). Due to power differentials and high stakes (i.e. student grades), contact between US undergraduates and their ITAs may lead to more negative perceptions of ITAs in general, causing students to avoid cross-cultural interactions altogether. Bresnahan and Sun Kim (1993: 348) remark that, 'forcing reluctant intercultural contact between U.S. undergraduates and ITAs, without some positive preparation and intervention for both parties, may be counterproductive to the very goals of greater diversity which universities are trying to achieve.' They continue by questioning the fairness of placing 'minimally prepared' ITAs in classes with US undergraduates who are anxious about international instructors, claiming that the negative experience that likely ensues teaches undergraduate students to henceforth avoid any dealings with foreigners (Bresnahan & Sun Kim, 1993).

Potential solutions focused on US undergraduate students

Despite the ITA-as-deficient-model currently in practice at most HEIs, scholars in the disciplines of education and human development, communication arts and sciences, and applied linguistics have begun to argue for increased training of US undergraduate students (Ates & Eslami, 2012; Bresnahan & Sun Kim, 1993; Fitch & Morgan, 2003; Jenkins & Rubin, 1993; Meyer & Mao, 2014; Plakans, 1996; Rubin & Smith, 1990; Subtirelu, 2017; vom Saal, 1987). While not specific to ITAs, Subtirelu and Lindemann (2016) categorized three ways in which native English speakers could improve their communication with speakers from other varieties: training in cross-cultural communication strategies, perspective-taking and inter-group interventions based on the Contact Hypothesis. The third suggestion (i.e. Contact Hypothesis-based interventions) is focused on for the remainder of this chapter.

The Contact Hypothesis

Subtirelu and Lindemann (2016) noted the promise of interventions that hailed from social psychology, in particular, Contact Hypothesis interventions. The Contact Hypothesis theorizes that prejudice can be reduced when interaction between contact groups occurs in ideal conditions. First proposed by Allport in 1954, it has remained robust in its results. In fact, a meta-analysis of 515 studies conducted by Pettigrew and Tropp (2006) showed that structured contact has reliably promoted increased tolerance towards members of the out-group. The research literature on intergroup contact reveals specific conditions of intergroup contact that are necessary (if not always sufficient) to reduce prejudice (Pettigrew & Tropp, 2006; Rubin & Lannutti, 2001). Accordingly, there is some consensus among researchers with regard to factors that influence successful contact outcomes. They are: (1) equal status between the groups in the contact situation; (2) common goals; (3) cooperative interdependence but no competition between the groups; (4) authority sanction or promotion (supportive norms) for the contact; (5) opportunities for person-to-person interaction; and (6) appropriate context to allow for friendship potential (Brown & Hewstone, 2005). Additionally, intergroup contact at more personal levels is strongly encouraged, because it allows participants to see the 'other' as more than just a member of an out-group (Tredoux & Finchilescu, 2007). However, it is important that 'others' are not so individuated that they are taken as exceptions to their groups. Moreover, participants should be seen as fairly typical of their respective groups in order to obtain the desired impact on social prejudice through the contact exercises (Hewstone & Brown, 1986). It has been found that the quality of the contact (i.e. implementation fidelity to each of these features) has a more profound effect than duration or intensity of the contact (Dovidio et al., 2003; Pettigrew, 1998). Moreover, the institutional support condition may be especially important in facilitating positive contact effects (Pettigrew & Tropp, 2006).

In the past, Contact Hypothesis studies have targeted various groups in order to reduce real-world and high-stakes prejudices, such as school students in Bosnia and Herzegovina (Becker, 2017), persons with and without HIV (Chan & Tsai, 2017), American and Mexican students (Mickus & Bowen, 2017), and abled versus disabled persons (Wickline et al., 2016), among many others. However, the Contact Hypothesis had not been drawn upon as an explicit theoretical framework to lessen tensions between ITAs and US undergraduate students until more recently with the incorporation of jigsaw classroom activities as part of a course (Smith et al., 2005). Jigsaw classroom activities involve the strategic dispersal of information to students with the aim that students must share their unique information in order to 'build' a cohesive discourse. In Smith et al.'s (2005) rendition, undergraduate students had to gather information from international partners to complete assigned tasks (and vice versa). The researchers hypothesized that undergraduate students who completed the intercultural course should evaluate ITAs' English speaking and teaching skills better than those in a comparison group. Although the results were complex and seemed to be confounded by the timing of the evaluations (i.e. when in the semester students were asked to rate), this study was an important step in applying tenets of the contact intervention to the US undergraduate student/ITA dynamic.

In 1996, Altinsel and Rittenberg presented on a program that Michigan State University (MSU) had implemented. MSU had noticed that ITAs received no follow-up support after their week-long orientation (and, for some, a remedial English class) to help them deal with cultural factors during their time as an ITA. While not explicitly drawing on the Contact Hypothesis, MSU created a Buddy Program that paired undergraduate students with ITAs. Through this program, each ITA/undergraduate pair spent time together each week with a different theme (e.g. student employment or extracurricular activities). Unfortunately, Altinsel and Rittenberg's presentation focused more on the benefits of the Buddy Program to the ITAs (as opposed to the undergraduate Buddies), such as 'dispel[ing] ITAs' uncertainties and build[ing] their confidence,' 'strengthen[ing] their sense of connection to the MSU students,' and 'help[ing] them feel part of the university community.' The one paragraph that touted the benefits for the undergraduates mentioned the large impression the experience made on them, especially hearing about the ITAs' experiences and accomplishments. The students were impressed and inspired by the hard work ethics and accomplishments of the ITAs, which led them to become critical of their peers' complaints about ITAs.

When fitted retroactively on Altinsel and Rittenberg's (1996), it can be seen that MSU's Buddy Program fit many of the parameters for optimal intergroup contact. Each ITA was placed with an undergraduate buddy, with each dyad absent of any markers of authority. The explicit goal was to learn more about each other's culture, and to do so, the participants needed to be cooperative in sharing information. A committee had been established within the university to create and promote this program, and the required frequent check-ins were indicators that the program was well-structured and well-supported by members of the HEI faculty. Finally, the eight weeks of sessions with carefully crafted activities aimed to reveal the behind-the-scenes thoughts and behaviors of the participants elicited the potential for friendship.

What is especially promising about well-structured intergroup contact is that prejudice reduction has been shown to go beyond the specific outgroup member and generalize to the entire outgroup (Pettigrew, 1998). Even more, it can sometimes generalize to other outgroups (Pettigrew & Tropp, 2006). Thus, in an ITA setting, an undergraduate student who has structured contact with a Chinese ITA might not only feel more positive about that ITA by the end of the session but may also feel more positive about other Chinese ITAs and ITAs of other nationalities. Beyond its repeated successes, another benefit of intergroup contact is that it is easy and inexpensive to facilitate logistically. Incoming college freshman generally receive an orientation, into which cross-cultural communication training could be included. Resident Assistants could conduct workshops with the undergraduates in their dormitories easily and cheaply to promote intercultural understanding (Bresnahan & Sun Kim, 1993). Undergraduates could be involved in training courses for ITAs (Ross, 2007; Sarwark & vom Saal, 1989; Trebing, 2007) or in post-screening courses, such as the one at MSU (Altinsel & Rittenberg, 1996), either of which could involve structured inter-group contact. Also, as will be seen below, even very brief lengths of contact have been shown to improve undergraduates' attitudes. Creating hour-long meetings between ITAs and US undergraduate students with an exercise and refreshments would not put a burden on the HEI either logistically or financially.

In the following section, we introduce three successful studies that utilized structured contact activities designed by the first author and her colleagues: (1) a single one-hour culture-sensitization activity; (2) a semester-long institutionally supported cultural partner program; and (3) three sessions of structured activities embedded in an intercultural communication course. It is beyond the scope of this chapter to provide methodological and statistical details of the assessments that we conducted to demonstrate that the inter-group contact interventions exerted an impact on undergraduates' attitudes toward ITAs. Our primary aim was to mitigate negative attitudes that US undergraduates often have toward ITA oral proficiency and teaching competence.

The ITA-Undergraduate Contact Interventions: Synopses of Three Studies

Study 1: One-hour culture-sensitization contact activity

The primary goal of this one-hour activity (Kang *et al.*, 2015) was to maximize undergraduate participation in the intervention while also testing the intervention's portability and sensitivity to a short duration. The activity was designed to be fun and enjoyable, and at the same time to fit into a one-hour class block. The circumstances were friendly with low anxiety, and refreshments were provided throughout the whole session. According to Stephan and Stephan (1985), anxiety is a common impediment to successful intergroup contact and it is a factor that can cause students' antipathy toward ITAs. The non-threatening environment created could also enhance the friendship potential contact condition suggested by Pettigrew (1998).

The contact activity comprised approximately two ITAs and four to five undergraduate students. They were recruited by advertising this event in the campus newspaper and in world languages classes on campus. Undergraduate students were expected to engage one-on-one with ITAs who might challenge their stereotypes. None of the ITAs had previous contact with the undergraduate student participants. In addition to informal conversation, the core part of the contact intervention involved mystery puzzle activities in which clues were distributed among members of small groups, with each group having to cooperate in sharing the clues and synthesizing them without the help of written media. Each mystery consisted of about 40 clues.[1] This type of activity was especially critical because it required input from all group members, and each individual's contributions were equally important for a successful outcome. This activity was therefore rich in cooperative talk; the structure of it necessitates that all participants speak or else the mysteries cannot be solved. Solving each puzzle generally took approximately 20 minutes. During the single session, undergraduate students participated in two different groups, rotating between different puzzles and ITAs. After both puzzles were solved, groups were encouraged to spend additional time discussing cultural differences. The entire session lasted for about an hour.

The contact meeting attempted to operationalize previously established conditions for prejudice reduction (Dovidio *et al.*, 2003; Pettigrew, 1998). First of all, *equal status* aspect was afforded, given that both ITAs and undergraduate raters were equally integral to solving the mystery puzzles with distributed clues. They pursued a *common goal* by solving a mystery puzzle and exchanging information regarding culture-specific non-verbal communication skills. In addition, the mystery puzzle task required *group cooperation*; i.e. all group members were required to share their pieces of their information to solve the mystery. Each participant was served refreshments and introduced themselves to other group members before they started the puzzle solving task. Consequently, group members established *interpersonal acquaintance* between members. Finally, participants in the intervention meeting were presented to each other as *typical groups* of ITAs and US undergraduates.

This one-hour culture-sensitization activity was designed to mitigate negative attitudes that US undergraduates often have toward ITA oral proficiency and teaching competence (Rubin, 2002). In order to evaluate those specific language attitudes, undergraduate students were asked to rate 11 audio recordings of ITAs presenting a 5-minute mini-lectures. (Note that these recordings were recorded by a separate group of ITAs than those who participated in the contact activities, supporting the idea that improved evaluations can expand beyond the actual ITA contact participants.) Sixty-three undergraduates first rated those ITAs' speech samples along four dimensions: comprehensibility, overall oral proficiency, degree of accentedness and teaching competence. Twenty-nine of these undergraduates were then randomly selected to participate in the inter-group contact intervention described below, while the remaining 34 students did not. After several weeks, during which the contact activity took place, these students were asked to rate the same speech samples a second time.

Results showed that students who engaged in the culture-sensitization activity for an hour were more positive in their evaluations of the ITAs' comprehensibility and teaching competence, whereas those who did not engage in the group activity did not change their ratings. In fact, the positive change was most dramatic among those students participating in the intervention who had indicated that their grades had been hurt in the past by poor teaching on the part of ITAs. Comments from participants on our open-ended questionnaires supported our findings that the intervention did influence students' perceptions of ITAs' oral performances. For example, one US participant wrote, 'because I met ITAs at the informal meeting or something, I kind of felt a bit more comfortable with the ITAs' accent' (from Kang et al., 2015: 14).

This study (Kang et al., 2015) does lend support to the Contact Hypothesis (Allport, 1954; Pettigrew, 1998), which argues that structured intergroup contact can mitigate intergroup prejudices. Informal and pleasant contact with interpersonal intimacy and equality could bring a positive change in undergraduate attitudes toward ITAs and consequently influence undergraduates' perceptions of ITA speech performances. This impact of the contact experience on rating behaviors is especially remarkable because the intervention was so short in duration (i.e. only one hour) and limited in intensity. The potency of the intervention, notwithstanding its brevity, may have been due to the fidelity of its design features to principles of effective intergroup contact. In fact, participants who experience carefully structured contact situations that are designed to meet the Contact Hypothesis's optimal conditions achieve a markedly higher mean effect size than do other participants in contact interventions (Pettigrew & Tropp, 2006). The current study offers a good example that shows a case of improving undergraduates' comprehension of accented English, and for the broader goal of enhancing students' global citizenship without ever leaving their home campuses (Davies & Pike, 2009).

Study 2: Institutionally supported contact activities

Unlike the one-hour contact activity above (i.e. Kang et al., 2015), this study (Staples et al., 2014) focuses on a semester-long program designed to provide optimal contact conditions to improve communication between US undergraduate students and ITAs. It similarly investigates the impact of this contact on US students' perceptions of ITAs' speaking performance, accent, comprehensibility and teaching ability within a university wide, institutionally supported program. That is, this study receives explicit institutional support as the program is connected with a specific organization or official entity and yields strong findings.

Ninety-four native English-speaking undergraduates from a state university were recruited through a director of a language partner program and through university instructors. The group that participated in the contact scenario contained 58 participants and the non-contact group contained 36 participants. Fifty-eight international partners participated in the study. They were predominantly from China and all but two of the partners were from Asian countries. Contact group participants interacted with their international partners once per week for eight weeks for one hour each time. Participants and their international partners chose the time and location for the meeting. They primarily chose their own topics for discussion, but activities were suggested at five points in the semester.

The five activities designed for 50-minute encounters incorporated principles recommended in the literature (e.g. Rubin & Lannutti, 2001; Smith *et al.*, 2005) and focused on intercultural communication topics such as ITA issues (complete materials are available from the first author upon request). Each activity began with a discussion, had opportunities for collaborative participation in reaching a goal, and ended with reflection. The design of the program and the nature of the activities promoted an equal status between undergraduates and their international partners. The role of the undergraduate as fellow student and member of the academic community was emphasized over the role as a 'tutor.'

Starting with initial recruitment material, staff advertised the program as an opportunity for cross-cultural exchange and developing international friendships, rather than for teaching English. Applicants were asked to discuss their reasons for participation and most remarked on their desire to learn about other cultures through student contact. Following Rubin and Lannutti's (2001) principles for intergroup contact, the contact was extended over eight weeks, providing ample time for the activity, as well as *acquaintance potential*. *Mutually beneficial outcomes* and *equal status* were supported by the fact that both the undergraduates and international partners were motivated and interested to gain cultural knowledge from their partners. The activities provided at five separate points in the semester ensured that the partners participated in tasks where *input from both parties was essential*. Many of the activities chosen by the pairs also fulfilled this condition. Finally, a diverse pool of participants was recruited from across the university, ensuring that *participants were typical members of their group*.

What has been missing from inter-group contact studies in the past is ongoing *institutional support*. In this study (Staples *et al.*, 2014), the program itself is situated within the Center for American English Language and Culture (CAELC), a pan-university program under the auspices of the Vice President and Provost at a high research-oriented university in North-East regions. In contrast to many other universities which house their English language units within a particular department, CAELC is a non-proprietary program, serving the entire university and thus allowing for greater visibility, flexibility and wider contact. CAELC services, and by extension, the volunteer program, reach virtually every school in this decentralized university. Beyond the structure, which gives the volunteer program extensive exposure, there is also considerable non-tangible support for global education, which permeates the student body and motivates students to participate. A commitment to supporting international initiatives both on campus and abroad began as part of the university strategic mission to promote internationalization.

Participants in both the contact and non-contact group took a pretest survey at the beginning of the semester, which involved rating five ITA speech samples in random order and filling out a background questionnaire. Both groups also took a posttest approximately seven weeks later, which consisted of ratings of the same five ITA speech samples, using the same procedures as the pre-test. The online interview was conducted approximately ten weeks after the completion of the posttest survey. The results indicate that the contact had a positive impact on all three outcome ratings (accent, comprehensibility and teaching ability). The qualitative comments suggest that participants gained a deeper understanding, appreciation and respect for ITAs and international students through participation in the program. For example, one respondent wrote:

> I understand more about ITAs in particular. While we as students may be focused on our grades and learning, the ITAs not only have to figure out how to teach – often for the first time – they are also learning how to communicate with a non-native language as well as with students from drastically different backgrounds and styles of learning. (from Staples *et al.*, 2014: 61)

Thus, it seems that institutionally supported contact can mitigate undergraduates' evaluations of ITA speech and instructional competence. Along with efforts to improve the production of ITAs, undergraduates' contact with international students and ITAs seems an important factor in improving the communication between undergraduates and ITAs.

Study 3: Course-embedded contact activities

The following study (Kang & Moran, 2015) also examines the effects of contact interventions on undergraduates' perceptions of international students' and ITAs' oral performance. However, it expands the scope of the previous studies by investigating international students' and ITAs' perspectives as well as undergraduate students' perspectives. Further, while the previous studies (described above) have commonly employed an intervention that is independent of the curriculum, the current study explores the feasibility of embedding intercultural contact activities directly into the classroom.

Two hundred US undergraduate students participated in this study, split evenly between a control group (100 students) and an experimental group (100 students). These students were enrolled in two sections of *Anthropology 103: Culture in Communication*. The two sections of the course were taught by the same instructor with identical curricula. The actual number of participants varied for each of the three activities; it ranged from 72 to 101 due to attendance status. Additionally, an average number of 85 international students who were attending an intensive English program (IEP) participated.

Three times throughout the semester, the experimental group of students met with the international students and were placed in groups of 3–4, with 1–2 international students and 1–2 US students per group. Groups were randomly assigned for each activity. Once groups were formed with the assistance of the activity facilitators, an overview and directions for the activity were provided. During the first 50-minute session, each group was given pictures with non-verbal gestures (e.g. as used in Kang *et al.*, 2015 above). They were asked to discuss as a group what the gestures meant in American culture, whether they had a similar or different meaning in the culture of the international students, and any examples of other culture related gestures. In the second activity, several weeks later, the groups of students shared opinions about cultural values and proverbs. They each received a 'culture puzzle' as a prompt developed by the first author.[2] This provided a foundation for students to share customs from their own cultures and relate them to others in the group. The third session took place in a gymnasium with light refreshments to encourage participation and establish a fun and informal atmosphere. Varied groups of four to five students were first given a long dowel. They were instructed to place one finger each upon the dowel and attempt to lower it to the ground. This game, called Helium Stick, is an ice-breaker that encourages communication and teamwork in order for the team to achieve its goal.[3] The aim of the second activity of that day was for each group to build the tallest structure possible out of marshmallows and uncooked spaghetti.[4] Each of these activities combined a kinesthetic component to the US undergraduate and international student interaction. Activity facilitators circulated the gymnasium, monitoring and encouraging student progress.

The timeline for this project spanned across a 16-week academic semester. At the beginning of the semester, all Anthropology students (both control and experimental) completed the pretest (i.e. online ratings of comprehensibility, oral proficiency and linguistic stereotyping), which consisted of nine ITAs and international graduate students' speech samples describing a series of pictures for a minute. Undergraduate students participated in the intercultural contact activities in weeks five, nine and twelve. At the end of the semester, they completed the online posttest. The instructor of the courses took this task as part of the curriculum so that students were required to complete the survey and to reflect on their experience.

The results revealed that although all students were enrolled in an Anthropology class, students who participated in contact activities rated ITA speech as more comprehensible, more proficient, and less negatively stereotyped than those who took part in the traditional curriculum alone. In addition, US undergraduate students seemed to have an increased respect for people from other cultures. The following comment from one undergraduate student provides insight into the impact of the interventions:

> Growing up in the US, it was always very clear to me how different we were to everyone else in the world, through the media. But now that I've interacted with the students from other cultures, I realize that yes we are different in some ways, like our cultures, history, but we are more alike than the American media tends to portray. (from Kang & Moran, 2015: 190)

Thirty-two international students and three ITAs also completed the Language and Culture surveys at the beginning and end of the semester. This survey was composed of 10 (7-point Likert-scale) questions adopted from Neulip and McCroskey's (1997) ethnocentrism scale and the Bogardus (1925) social distance scale. Findings showed that students' willingness to interact or communicate with American students changed significantly toward the positive direction from before to after the intervention. Also, international students felt significantly more comfortable in collaborating with American students than they did before such experience. One ITA stated that she was surprised to see how supportive native English-speaking students were when communication breakdown happened and added the following comment: 'I think this kind of activity would help reduce stereotypes and negative perceptions that native speakers have towards non-native speakers and vice versa' (from the first author's unpublished source).

When it comes to undergraduate studies' course curriculum development, the current study is worthy of attention. As part of Liberal Arts requirements, it is common for undergraduate students to take an Anthropology 100-level (or equivalent) class, which intends to introduce various cultures and languages. However, the current study demonstrated that simply taking the class itself might not bring necessary or effective attitude changes to students. In contrast, students who participated in actual contact interventions revealed significant perceptual changes. This implies that it is important to incorporate hands-on contact experience in the curriculum, which can benefit undergraduate and intentional students as well as ITAs. What is also important is the positive impact of this contact on international students and ITAs. Participating in this constructive contact and interacting with US undergraduates in a structured manner has helped them positively change their attitudes toward US students. This finding suggests that this type of contact activity may be effective in promoting ITAs' interaction with US students in general.

Future Applications of Contact Activities

Due to the complex nature of 'the ITA problem,' researchers in several fields have observed and analyzed different facets of ITA/American undergraduate student interactions. It can be seen how a transdisciplinary approach could best address this multi-faceted issue that deals not only with oral proficiency and intelligibility, but also attitudes regarding people with non-native English accents, pedagogical skills and general dynamics of higher education. This chapter shows how researchers in the field of applied linguistics drew from social and educational psychology in order to ameliorate undergraduate students' attitudes towards ITAs.

Results showed that three sets of inter-group contact activities conducted between international students or ITAs and US undergraduate students could yield a measurable impact on certain attitudinal responses. At the same time, the successes of these various interventions lend credence to the view that comprehension of ITAs' speech is in part a function of the undergraduate's attitude toward ITAs and their willingness to communicate with international participants. These types of inter-group interventions might encourage undergraduate participants to individuate ITAs, and consequently detach the ITA group from negative stereotypes (Miller, 2002). Furthermore, undergraduates' contact with ITAs can help correct inaccurate information about ITAs that students often create (Pettigrew, 1998).

We have intentionally chosen three scenarios: (1) a single one-hour cultural-sensitization contact activity; (2) a semester-long institutionally supported cultural partner program; and (3) course-embedded contact activities. It is largely because they have the same fundamental idea in which US undergraduate students' negative attitudes toward ITAs can be mitigated by structured positive contact between students and ITAs (or international students), and in fact such interventions are practically feasible and achievable. Ultimately, these efforts can be well suited for the broader goal of enhancing students' global citizenship at large (Davies & Pike, 2009), which is what so many universities purport to do.

However, Subtirelu (2017) warns against minimizing the economic factors involved in ITA recruitment. HEIs save a great deal of money by having ITAs teach classes as they complete their graduate studies. With evidence that students avoid ITA-led classes at a mass level (e.g. Rubin & Smith, 1990), HEIs should be invested in creating more successful US undergraduate student/ITA encounters, at least from a financial motivation if not an altruistic one. HEIs are in need of intercultural training that has maximum impact for a minimum investment of time and capital. The studies summarized here offer options that could be implemented easily on a rather large scale. The first study took only one hour, a quick and casual implementation. The second and the third studies took place throughout the semester, but activities were embedded into already existing programs or courses. They can be easily adopted as models of approaches to improving US undergraduates' attitudes toward international peers and instructors. More specifically, inter-group contact activities like these can be incorporated into courses that now exist in intercultural communication, anthropology, linguistics and/or English departments, or adopted in orientation sessions or workshops that take place at the beginning of the school year.

The focus of our arguments in this chapter has been mostly on US undergraduate students and ITAs. However, a great number of studies about the Contact Hypothesis suggest that structured contact activities can also improve attitudes of other groups toward non-native speakers of English at large (see meta-analysis from Pettigrew & Tropp, 2006). Accordingly, the applications of this idea can certainly extend to other English for Specific Purpose (ESP) contexts. These types of activities can benefit overall communication between native speakers and non-native speakers in various workplaces (e.g. managers and employers in businesses or health care providers and patients). Corporations and medical hospitals could introduce intercultural contact to their diversity programs or consider modifying their existing activities by employing the contact principles presented in this chapter.

For concluding remarks, we would like to address a couple of caveats that one should be aware of when adapting and applying the contact activities. Perhaps the first caution goes with the administration itself. It is important for practitioners to provide systematic instruction of the contact invention. Anyone who plans to administer these contact activities should make sure to develop specific guidelines for each member of the contact group. Some of the activities can be piloted before the implementation. In addition, mediators or activity facilitators can ensure that each member of the group can participate in the activities after he/she fully understands the procedures. Finally, and most importantly, the activities should be enjoyable to all participants.

Another caveat would be activity-related; i.e. activities themselves need to be well thought out (see Kang & Moran, 2015). In fact, not all contact activities will lead to successful outcomes. Some may work better than others depending on the contexts of interventions or the size of participant groups. As Kang and Moran (2015: 195) confessed, their second day activity ('culture quizzes') was not well perceived by participants partially because the activity might have been too complex. They speculated that the activity was 'too advanced or vague' for international students to utilize. However, the non-verbal communication activity (Kang *et al.*, 2015) or the helium stick and spaghetti tower activities (Kang & Moran, 2015) were especially successful according to the authors. Therefore, it would be necessary to gain some insights into participants' reactions to some activities before any implementation.

Notes

(1) To see an example of the mystery puzzles, use the following link: www.edteck.com/rigor/lessons/detective/clues2.pdf.

(2) The complete version can be provided by the first author upon request.

(3) For more information on the helium stick activity, please see http://www.wilderdom. com/games/descriptions/HeliumStick.html

(4) For more information on the spaghetti towers activity, please see http://youthworkinit. com/spaghetti-and-marshmallow-tower/.

References

Ahn, J. and Moore, D. (2011) The relationship between students' accent perception and accented voice instructions and its effect on students' achievement in an interactive multimedia environment. *Journal of Educational Multimedia and Hypermedia* 20 (4), 319–335.

Allport, G.W. (1954) *The Nature of Prejudice*. Cambridge, MA: Addison-Wesley.

Altinsel, Z. and Rittenberg, W. (1996) Cultural support for international TAs: An under-graduate buddy program. Paper presented at the Conference of Teachers of English to Speakers of Other Languages (Chicago, IL, March 26–30).

Ashavskaya, E. (2015) International teaching assistants' experiences in the U.S. class-rooms: Implication for practice. *Journal of the Scholarship of Teaching and Learning* 15 (2), 56–69.

Ates, B. and Eslami, Z.R. (2012) Teaching experiences of native and nonnative English-speaking graduate teaching assistants and their perceptions of preservice teachers. *Journal on Excellence in College Teaching* 23 (3), 99–127.

Becker, M.T. (2017) Socializing with the out-group: Testing the Contact Hypothesis among school students in Bosnia and Herzegovina. *Politicka Masao: Croatian Political Science Review* 54 (4), 126–142.

Bogardus, E.S. (1925) Measuring social distances. *Journal of Applied Sociology* 9, 299–308.

Bresnahan, M.I. and Sun Kim, M. (1993) The impact of positive and negative messages on change in attitude toward international teaching assistants. *Folia Linguistica* 27 (3/4), 347–363.

Brown, R. and Hewstone, M. (2005) An integrative theory of intergroup contact. In M.P. Zanna (ed.) *Advances in Experimental Social Psychology* 37 (pp. 255–343). San Diego, CA, US: Elsevier Academic Press. doi: 10.1016/S0065-2601(05)37005-5

Chan, B.T. and Tsai, A. (2017) Personal contact with HIV-positive persons is associated with reduced HIV-related stigma: Cross-sectional analysis of general population sur-veys from 26 countries in sub-Saharan Africa. *Journal of the International AIDS Society* 20, 1–8. doi: 10.7448/IAS.20.1.21395

Chiang, S-Y. (2016) 'Is this what you're talking about?': Identity negotiation in international teaching assistants' instructional interactions with U.S. college students. *Journal of Language, Identity, & Education* 15 (2), 114–128. doi: 10.1080/15348458.2016.1137726

Compton, L.K.L. (2007) The impact of content and context on International Teaching Assistants' willingness to communicate in the language classroom. *TESL-EJ* 10 (4), 1–20.

Davies, I. and Pike, G. (2009) Global citizenship education: Challenges and possibilities. In R. Lewin (ed.) *The Handbook of Practice and Research in Study Abroad: Higher Education and the Quest for Global Citizenship* (pp. 61–78). New York, NY: Routledge.

Dovidio, J.F., Gaertner, S.L. and Kawakami, K. (2003) Intergroup contact: The past, present, and the future. *Group Processes & Intergroup Relations* 6 (1), 5–21.

Fitch, F. and Morgan, S.E. (2003) "Not a lick of English": Constructing the ITA identity through student narratives. *Communication Education* 52, 297–310.

Halleck, G.B. (2008) The ITA problem: A ready-to-use simulation. *Simulation & Gaming* 39 (1), 137–146.

Hewstone, M. and Brown, R. (1986) Contact is not enough: An intergroup perspective on the 'contact hypothesis.' In M. Hewstone and R. Brown (eds) *Contact and Conflict in Intergroup Encounters* (pp. 1–44). Cambridge, MA: Blackwell.

Isaacs, T. (2008) Towards defining a valid assessment criterion of pronunciation proficiency in non-native English speaking graduate students. *Canadian Modern Language Review* 64 (4), 555–580.

Jenkins, S. and Rubin, D.L. (1993) International teaching assistants and minority students: The two sides of cultural diversity in American higher education. *Journal of Graduate Teaching Assistant Development* 1, 17–24.

Jiang, X. (2014) Chinese biology teaching assistants' perception of their English proficiency: An exploratory case study. *The Qualitative Report* 19, 1–24.

Kang, O. and Moran, M. (2015) Enhancing communication between undergraduate students and International Teaching Assistants. *Studies in Graduate and Professional Student Development*, 169–201.

Kang, O. and Rubin, D.L. (2009) Reverse linguistic stereotyping: Measuring the effect of listener expectations on speech evaluation. *Journal of Language and Social Psychology* 28 (4), 441–456. doi: 10.1177/0261927X09341950

Kang, O., Rubin, D. and Lindemann, S. (2015) Mitigating U.S. undergraduates' attitudes toward international teaching assistants. *TESOL Quarterly* 49 (4), 681–706.

Kaplan, R.B. (1989) The life and times of ITA programs. *English for Specific Purposes* 8 (2), 109–124.

Lindemann, S. (2002) Listening with an attitude: A model of native-speaker comprehension of non-native speakers in the United States. *Language in Society* 31 (3), 419–441. doi:10.1017/S0047404502020286

Mayer, R.E., Sobko, K. and Mautone, P.D. (2003) Social cues in multimedia learning: Role of speaker's voice. *Journal of Educational Psychology* 95 (2), 419–425. doi: 10.1037/0022-0663.95.2.419

Meyer, K.R. and Mao, Y. (2014) Comparing student perceptions of the classroom climate created by U.S. American and International Teaching Assistants. *Higher Learning Research Communications* 4 (3), 12–22.

Mickus, M. and Bowen, D. (2017) Reducing the cultural divide among U.S. and Mexican students through application of the Contact Hypothesis. *Intercultural Education* 28 (6), 496–507. doi: 10.1080/14675986.2017.1388685

Miller, N. (2002) Personalization and the promise of contact theory. *Journal of Social Issues* 58, 387–410.

Monoson, P.K. and Thomas, C.F. (1993) Oral English proficiency policies for faculty in U.S. higher education. *Review of Higher Education* 16, 127–140.

Neulip, J.W. and McCroskey, J.C. (1997) The development of a U.S. and generalized ethnocentrism scale. *Communication Research Reports* 14, 385–398. doi:10.1080/08824099709388682

Pettigrew, T.F. (1998) Intergroup contact theory. *Annual Review of Psychology* 49, 65–85.

Pettigrew, T.F. and Tropp, L.R. (2006) A meta-analytic test of intergroup contact theory. *Journal of Personality and Social Psychology* 90, 751–783.

Plakans, B.S. (1997) Undergraduates' experiences with attitudes toward international teaching assistants. *TESOL Quarterly* 31 (1), 95–119.

Purdue University (2017) Purdue Liberal Arts: Oral English Proficiency Program. Accessed 29 January, 2018 from http://www.purdue.edu/oepp/

Ross, C. (2007) Paper presented as part of the InterSection on *Intercultural communication/international teaching assistants: Redirecting the flow of university intercultural responsibility* at the 41st Annual Teaching English to Speakers of Other Languages Convention in Seattle, WA.

Rubin, K.D. (1992) Nonlanguage factors affecting undergraduates' judgments of nonnative English-speaking teaching assistants. *Research in Higher Education* 33 (4), 511–531.

Rubin, D.L. (2002) Help! My professor (or doctor or boss) doesn't talk English! In J. Martin, T. Nakayama and L. Flores (eds) *Readings in Intercultural Communication: Experiences and Contexts* (pp. 127–137). Boston: McGraw-Hill.

Rubin, D.L. and Lannutti, P.J. (2001) Frameworks for assessing contact as a tool for reducing prejudice. In V.H. Milhouse, M.K. Asante and P.O. Nwosu (eds) *Transcultural Realities: Interdisciplinary Perspectives on Cross-Cultural Relations* (pp. 313–326). Thousand Oaks, CA, US: Sage Publications, Inc. doi: 10.4135/9781452229430.n18

Rubin, D.L. and Smith, K.A. (1990) Effects of accent, ethnicity, and lecture topic on undergraduates' perceptions of non-native English speaking teaching assistants. *International Journal of Intercultural Relations* 14, 337–353.

Sarwark, S. and vom Saal, D. (1989) Strengthening the international teaching assistant program through the involvement of undergraduates. Paper presented at the second National Conference on the Training and Employment of Graduate Teaching Assistants, Seattle, WA.

Smith, R.A., Strom, R.E. and Muthuswamy, N. (2005) Undergraduates' ratings of domestic and international teaching assistants: Timing of data collection and communication intervention. *Journal of Intercultural Communication Research* 34 (1/2), 3–21.

Staples, S., Kang, O. and Wittner, E. (2014) Impacting undergraduates' perceptions of ITAs through institutionally supported contact. *English for Specific Purposes* 35, 54–65.

Stephan, W.G. and Stephan, C. (1985) Intergroup anxiety. *Journal of Social Issues* 41, 57–176.

Subtirelu, N.C. (2017) Students' orientations to communication across linguistic difference with international teaching assistants at an internationalizing university in the United States. *Multilingua* 36 (3), 247–280.

Subtirelu, N.C. and Lindemann, S. (2016) Teaching first language speakers to communicate across linguistic difference: Addressing attitudes, comprehension, and strategies. *Applied Linguistics* 37 (6), 765–783.

Trebing, D. (2007) International teaching assistants' attitudes toward teaching and understanding of U.S. American undergraduate students. Unpublished doctoral dissertation. Southern Illinois University, Carbondale.

Tredoux, C. and Finchilescu, G. (2007) The Contact Hypothesis and intergroup relations 50 years on: Introduction to the special issue. *South African Journal of Psychology* 37 (4), 667–678.

Temple University (2018) Intensive English Language Program. Accessed 29 January, 2018 from https://ielp.temple.edu/find-program/international-graduate-students/international-teaching-assistant-program

Wickline, V.B., Neu, T., Dodge, C.P. and Shriver, E.R. (2016) Testing the Contact Hypothesis: Improving college students' affective attitudes toward people with disabilities. *Journal on Excellence in College Teaching* 27 (2), 3–28.

Yook, E.L. and Albert, R.D. (1999) Perceptions of international teaching assistants: The interrelatedness of intercultural training, cognition, and emotion. *Communication Education* 48 (1), 1–17.

vom Saal, D. (1987) The undergraduate experience and international teaching assistants. In N. Van Note Chism and S.B. Warner (eds) *Institutional Responsibilities and Responses in the Employment and Education of Teaching Assistants* (pp. 267–274). Columbus, OH: The Ohio State University.

6 Examining Rater Bias in Scoring World Englishes Speakers Using a Transdisciplinary Approach: Implications for Assessing International Teaching Assistants

Jing Wei

This chapter takes a transdisciplinary approach to examine how linguistic stereotypes – a critical concept in research studies on international teaching assistants – play a role in raters' scores of test takers of a variety of language backgrounds (Fir Group, 2016). It employed a mixed-method design that involves an experimental component to examine the impact of a special training package on raters' scores and the rationale for why such changes occurred. The findings from the study showed that raters' judgment of test takers' responses was not just engagement of semiotic resources at the micro level, but rather a complex linguistic behavior conditioned by social identities that were developed through sociocultural institutions and communities at the meso level.

Introduction

As English is spreading globally, new linguistic features that deviate from the Inner Circle English forms start to emerge (Kachru, 1982, 1985). Although features characterizing the target language use domain have changed, English language tests still remain unchanged, which causes a mismatch between the forms that are tested and the forms that are required for successful communications in the real world. Tests that continue to target Inner Circle English varieties are biased against users of other English varieties, as their test scores do not reflect their true communicative competence.

Given the mismatch between what is tested and what is required for real-world communications, World Englishes (WE) scholars (e.g. Elder & Davies, 2006) call for a revolution in language tests so that constructs other than native English varieties can be assessed. They argue that instead of using Inner Circle native English varieties as the standard, language tests should be normed on Outer and Expanding Circle English varieties (traditionally labeled as non-native English varieties). On the other hand, researchers on English as a Lingua Franca (ELF) (e.g. Jenkins, 2006; Jenkins & Leung, 2013, 2017) argue for a different approach to revamp the current language testing practice. They contend that English use has transcended the boundaries of language varieties. English language users are constantly shuttling between different varieties of English or between different languages. Therefore, the knowledge/ability to use one single variety or language is not sufficient to meet the communicative demands in the current world. One needs to be proficient in multiple languages and language varieties as well as to have the ability to make the appropriate choice about which language or variety should be used based on a communicative context.

In a different context, there has been a similar concern about test bias in Native Speaking (NS) undergraduate students' judgment of international teaching assistants (ITAs). University campuses in the US have become increasingly diverse with the influx of international students to higher education. According to National Center for Education Statistics, 27.1% percent of teaching assistants are international students (Kang et al., 2015). As more international students serve as teaching assistants, they are often perceived by NS undergraduate students as lacking the necessary English language proficiency to explain the academic contents clearly (Lindemann, 2002). Undergraduate students' linguistic stereotypes about ITAs have been shown to negatively affect their ability to comprehend instructions delivered by ITAs and their ratings of ITAs' oral proficiency levels (Rubin, 2002). Linguistic stereotypes have become the focus of research in ITA studies. However, very few studies have been conducted to look at whether linguistic stereotypes exist in trained raters in the standardized assessment setting and how raters' linguistic stereotypes affect their scores of test takers of a variety of language backgrounds.

In light of these gaps, the purpose of this chapter is to take a transdisciplinary approach to examine how linguistic stereotypes – a concept key in ITA research – play a role in raters' scores of test takers of a variety of language backgrounds (Douglas Fir Group, 2016). It is particularly valuable to take a transdisciplinary approach to investigate rater issues, because raters' judgment of test takers' responses are not purely linguistic in nature, but rather an reflection of their identify that is shaped by the sociocultural institutions and communities in which raters participated as well as influenced by larger societal value systems (Douglas Fir Group, 2016).

Literature Review

Debate on World Englishes assessment

According to WE scholars (Canagarajah, 2006; Davies, 1999; Davies *et al.*, 2003; Lowenberg, 1993, 2000, 2002), the primary reason for proposing a WE test is that: Native English (NE), the construct that is being assessed by current international English tests, has been challenged by the changing order of communication in our postmodern era: English is increasingly used as an instrument of communication by people who were traditionally labeled as non-native speakers. Continuing to use NE as the norm for language tests may result in test bias. While admitting that Standard English or Native Speaker is the norm that guides international English tests, language testers defend that resorting to the NS norm is not driven by a political agenda of representing the interests of the Inner Circle countries, but by a practical concern of developing valid, fair tests that can be held accountable to all test takers (Elder & Davies, 2006; Elder & Harding, 2008).

Elder and Harding (2008) have named four major obstacles that are faced by test developers in developing WE tests: first, the construct of WE test is fluid, which refers to the fact that many of the local varieties of English that are spoken by the Outer and Expanding Circles countries have not yet been fully codified. It is therefore not possible to develop a test based on a changing construct. Second, it is the purpose of the test that dictates what construct should be tested. One cannot pre-specify WE as the construct to be assessed across all contexts of assessment. Third, limited by the practical constraint of not being able to sample representatively from English varieties spoken by all test takers, including only a few varieties will not be fair to test takers who are not familiar with the varieties that are sampled. Finally, tests that only assess proficiency in local varieties of English may not adequately serve the interests of test takers who aim to migrate beyond the local contexts. Also, English speakers from the Outer and Expanding Circles often have negative attitudes towards the local forms of English, and prefer to be tested by an international English test than by a local test. All the constraints that are involved in test development make it difficult for language testers to fully embrace the assessment of WE as an alternative to the current testing practice. Among all the constraints identified, none of them were related to rater issues and the potential problem of linguistic stereotypes in raters.

Rater training

Training has been recommended as the standard procedure in large-scale standardized tests because training helps raters better understand rating scales and test tasks, which reduces rater variation (Weigle, 1994). On the other hand, there have been reports that the effects of training tend to be rather short-lived (e.g. Lumley & McNamara, 1995) or limited to internal consistency (e.g. Weigle, 1998). Among all the rater training studies, none of the rater training programs aimed to reduce linguistic stereotypes, with the exception of ITA studies conducted by Kang and her colleagues that examined how inter-group contacts helped ameliorate undergraduate student's linguistic stereotypes (Kang, 2008; Kang et al., 2015).

Kang (2008) examined how undergraduate raters' language background and linguistic stereotypes are associated with their ratings of ITAs. She recruited 70 US undergraduate students as raters and asked them to rate ITAs' speech samples. Then, she administered a socio-psychological intervention in which a subgroup of raters was asked to solve mystery puzzles with ITAs. After six weeks, all raters were invited to rate the same batch of speech samples again. A two (time of training) by two (training group) mixed factorial analysis of variance (ANOVA) was conducted on each dependent variable (i.e. ratings of oral proficiency, instructional competence, comprehensibility, accent standardness, superiority, social attractiveness and rater leniency) in order to understand the impact of the intervention on each type of rating. The results showed that the socio-psychological intervention was particularly effective in improving undergraduate students' ratings of ITAs' instructional competence and comprehensibility.

Focusing on a similar research question, Kang et al. (2015) reported on two studies that looked at the impact of inter-group contact activities on undergraduate students' ratings of ITAs' language and teaching proficiency. Using slightly different research designs, both studies revealed that inter-group contact as brief as one hour resulted in statistically higher ratings of ITAs' language and teaching proficiency in the treatment group than ratings of ITAs in the control group. Although inter-group contact intervention has been shown to be effective in reducing undergraduate students' linguistic stereotypes, it has limited applications in the context of standardized assessment, as it is not practical to have raters participating in inter-group contact activities with test takers. Therefore, this study proposes an alternative method for reducing raters' linguistic stereotypes, that is, through modifying standard rater training programs.

The purpose of the current study is to explore the possibility of implementing alternative rating criteria that are different from standard Inner Circle English in large-scale international English language tests through a special training package and to investigate the role that linguistic stereotypes play in the rating process. It focuses on the following research question:

> How did a special training program that targets Outer and Expanding Circle varieties of English affect raters' scores?

This question can be broken into two sub-questions:

> i) *How did raters' scores in the special training program change from pre- to post-training, compared to raters' scores in the regular training program?*
>
> ii) *Why did such changes occur after raters participated in the special training program?*

Methods

This study employs a mixed-method design that involves an experimental component to examine the impact of a special training package on raters' scores and the rationale for why such changes occurred. Indian, Chinese and American raters were selected as the participants of this study because they represented three different language backgrounds from Kachru's model of three concentric circles (Kachru, 1985). Specifically, Indian raters represented the Outer Circle English speakers, Chinese raters represented the Expanding Circle English speakers, and American raters represented the Inner Circle English speakers. Raters of the three language backgrounds were randomly assigned into an experimental group that used the special training package and a control group that was trained with the regular training package. In order to measure the effects of training on raters' scores and awareness of World Englishes features, both the special and regular training groups scored a set of speaking responses after the training. In order to examine why changes in raters score occurred, raters also performed think-aloud on a subset of responses to demonstrate the decision-making process and the criteria they applied in assigning scores.

Participants

Thirty Indian, Chinese and American raters participated in this study. They were consisted of 10 raters born and raised in India, 10 raters born and raised in China, and 10 raters born and raised in the US. Almost all of the raters were graduate students from New York University and Columbia University with backgrounds in TESOL, English education or a related field. The raters' ages ranged from 21 to 63, with a mean of 29.29. Of these, seven were male and 23 were female. Each language group has a mix of experienced and novice teachers, whose teaching experience ranged from 0 to 6 years.

TOEFL iBT task prompts

The speech samples included test takers' responses to four prompts of two task types. Prompts 1 and 3 were independent tasks that required test takers to use their own knowledge, information, or personal opinion to answer questions without having to synthesize any reading or listening source material. Prompts 2 and 4 were integrated tasks that assessed test takers' ability to summarize and compare ideas based on what was learned from a listening and a reading passage. The independent tasks asked test takers to clearly state their opinion about a familiar topic (i.e. 'which is the best way to relax' for prompt 1 and 'getting up early versus getting up late' for prompt 3) and to explain their reasons for that opinion. For both prompts, test takers had 15 seconds to prepare and 45 seconds to complete their responses. The two integrated tasks were based on a campus life situation and an academic lecture respectively. For prompt 2, test takers were asked to summarize a conversation between two students talking about renovating a school library. For prompt 4, test takers were required to first listen to a biology professor's lecture on allergies and then explain what causes an allergic reaction by using the example given by the professor. For the two integrated tasks, test takers were given 30 seconds to prepare their responses and 60 seconds to complete the tasks.

TOEFL iBT scoring rubrics

There was a separate rubric for each type of task, but both rubrics evaluated test takers' responses in terms of delivery, topic development and language use. Delivery refers to the pace, clarity and intelligibility of the speech. In assessing delivery, raters had to take into account pronunciation, intonation patterns, rhythm/pace and fluidity of expressions of test takers' responses. Language use refers to the range, complexity and accuracy of the use of grammar and vocabulary. The third dimension – topic development – differs slightly for the independent task than for the integrated task. For independent tasks, topic development evaluates test takers on the development and coherence of their responses and the clarity of the relationship between the ideas presented. For integrated tasks, topic development also assesses the accuracy, relevance and completeness of the ideas as required by a task prompt. There were five levels in each rubric, and test takers' responses were rated holistically on a scale of 0 to 4. In order to achieve level 4 – the highest level, test takers' responses had to fulfill the descriptions of all three criteria. However, to obtain a score of 1 to 3, their responses only needed to match the descriptions for two out of three criteria. Score 0 was only given to people who did not make any attempt to answer a question. Since the TOEFL public data set does not contain any response of this type, level 0 was removed from the rubric for the current study.

Speech samples

The speech samples rated by raters were drawn from a data set provided by Educational Testing Services (ETS). The entire data set consisted of 240 candidates' responses to six tasks. However, for the purpose of the current study, only 20 Chinese and 20 Indian test takers' responses to two independent tasks and two integrated tasks were selected as speech samples for scoring and training. When sampling test takers, a systematic approach was taken to ensure that the selected samples were representative of the levels of speaking proficiency of the entire public data set. Specifically, test takers of each language group were first divided into four quartiles based on their overall speaking scores. Then, a fixed number of test takers were randomly selected from each quartile. Although this approach cannot guarantee that the Chinese and Indian test takers were matched in their proficiency levels (i.e. in the large data set, the Indian test takers have higher overall speaking scores than Chinese test takers), it ensures that the selected sample properly represents the large data set.

Data collection

All of the scoring sessions were conducted face-to-face and monitored by the researcher. Raters were requested to bring their own laptops in order to complete all the instruments that were delivered online. They first convened in a seminar room to complete training and scoring, and then broke into individual rooms to conduct think-aloud protocols.

First, raters from each language background group were randomly assigned to a treatment and a control group, resulting in five Indian, five Chinese and five American raters in the treatment group, and five Indian, five Chinese and five American raters in the control group. The treatment group received a 60-minute special training conducted by the researcher for each task. Raters listened only to Chinese and Indian test takers' speech samples, and read explanations of each benchmark sample in which varietal features in the Chinese and Indian test takers' responses were highlighted. On the other hand, raters in the control group received regular training from the researcher for the same two tasks. The difference was that the speech samples used in regular training were sampled from test takers speaking various L1s, and the raters were only provided with topic notes and annotations to benchmark samples. No explanations were given about features of English unique to Chinese and Indian test takers. The complete list of features of Chinese and Indian English can be found in Appendix B.

After the training, both groups participated in a scoring session in which they rated the same set of 40 speech samples. At the end of scoring, raters participated in a 15-minute tutorial on think-aloud protocols (TAPs) and spent 45 minutes to an hour rating an additional set of 8 speech samples that were selected by the researcher and conducting think-aloud while rating them. The think-aloud was conducted independently by raters in separate seminar rooms with the guidance of a list of questions prepared by the researcher (see Appendix C for a sample list of questions used in TAPs). A digital recorder was set up in each seminar room to record the verbal protocols and the recordings were later transcribed verbatim by the researcher.

Data analysis

To address Research Sub-Question 1, the researcher conducted two separate Multifaceted Rasch Model (MFRM) analyses on rater scores from the special training group and the regular training group after training. For each MFRM analysis, the model included five main facets (i.e. rater, test taker, item, rater group and test taker group) as well as the interaction between rater and test taker group.

The effect of training on scores was measured by comparing the special and regular training group in their post-training score internal consistency and severity spread. Four statistical indices were used in judging internal consistency: test taker fixed chi square value, test taker separation ratio, and the reliability of the test taker separation index (Knoch *et al.*, 2007). Severity spread was examined by rater fixed chi-square value, rater separation ratio, rater separation strata, the reliability of rater separation index, and the number of raters with severity measures moving closer to the mean of zero (Elder *et al.*, 2007; Knoch *et al.*, 2007).

To investigate Research Sub-Question 2, that is, the effect of special training on raters' awareness of Chinese and Indian varietal features, the researcher examined the verbal protocol data from raters of each training group using content analysis (Strauss & Corbin, 1998). The researcher transcribed the recordings and coded the data thematically. Since no existing coding scheme fit the purpose of the current analysis, the codes were extracted from the data using a grounded theory approach, i.e. open coding, memoing and sorting (Strauss & Corbin, 1998). Particular attention was paid to raters' ability to interpret Chinese and Indian varietal features that were highlighted in the special training package, with additional focus on raters' attitudes towards Chinese and Indian English.

Findings

Training effects on scores

This section first reports the quantitative analysis of rater scores – comparing the internal consistency and severity spread of the rater scores between the special and regular training groups. The hypothesis of this study was that raters who participated in the special rater training program would be more lenient in scoring Chinese and Indian English speakers than those who participated in the regular training program. The training outcome was measured by the internal consistency and severity spread of scores of a group. Then, findings from the verbal protocol analysis were drawn on to explain the underlying rationale for the reported change in raters' scores.

Training group difference in internal consistency

Group difference in internal consistency was investigated by examining the separation statistics of test takers' scores, i.e. chi-square, separation ratio, separation strata and separation reliability (Knoch *et al.*, 2007). When test takers cannot be separated into distinguishable strata, it shows that raters as a group have low internal consistency in scoring.

Table 6.1 displays the values of test taker separation indices. The first index, test taker fixed chi-square tests the assumption that all test takers have the same level performance after accounting for measurement errors (Knoch *et al.*, 2007). The fixed chi-square values for both special training and regular training groups indicate that in both conditions test takers can be separated into different levels of performances, which shows that all raters scored consistently after they received training. Furthermore, the test taker separation ratio and strata indicate the number of statistically distinguishable levels of performance into which test takers can be separated. Similar to the conclusion made from fixed chi-square values, both separation ratio and strata suggest that test takers can be separated into statistically distinguishable levels (indicating that raters scored consistently in both conditions). Finally, the separation reliability values, as shown in Table 6.1, were very high, i.e. close to 1, which shows that raters from both groups scored consistently after the training. Although the four indices above show that both groups of raters scored consistently internally, the values of those four indices for the special training group were slightly larger than the values for the regular training group. This suggests that internal consistency of raters for the special training group was slightly higher than that of the regular training group.

Training group difference in severity spread

One way to assess whether the severity spread was different for the special training group than for the regular training group is by comparing the value of fixed chi-square statistic in the post-training condition. The fixed chi-square tests the hypothesis that all raters in the group exercised the same level of severity during the rating. A significant value means that at least the most severe and the most lenient raters from a group had shown different levels of severity when rating test takers. Suppose that

Table 6.1 Test taker separation statistics

	Special training ($n = 15$)	Regular training ($n = 15$)
Fixed chi-square	420.8, df = 19, $p = 0.00$	389.1, df = 19, $p = 0.00$
Separation ratio	4.61	4.20
Separation strata	6.48	5.93
Reliability	0.96	0.95

Table 6.2 Rater severity measures

	Special training	Regular training
Fixed Chi-square	94.4, df = 14, p = 0.00	42.7, df = 14, p = 0.00
Separation ratio	2.48	1.51
Separation strata	3.63	2.34
Reliability	0.86	0.69

raters who received special training had shown smaller spread in rating severities than raters who were regularly trained, the fixed chi-square statistic in the special training group should be smaller than that in the regular training group. Table 6.2 shows that for the special training group, the value of fixed chi-square statistic was actually larger than that of the regular training group, which indicates that raters in the special training group varied more in severity.

Similar findings about rater severity spread were revealed by separation ratio and separation strata. Separation ratio and separation strata assess the distribution of scoring severity of a rater group (Knoch *et al.*, 2007). Separation ratio measures 'the spread of the rater severity measures relative to the precision of those measures', and separation strata shows 'the number of statistically distinct levels of rater severity among the sample of raters' (Knoch *et al.*, 2007: 32). If raters in a group move closer in their scoring severity after training, their separation ratio and separation strata should become smaller. Table 6.2 shows that the separation ratio and separation strata statistics of the special training group were larger than the same statistics of the regular training group. After training, raters from the special training group were divided into three and a half distinct level in their scoring severity, as indicated by their separation strata, whereas raters from the regular training group were separate into two and a third statistically distinct levels. The rater separation reliability index is a measure of the reproducibility of rater severity estimates (Winke *et al.*, 2013). In the case of special training group, the separation reliability index was 0.86, suggesting that the same rater scoring severity distribution would happen again if the same data collection procedure was repeated. However, for the regular training group, the separation reliability index was relatively low at 0.69, which indicates that raters' severity estimates might not be reproducible.

To address Research Sub-Question 1 – *How did raters' scores in the special training program change from pre- to post-training, compared to raters' scores in the regular training program*, the FACET results show that there was more variation in raters' scores after they received the special training than after they received the regular training. Analysis of TAP data shed light on why raters in the special training group had more variance in their ratings than those in the regular training group.

Insights from verbal protocol data

The analyses of TAP data revealed a possible source of rater variations after they received the special training: raters showed a different degree of acceptance of the language features that are unique to Chinese and Indian English varieties. In other words, most of the raters became aware of those varietal features after the special training, but not all of them regarded the use of those features as grammatically accurate. This in turn implies that raters might have different attitudes towards the legitimacy of the Chinese and Indian English varieties and those attitudes were resistant to the special training they received. Here are some examples that illustrate rater differences in whether they accepted Indian and Chinese English varietal features.

In the special training, raters were told that the phrase 'more better' was frequently used by Indian English speakers and was acceptable in that variety. However, in the TAP data, raters made different comments on whether they thought it was appropriate to use 'more better.' Four out of 15 raters commented that 'more better' was grammatically incorrect whereas 5/15 raters said that they were fine with this usage. The remaining raters did not explicitly express how they would score this feature. For example, Rater A-1 said: 'I think there is something in the explanation about "more better." Even before that, this wasn't something that would bother me.' Similarly, Rater I-9 commented: 'I think er he uses a very typical phrase. He uses "more better." I think I heard quite a few of my Indian friends used that. Even it is not grammatical I feel Indians do think it is [grammatical] though. It can be excused.' On the other hand, some raters explicitly pointed this out as a grammatical error. Rater I-2 said: 'Here he says "it is more better to get up early" which is grammatically incorrect.'

The same pattern was detected with raters' comments about Chinese test takers' responses. Not all raters in the special training group accepted Chinese English features that were highlighted in the training materials. When responding to the prompt of what is the best way to relax after studying, a Chinese test taker talked about the importance of relaxation by citing a Chinese idiom: 'If we take the time to sharpen our knife, we will cut the wood more efficiently.' Although raters were able to understand why Chinese test takers used idioms in their responses, not all raters considered using idioms as acceptable. Among the 15 raters, five raters said that it was legitimate to use Chinese idioms while three raters had a different opinion. For example, Rater C-8 was concerned that the use of Chinese idioms might cause intelligibility problems for raters who were less familiar with Chinese language background: 'So it's pretty easy for Chinese, for speakers with Chinese native background to understand that idiom, but I don't know if it applies to people from other cultural backgrounds.' Similarly, another rater, Rater C-6 commented that the idiom use was not 'native-like': 'But this is just direct translation from Chinese to English. I don't think it's native-like

[...] I don't like the way she used that proverb, coz as a Chinese I can understand her but for readers from a totally different background, I don't think they will understand what she is talking about.' On the contrary, Raters C-9 and I-1 complimented the test taker on the same response. C-9 said: 'This student is really smart, because it showed that she was able to use metaphor to illustrate why people need to have a rest or need to relax.' I-1 commented: 'This person is very creative.'

To summarize, compared with raters who received regular training, raters in the special training group showed lower internal consistency and higher severity spread after they were normed on rating materials that highlighted Indian and Chinese English features. Analyses of raters' TAP data revealed that such variances in specially trained raters' scores might be attributed to their different attitudes towards those language varieties.

Discussion

The purpose of this study was to take a transdisciplinary approach to investigate the effects of a special rater training package on raters' scores and their rating criteria. The analyses revealed that raters who were normed on features unique to Chinese and Indian English varieties had slightly higher internal consistency but larger spread in severity measures compared to those who were normed on standard American English. Such results may on appearance suggest the 'ineffectiveness' of the special training package. However, the researcher would argue that it is far more superior to have less than consistent scores by implementing the appropriate scoring criteria than aiming for a false cleanness in scores. The purpose of rater training should be to train raters to score test takers based on their real communicative competence. In our current world, that is manifested by a multilingual multicultural competence (Jenkins & Leung, 2013). Using standard Inner English as the norming criteria might achieve uniformity in raters' scores, but it essentially is teaching raters to uniformly apply the erroneous rating criteria. Therefore, test developing companies and the test research community should not be intimidated by the appearance of messiness in rater scores and start to explore the possibility of assessing test takers using the appropriate criteria.

Another significant finding from the study was that not all raters who received the special training accepted the features of Chinese and Indian Englishes in spite of being aware of those features. This finding shows that scoring is not merely raters' engagement with semiotic resources at the micro level. Raters' scores are conditioned and shaped through a variety of sociocultural institutions and communities at the meso level (Fir Group, 2016). This finding also speaks to the importance of making the distinction between rater awareness and rater acceptance. Previous studies on shared L1 effects in raters and listening comprehension tests have mixed findings about the existence of shared L1 effects (Bent & Bradlow, 2003;

Carey *et al.*, 2011; Harding, 2012; Stibbard & Lee, 2006). For example, Carey *et al.* (2011) found that raters who were familiar with test takers' accents were more lenient towards that group of test takers in scoring. On the other hand, Bent and Bradlow (2003) reported that shared L1 advantage in listening test only appeared when the listening materials were read by heavily accented speakers. The TAP analyses in the current study provided a reasonable explanation of why the body of literature on shared L1 effects had mixed findings: raters might be able to understand features of Outer and Expanding Circle English varieties, but they might not accept them as accurate in scoring. Therefore, the shared L1 effects in scoring appeared in some studies but not all of them, depending on the language attitudes of raters used in a particular study.

Conclusions

The current study has significant theoretical and methodological implications for language assessment. Theoretically, the result of the study has implications for the conceptualization of rater training. In previous rater training studies (e.g. Elder *et al.*, 2007; Knoch *et al.*, 2007), scoring consistency seems to be the only target that is to be attained. However, the current study shows that as raters were first normed on new scoring criteria, they might show different degrees of resistance towards those criteria and their scores would become less consistent than before. Such messiness in scores is far more desirable than a false uniformity with the wrong scoring standard being implemented.

Methodologically, this study shows the importance of employing a mixed-method design to investigate training effects both in terms of their scores and scoring criteria. The analyses of scores showed that raters from the special training group scored less consistently than raters from the regular training group. Such finding of rater scores can be supported by TAP data which showed that not all raters who received the special training accepted Chinese and Indian English variety features in spite of being aware of them. The employment of both qualitative and quantitative methods provides data triangulation that would not be possible if only quantitative method were used (Wei & Llosa, 2015).

References

Bent, T. and Bradlow, A.R. (2003) The interlanguage speech intelligibility benefit. *Journal of the Acoustic Society of America* 114 (3), 1600–1610.

Canagarajah, S. (2006) Changing communicative needs, revised assessment objectives: Testing English as an international language. *Language Assessment Quarterly* 3, 229–242.

Carey, M.D., Mannell, R.H. and Dunn, P.K. (2011) Does a rater's familiarity with a candidate's pronunciation affect the rating in oral proficiency interviews? *Language Testing* 28 (2), 201–219.

Davies, A. (1999) Standard English: Discordant voices. *World Englishes* 18, 171–186.

Davies, A., Hamp-Lyons, L. and Kemp, C. (2003) Whose norms? International proficiency tests in English. *World Englishes* 22 (4), 571–584.

Douglas Fir Group (2016) A transdisciplinary framework for SLA in a multilingual world. *The Modern Language Journal* 100, 19–47.

Elder, C. and Davies, A. (2006) Assessing English as a lingua franca. *Annual Review of Applied Linguistics* 26, 282–301.

Elder, C., Knoch, U., Barkhuizen, G. and Randow, J. (2007) Evaluating rater responses to an online training program for L2 writing assessment. *Language Testing* 24 (1), 37–64.

Elder, C. and Harding, L. (2008) Language testing and English as an international language: Constraints and contributions. *Australian Review of Applied Linguistics* 31 (3), 1–34.

Harding, L. (2012) Accent, listening assessment and the potential for a shared-L1 advantage: A DIF perspective. *Language Testing* 29 (2), 163–180.

Jenkins, J. (2006) The times they are (very slowly) a-changin'. *ELT Journal* 60 (1), 61–62.

Jenkins, J. and Leung, C. (2013) English as a Lingua Franca. *International Journal of Applied Linguistics (United Kingdom)* 23 (3), 396.

Jenkins, J. and Leung, C. (2017) *English as a lingua franca* 3 (3), 30–51.

Kachru, B.B. (1982) *The Other Tongue: English Across Cultures*. Urbana, IL: University of Illinois Press.

Kachru, B.B. (1985) Standards, codification and sociolinguistic realism: The English language in the outer circle. In R. Quirk and H.G. Widdowson (eds) *English in the World: Teaching and Learning the Language and Literatures* (pp. 11–30). Cambridge: Cambridge University Press.

Kang, O. (2008) Ratings of L2 oral performance in English: Relative impact of rater characteristics and acoustic measures of accentedness. PhD thesis, University of Georgia.

Kang, O., Rubin, D.L. and Lindemann, S. (2015) Mitigating U.S. undergraduates' attitudes toward international teaching assistants. *TESOL Quarterly* 49 (4), 681–706.

Knoch, U., Read, J. and Randow, J. (2007) Re-training writing raters online: How does it compare with face-to-face training? *Assessing Writing* 12, 16–43.

Lindemann, S. (2002) Listening with an attitude: A model of native-speaker comprehension of non-native speakers in the United States. *Language in Society* 31, 419–441.

Lowenberg, P.H. (1993) Issues of validity in tests of English as a world language: Whose standards? *World Englishes* 12 (1), 95–106.

Lowenberg, P.H. (2000) Assessing English proficiency in the global context: The significance of non-native norms. In H.W. Kam (ed.) *Language in the Global Context: Implications for the Language Classroom* (pp. 207–228). Singapore: SEAMEO Regional Language Center.

Lowenberg, P.H. (2002) Assessing English proficiency in the expanding circle. *World Englishes* 21, 431–435.

Lumley, T. and McNamara, T. (1995) Rater characteristics and rater bias: Implications for training. *Language Testing* 12, 54–71.

Rubin, D.L. (2002) Help! My professor (or doctor or boss) doesn't talk English! In J. Martin, T. Nakayama and L. Flores (eds) *Readings in Intercultural Communication: Experiences and Contexts* (pp. 127–137). Boston, MA: McGraw-Hill.

Stibbard, R.M. and Lee, J. (2006) Evidence against the mismatched interlanguage speech intelligibility benefit hypothesis. *Journal of the Acoustic Society of America* 120 (1), 433–442.

Strauss, A. and Corbin, J.M. (1998) *Basics of Qualitative Research: Techniques and Procedures for Developing Grounded Theory*. London: SAGE publications.

Wei, J. and Llosa, L. (2015) Investigating differences between American and Indian raters in assessing TOEFL iBT Speaking Tasks. *Language Assessment Quarterly* 12 (3), 283–304.

Weigle, S.C. (1994) Effects of training on raters of ESL compositions. *Language Testing* 11, 197–223.

Weigle, S.C. (1998) Using FACETS to model rater training effects. *Language Testing* 15 (2), 263–287.

Winke, P., Gass, S. and Myford, C. (2013) Raters' L2 background as a potential source of bias in rating oral performance. *Language Testing* 30 (2), 231–252. https://doi.org/10.1177/0265532212456968

Appendix A: Examples of Anchor Justifications

Special training anchor justification

This is another response from an Indian test taker. In this response, vocabulary and grammar are used effectively and accurately for the most part. The phrase 'more better' is an expression that is created, used and accepted in all India (although it is considered as a grammatical mistake in American prescriptive grammar). It means 'better than better'. For example, people would say: 'I like iPhone better than my old Nokia, but Raj says that Samsung Galaxy is more better.' The speaker demonstrates considerable automaticity at the phrasal and sentence level, although the range of the structures used is somewhat limited. The information the speaker communicates is clearly relevant to the prompt. She uses her personal example to discuss why she prefers early morning and early night. Although she clearly indicates a preference, her reasoning to back up the preference lacks elaboration.

Regular training anchor justification

In this response, the speech is generally clear and the pacing is fluid. The speaker demonstrates a fairly good use of grammatical uses and vocabulary, though minor lapses do exist. The speaker starts by saying she personally prefers getting up early and going to bed early. Her reasons are quite simple. Then she uses 'however' to signal a transition, but the content followed does not match the expectation of the listener (she does not say anything that contrasts with 'my reasons are quite simple'). Later, she compares her personal experience of two opposite life styles and her own feelings, and uses that as the reason to support her preference. Because of the lack of coherence at the beginning, this response gets a THREE.

Appendix B: Examples of Indian and Chinese English Highlighted in the Training

The following examples show how features of Indian and Chinese English were highlighted in explanations for training samples in the specialized training group.

Indian test taker

(1) This response from an Indian speaker is sustained and the content is well-developed. The speech is clear, pacing is fluid and intonation is used to help convey this speaker's attitude towards the question. Some of the information that the speaker provides is clearly incidental (e.g. he does exactly the opposite). Although this information is not directly relevant to the main argument, this does not detract from the coherence of this response. This speaker clearly indicates his preference and provides two reasons to back up his opinion. His arguments about 'the mind works best in the morning' and 'getting up early helps your body cycle works properly' are common beliefs in the culture and functions to support his argument.

(2) This is another response from an Indian test taker. In this response, vocabulary and grammar are used effectively and accurately for the most part. The phrase 'more better' is an expression that is created, used and accepted in all India (although it is considered as a grammatical mistake in American prescriptive grammar). It means 'better than better'. For example, people would say: 'I like iPhone better than my old Nokia, but Raj says that Samsung Galaxy is more better.' The speaker demonstrates considerable automaticity at the phrasal and sentence level, although the range of the structures used is somewhat limited. The information the speaker communicates is clearly relevant to the prompt. She uses her personal example to discuss why she prefers early morning and early night. Although she clearly indicates a preference, her reasoning to back up the preference lacks elaboration.

(3) In this response by an Indian test taker, even though words and phrases can be easily understood, the response is very limited. Much of the speaker's language is directly repeated from the prompt ('go to bed early at night and wake up early'). The delivery is choppy, fragmented and telegraphic, with frequent long pauses and incompleteness. The speaker lists out two reasons for getting up early: 'give us relaxation' and 'good discipline', neither of which is elaborated. Implied in his response are cultural beliefs that getting up early and going to bed early is a healthy life style, and indicates self-discipline (i.e. waking up early shows you are lazy). The relevance of the response may depend on to what extent the rater/scorer endorses these beliefs. Also, there are places with missing articles (e.g. 'agree with opinion'), which is because definite articles are used as if conventions are reversed in Indian English. For example, 1) *It is the nature's way.* 2) *Office is closed today.*

The pronunciations of the first vowels in 'opinion' and 'early' are also typical of Indian English. /ɒ/, /ɔː/ and /ə/ are merged (as in cot, caught, courtesy). Also, the r-sound in 'early' is not rhotic (contrasted with American pronunciation of 'early').

(4) This is another response from an Indian test taker (South India). Speech is basically intelligible, though listener effort is needed primarily because of its intonation pattern and rhythm. Most of the Indian languages are 'syllable-timed' (meaning each syllable lasts about the same time). However, English is a 'stress-timed' language (i.e. syllables may last different amount of time and only content words are stressed). The test taker's first language, Telugu, gets transferred to English speaking. Because every word is having the same stress, the speech has a 'sing-song' nature. There are instances where problems with articulation obscure meaning ('exam', 'got good results' 'improve health'). In terms of content, the response is related to the task. The test taker prefers going to bed early and getting up early because he works more efficiently in this way. He uses a personal example to support this argument: he got up early one time and studied for an exam, and got good results. However, parts of the response sound very repetitious: he starts by repeating the prompt, not presenting his opinion.

(5) This speech is generally clear. Pacing is fluid. The overall intelligibility is high. He uses intonation patterns effectively to persuade the listeners (e.g. 'I would know like 'come on' I have something like…').

The speaker does not start the response by clearly expressing an opinion. Rather, at the beginning his preference is implied through a personal example. Only at the end is his preference explicitly stated. This is consistent with characteristics of discourse structures of Indian English. Based on argument of contrastive rhetoric, instead of following a linear progression of content development (first expressing an opinion and then support the opinion), Indian English speakers sometimes would like to set up a background for what is to be expressed, and reveal their position explicitly at the end.

The ending has parts that are less relevant to the prompt (therefore less convincing). He talks about sleeping late at night to prepare for exam and getting up **on time** for exam. This is not the same as getting up late, as the exam can be scheduled any time during the day.

(6) This response from an Indian test taker is sustained and the content is well-developed. The speech is clear, pacing is fluid and intonation is used to help convey the speaker's preference for getting up early and going to bed early. He demonstrates a good control of both simple and complex words and sentence structures. The content is also very rich: the speaker lists two reasons for getting up early ('not disrupt physical system of our body' and 'more energy during the day') and provides elaboration for each point. His pronunciation of /θ/ as [t̪ʰ] , which is typical of Indian speakers from the north, as in the word 'lethargic' may require some listener effort. His use of display question and self-answer as in 'why? Because…' is a literal translation from Hindi.

Chinese test takers

(1) The speech in this response is quite intelligible, in spite of one or two brief moments where the speaker has to pause and search for the right expressions. Although the speaker shows reasonable control of grammar and vocabulary, the range of vocabulary and grammar is quite limited. Some of the uses that might be considered as ungrammatical in American prescriptive grammar are actually literal translation from Chinese. For example, 'keep fresh brain to study'. Also, some English speakers from China have difficulty distinguishing 'sleep' from 'go to bed', as they both correspond to the same Chinese words (睡觉). In terms of content, the response is connected to the task, but the reasons are vague and not well developed (e.g. 'good for my health', 'keep fresh brain').

(2) This speaker is from China. She clearly states a preference and uses three reasons to support her preference. However, the extent to which one agrees with / is able to understand her argument also depends on the listener's cultural background. Her first reason – it is common sense that go to bed early is good for health – represents an Asian view of a healthy lifestyle. Her second reason that class and work start at 8:00 is typically true for most schools and jobs in China (but not necessarily true in other parts of the world). Her third reason – good sleep is during the night (one sleeps better at night) – is also universally accepted in China, but is more subject to debate in other cultures (some people believe the number of hours slept is more important than when you sleep).

Her speech is generally clear and intelligible, although her pronunciation of the word 'night' as 'light' reflects the difficulty that some Chinese English speakers have with /l/ /n/ distinction.

Her control of grammar and vocabulary is basic. Short sentences are mostly used, and some words lack preciseness (e.g. 'psychological evidence', 'society, environment, life').

(3) This speaker is also from China. He clearly expresses an opinion at the beginning and lists three reasons to argue for his preference. However, most of his reasons lack development. For example, he says 'it is a good habit' without adequate explanation of why it is so. His control of grammar and vocabulary is very limited. Most of the words he uses correctly are very basic, and all the complicated ones he uses are incorrect (e.g. he uses 'sterned' to mean 'alert', 'efficient' without 'ly', 'obey/observe...' without finishing the object of the verbs).

His response also reflects Chinese values about 'scheduling work for the day/not postponing work to the night' 'people's brain works best in the morning', 'we should obey our parents' orders and conform to their life styles' etc.

(4) In this Chinese speaker's response, the speech is very clear and intelligible. Pacing is fluid. The response is sustained and coherently most of the time. The speaker first explicitly states what is valued in Chinese culture (which suggests a good sense of audience – she assumes that the listeners/raters may not come from the same background as her), and then expresses her agreement with those cultural values. Although her sentences and vocabulary are rather simple, they are used mostly correctly.

(5) This speech by a Chinese test taker is intelligible, in spite of one or two brief moments where pronunciation obscures meaning. At the beginning, she intends to quote the saying 'it's the early bird that can catch the early worm' but doesn't recall/express correctly. Many places in her response reflects characteristics of Chinese English. (1) Her pronunciation of the word 'because' at the beginning (i.e. she rolled the tongue here) represents an over-application of rhotic sounds /r/ as in American English. (2) She omits subject in one place ('very important'), and in Chinese, subject is optional in a sentence. (3) Some phrases and words are direct word-by-word translation from Chinese, and may sound ungrammatical in prescriptive grammar. e.g. 'Keep your energy all day' (保持精力一整天) 'so you can do anything in spirit' (做任何事都有精神). (4) The presentation of the second argument 'your day will be night' may sound vague, because embedded in this is the Chinese cultural value for 'not doing at night what you are supposed to do in the day' (不要黑白颠倒).

Appendix C: Think-Aloud Questions

Play a speech sample once, and pause at the end. The researcher will ask:

(1) What score are you going to give to this response? OR
In general, how well do you think this person has performed on the task?
(2) Why are you giving this score? OR
Why do you think so?
Let the rater rewind and replay the same sample as many times as they want, and pause whenever he/she has a comment to make. If the rater does not speak much, the researcher will probe with the following questions:
(3) Can you tell me more about why you find that part of the response interesting?
(4) What do you think the test taker was trying to say?
(5) Can you say a little more about why you were having trouble understanding that part of the response?
(6) Can you tell me more about why you find it difficult to give a score to this response?

7 A Community of Practice Approach to Understanding the ITA Experience

Shereen Bhalla

The Community of Practice (CoP) framework is a practice-based approach which examines social learning through a process of mutual engagement. A CoP is a group of people who are mutually engaged in a set of relations and who are working towards a further attainment of knowledge (Lave & Wenger, 1991: 98). The main goal for this chapter is to examine how ITAs make sense of their own experiences as experts in the course material, as they are challenged with the struggles of being foreigners to the county in which they are instructing. As India has a long-standing history with English, many of the South Asian ITAs have spent a large part of their education learning English and thus, have achieved Indian English proficiency. This chapter examines the ITA experience from their perspective gathered by focus group narratives and individual interviews focused on linguistic and cultural issues which have arisen in the classroom and university setting, and the professional socialization of the ITA position.

Introduction

According to the United States Census Bureau, there are over 2.57 million South Asians from India in the United States, making them one of the fastest-growing ethnic groups (Bureau, 2000). When examining this population in further detail, it has been estimated that 69% of South Asians from India have at least a college degree (Bureau, 2000; Roy, 2009). In the 1960s and 1970s, many of the South Asian[1] students who arrived from the Indian subcontinent to study in the United States were men attaining higher education (Kurien, 1999). However, the 1980s saw waves of both South Asian men and women coming to the United States to pursue undergraduate and graduate degrees (Kurien, 1999). With this number constantly growing, many seek degrees in science, technology, engineering, mathematics (STEM) and teach undergraduate courses in these respective disciplines (Bailey, 1983; Gorsuch, 2003). This chapter examines how South Asian international teaching assistants (ITAs) participate in communities of practice as they navigate tensions between their professional identities and globalizing ideologies of English.

Professionalization and Professional Identities

The teaching assistant (TA) experience for many students is a challenging progression as they must balance being the teacher and expert in the course content in their classrooms, alternating between being a student and a learner while working with and under senior faculty and professors (Bailey, 1983; Jia & Bergerson, 2008). This creates tension for TAs that can often be difficult to balance, especially for ITAs. Without knowing the culture of American classrooms, ITAs may not have a clear understanding of their roles within the educational system in the United States, therefore linguistic and cultural differences in interactions between ITAs and their students can become 'complicated and sometimes problematic' (Bailey, 1984: 3).

Though research focused on ITA and professional identity is limited, there have been several studies which examine the professional socialization process through TA and ITA training (Jia & Bergerson, 2008; Mehra & Papajohn, 2007; Rounds, 1987; Tillema, 1994; Twale et al., 1997). While becoming socialized in an American university, there is encouragement for ITAs to participate in two types of socialization – academic discourse and university norms. Academic discourse is defined as 'a dynamic, socially situated process that in contemporary contexts is often multimodal, multilingual and highly intertextual as well' (Duff, 2010: 169). This process would introduce and disseminate commonly used academic language and jargon. However, a familiarization of academic norms and university customs is also an integral part for newcomer ITAs. As Trebing (2007) explains, it is often expected that ITAs understand US university and departmental norms in addition to knowledge of popular pedagogical practices and 'standard' classroom behavior. An ITA's ability to gauge the knowledge and learning styles of their students might be just as important as their communication skills with them (Hoekje & Williams, 1992). If an ITA is a novice teacher or has already taught in a country other than the United States, new role relationships must be learned. Therefore, ITAs must learn the norms and/ or reciprocity for that particular cultural context in which they find themselves and what the students' expectations are for ideal and normative TA behavior. In this chapter, we will examine how participation in the professional ITA position impacts identity construction.

A Community of Practice Approach

The Community of Practice (CoP) framework is a practice-based approach, which examines social learning through a process of mutual engagement (Lave & Wenger, 1991). Simply put, a CoP is a group of people who are in a shared assignment with a set of relations and are working towards a further attainment of knowledge (Lave & Wenger, 1991: 98). CoP studies seek to clearly address theoretical tensions between groups and individuals that are generated by such pairings as structure and agency, collectivity and subjectivity, and power and meaning. Thus, practice is a socially constituted way of engaging with the world and identity is a function of the mutual constitution of group and self (Garrett & Baquedano-Lopez, 2002; Wenger, 1998).

CoPs are organically formed by people who are engaging in a process of collective learning in a shared field. The members of this group are involved in a set of relationships over time and, therefore, a community develops around things that matter to this particular group of people (Lave & Wenger, 1991; Wenger, 1998). A CoP encourages the members to collaboratively learn as they take collective responsibility for managing the knowledge they need. In order to do that, there are three salient features of a CoP: (1) there is reciprocated commitment in a set of relations; (2) they share a mutually negotiated venture as they work towards the acquisition of knowledge; and (3) they make use of a shared inventory of knowledge and vernacular (Wenger, 1998: 73). In this chapter, South Asian ITAs are the CoP being examined. As they work towards professional identity acquisition and acceptance into American classrooms, this becomes their cooperative endeavor. Tools from their department as well as other university services and discussions with fellow ITAs help formulate their shared repertoire.

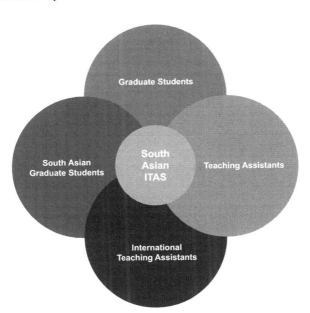

Figure 7.1 The South Asian International Teaching Assistant Community of Practice

A CoP defines a community in terms beyond regional origins, linguistics and race but in terms of communal and interactive engagement (Wenger, 1998). Often, a CoP goes beyond a group of people of the same race, instead recognizing that a joint goal can help bind them as they work together. What makes this framework best suited for this study is the idea that with mutual engagement, jointly negotiated enterprise and shared repertoire, a CoP is formed. Similarly, within that CoP other more specialized CoPs can exist. For this study, the South Asian ITAs would be a specialized CoP in the larger sphere of a TA CoP, indicated in Figure 7.1 below:

ITA professional socialization

While some ITAs may have a strong command of the English language, they may not be aware of the nuances or specific practices associated with teaching in the US university setting. Fox and Gay (1994: 21) found that,

> ITAs who successfully adjust to the United States university system, communicate effectively in the classroom, and understand the cultural characteristics of their students, will increase the quality of the educational opportunities, experiences and the outcomes that undergraduates receive.

LoCastro and Tapper's (2006) work with ITAs examined how they handled the pressure to accommodate to United States academic norms while constructing their pedagogical identities. Using ITAs' academic perspectives from their home cultures, notions about US pedagogical norms received from ITA training and their ways of knowing to create an environment of learning for their own students, they focused on how ITAs constructed their teacher identities at their university (LoCastro & Tapper, 2006). They recognized that in order to move away from a deficit view of ITAs, there needed to be an augmented consciousness of World Englishes and for teacher training to incorporate diversity for both ITAs and United States based TAs.

As mentioned above, the South Asian ITAs in this study are viewed as constituting a broader CoP with participants mutually engaging with one another in a jointly negotiated enterprise, drawing on a shared set of negotiable resources (Mullany, 2006). Simply put, with the South Asian ITAs in this study, this means the university helped facilitate the process of a professional educator identity. The resources in developing this identity were shared among ITAs through professional development meetings and conversations with other ITAs, which constituted the mutual engagement aspect of a CoP.

Learning as a social process

A central component of CoP is that learning is a holistic process, with social practice playing a large role in the method. In a CoP, 'the concept of identity serves as a pivot between the social and the individual, so that each can be talked about in terms of the other' (Wenger, 1998: 145). In a CoP, members share ways of going about things, and their social actions are internalized and form part of their habitus (Bourdieu, 1991). The CoP is a process of sharing information and experiences in a group, in which the members learn from each other and have an opportunity to develop themselves personally and professionally (Lave & Wenger, 1991).

Interactions among other members of a CoP also help demonstrate the social nature of the learning. As articulated by Lave and Wenger (1991: 35), 'learning is an integral part of generative social practice in the lived-in worlds.' Therefore, it is the learning and shared knowledge among individuals, which helps enforce a connection among the members (Lave & Wenger, 1991). This is a recurring theme in a CoP, where the members' interactions are intertwined with a particular social or learning context as these complex interactions between different features prevent them from being accomplished individually. One clear indicator of how learning is a social process and practice is evident in the role of participation and non-participation as well as membership and non-membership, which will be explored in the subsequent section.

Participation

Learning is more than the transmission of knowledge, as it becomes a social process where knowledge is co-constructed, and membership is mutually engaged. Although there are varying degrees of membership, participation facilitates the relationship between identity and practice, which is a crucial element to a CoP (Wenger, 1998: 149). Therefore, learning involves participation in a CoP and that participation 'refers not just to local events of engagement in certain activities with certain people, but to a more encompassing process of being active participants in the practices of social communities and constructing identities in relations to these communities' (Wenger, 1998: 4). However, identities are also enacted by non-participation in practices as well as our participation in them, which is referred to as peripherality and marginality (Wenger, 1998: 165).

When examining a peripheral participant, there is a stipulation that some degree of non-participation is necessary to demonstrate that the participation is adequate at best (Wenger, 1998). However, the participation component reigns over the non-participation aspect and, within a CoP, the inside signals a movement towards active participation, thus making them a core member, whereas with marginality, the non-participation overshadows, preventing full participation (Wenger, 1998: 166). The role of participation in a CoP can be summarized as 'peripherality may be a mix of participation and non-participation, where non-participation is characterized by observing or being told what to do' (Martin, 2005: 154). This would then signify that non-participation may indicate participation at the direction of others. For example, an individual may be passively participating in a professional role, such as the TA for a biology laboratory where experiments are being conducted by undergraduate students. In this lab, a supervising professor may assign the TA a list of tasks for the students to complete so that their experiments are successful. Through the administration and oversight of these tasks, the TA is then participating in the job that they are assigned, even if their participation is subsidiary.

Data Collection

This chapter derives from a larger study on the experiences of South Asian ITAs at a US university. Data for this study were collected between August 2010–August 2011 at Southern Texas University[2] with a total of 17 South Asian participants between the ages of 23–34, nine of whom were male and eight were female. On average, the amount of time spent in the US was 1.5 years, with one participant having resided here for over 10 years. Several of the participants had only been in the US for a semester prior to partaking in this study. Data were collected through focus groups, interviews and classroom observations. Participant demographic information is presented in Table 7.1.

Data Analysis

The following sections will discuss the data through the lens of the CoP framework. Individual preferences of how the ITA identity is enacted as well as the influence of timescales on the development of and the performance of the teacher role in the classroom in relation to the CoP framework will be discussed in the follow sections. This is particularly an interesting angle as many of the ITAs also discuss the role English proficiency plays in their experience. Similarly, an analysis is made of how

Table 7.1 Participant demographic information

Name	Age	Time in the US	First language(s) (L1)	When/Where did they learn English	Career goals
Ashlesh	34	9 years	Kannada, Hindi, Telugu	Bangalore, at home	Academic faculty
Boomika	24	1 year	Tamil	Childhood	Teach Science in India
Kalpana	23	2 years	Telugu, Hindi	From Grade '1' & India	Pursue PhD
Neil	27	3 years	Telugu	Since 2nd Grade	R & D work
Pradeep	30	4+ years	Telugu	At age 5, school	Open up my own business
Rajesh	26	1 year	Konkani	6, India	Research
Reshma	25	3 years	Gujarati	All my school life	Teaching high school
Sindhura	23	1 year	Telugu, Hindi, Tamil	Childhood & school India	Teaching full time

much the ITAs in this study participated (or did not participate) in the duties and the roles that are aligned with the position.

Individual preferences

While several of the study's participants, e.g. Sindhura and Pradeep, offer extreme participations in the ITA CoP, others consistently strived to maintain a balance. This was often demonstrated in the flexibility they portrayed in classroom management styles, particularly when examining the ITA practices of Kalpana and Reshma. Sindhura, Kalpana and Reshma were the ITAs for a biology course, which had a large classroom styled lecture and then a smaller break-out laboratory component. So once a week for five hours, they were in charge of administering, conducting and overseeing a biology experiment with about 20–25 students in a lab. Similar to other biology laboratory practices, a quiz is administered within the first five minutes of class prior to the experiment. In Excerpt 1, Reshma recalls her positioning on the administering the quiz:

Excerpt 1

1   Sometimes when the students are coming in, it's 8 o'clock. If I see that there is an
2   accident on the freeway, the first half an hour I won't start the class because somebody
3   might be stuck in the traffic and I have to give a quiz like in the first five minutes, after
4   that, I'm not supposed to but I will give.

Reshma's admission of her flexibility in administering the quiz, allows her to develop an ITA identity, which takes into account the personal aspects of her students' lives. By giving them leeway in the departments' strict tardiness policy, she is asserting authority in her classroom, balancing what the department stipulates and what she feels is reasonable. This is in stark contrast to Sindhura who felt that it was her responsibility to maintain the provisions set by the department and began the quiz promptly at class time. As she explained, 'the class starts on time and so I make an effort to have the materials ready before the start time so it lets students know they need to be ready to start on time.' As identities within a CoP can be negotiated, Reshma is comfortable incorporating her element into the interaction order of the classroom, whereas Sindhura felt it was more important to reflect the interaction order set by the department (Scollon & Scollon, 2004). Their respective decisions signals Reshma's transition from a peripheral member into a core, as she is constructing a professional identity based on her own experiences as a student. Her confidence in being flexible and in not disrupting her professional identity establishes her professional identity practices and the boundaries that she wishes to maintain.

Though Sindhura and Reshma worked for the same lead professor and administered the same laboratory experiments, their positionality in the classroom was quite different from the other. As Nexus Analysis explains 'different people play the same role differently depending on their history of personal experience' (Scollon & Scollon, 2004: 13). As both of these ITAs navigated their classroom practices to best fit their imagined identity, they are both actively participating in the ITA CoP. Sindhura's historical body of her teaching experience in India coupled with her desire to maintain the department rules was implemented in a manner that she was comfortable with. While Reshma, who had no prior teaching experience, was still actively constructing her professional identity, she was demonstrating flexibility in her practices as particular situations arose.

While Pradeep uses elements of his social life to maintain a peripheral membership into the student CoP, Reshma similarly positions herself the same way. However, Reshma references her own experiences as a current student to help facilitate classroom management as opposed to gaining entrance into the student CoP. This tactic explains that 'one can be sustained within their group and represent that group, but they may have to borrow from other groups to embellish their notion of membership and coolness across groups' (Morgan, 2001: 2). Therefore, Reshma is able to access components of her student CoP to help her develop her ITA identity, without leaving the boundaries of the ITA CoP.

Development and time scales

The length of time as a TA was also a factor in how the ITAs performed classroom management. This was evident in the case of Rehsma and Kalpana, as Reshma was in her first semester of TAing and Kalpana was in her second year of being an ITA. Both of these females were less strict than Sindhura, and this was demonstrated through their varying degrees of flexibility in their classroom management style. This consistent adaptability was prevalent in how Kalpana would often let students bring in other assignments to work on as well as let them leave to go get food while their experiments were being conducted. In Excerpt 2, Kalpana discusses trying to locate a balance:

Excerpt 2

1   My first semester I was really serious with them. I just wanted them to study not play in

2   the class and they were like oh please let us, it's like a five-hour long class so. And now I

3   am like letting them just go whatever you want to do but just finish this experiment and

4   do whatever you want.

As Kalpana's professional identity practices develop over the two years that she had been an TA, she begins to adopt elements of local practice into her historical body. This allows her to further construct an identity, which combines the influences of local culture with the professional practices of the TA position. In the concept of timescale, this process becomes dependent on the time the participant has to construct the identity they wish to be seen as and the length of time that individual may want to be a part of the group (Blommaert, 2005). Kalpana's two-year time period at STU has allowed her to determine the best way to handle her own classroom. Through timescale movement, she has been able to 'try on' different ITA identities — initially starting off as a serious teacher and then finding a space in which she was comfortable in. This shift signals a move from the peripheral to a more core role, as she is still actively participating in the ITA CoP. However, the boundaries of the role become negotiable as she constructs her professional ITA identity.

English familiarity

One way in which the South Asian ITA experience is different than ITAs from other countries, is India's long-standing history of English. For the ITAs, they recognize English as being a part of their bilingual repertoire or their second language. Therefore, there was already an awareness and comprehensibility with the dominant language. Rajesh, one of the two participants who learned English when he was six years old, pointed out that 'when I came here, if I had a question….I feel comfortable with my English to ask someone or to try and find out the answer.' Rajesh felt that his familiarity with English was beneficial, making the newness of America seem less daunting despite linguistic features and nuances of American English with which he was unacquainted with.

Wanting to return to India to teach science, Boomika often remarked that she found it difficult to feel connected to the university culture at STU, noting that 'thank god, I speak English […] otherwise sometimes I think that I would really hate it here.' As identity is a development rather than a result (Bourdieu, 1991: 248), a move into an environment, which their second language dominates, is tricky. Often times in a CoP, experiences and members' own identities become a process of negotiation and the ITAs can struggle to reach a balance (Wenger, 1998). In Boomika's comment, we see that she recognizes that being proficient in English helps make her experience more positive than if she were far more unfamiliar with the dominant language.

Any experience abroad is technically considered a negotiation. Particularly when taking into consideration the generating, regulating and modification that a second language environment results in a second language identity where certain cultural capital influences particular choices, or, knowledge of the existence of particular ideas (Mathews, 2000).

Therefore, for Boomika and Rajesh, their proficiency in English provides a type of commodity to mediate for their experience. This allows them to access the dominant language of the CoP at STU. English proficiency also allows them to make particular choices as to how they want their own identity to be constructed or portrayed. This type of symbolic competence permits the ITAs 'to display a particularly acute ability to play with various linguistic codes' (Kramsch & Whiteside, 2008: 664). Therefore, the South Asian ITAs are able to use English to enact an identity that they wish to portray, which allows them to play an active role in their positioning (Kramsch, 2006). Additionally, in the South Asian ITA CoP, members become resources for one another as they all have one another, and are possibly encountering similar difficulties. The CoP further becomes a support system for the ITAs as they are able to communicate (whether in English or a South Asian dialect) their frustrations and troubles with each other. This then also allows other members who have built an identity around their experiences (Wenger, 1998), as resources to depend on and gather advice from (Wenger, 1998).

Participation in the ITA CoP

Across all universities, TA roles and duties are varied according to the course content and structure as well as the lead teacher they work with. These factors also impact TA involvement and participation levels in the position itself. For the ITAs at STU the TA position was a desired source of employment for many graduate students in the Biology department, particularly so for the international students at STU as there were many advantages. Employment in a TA or GA position is a 20-hour per week position, allowing for in-state tuition rates as opposed to the astronomical rates of international student tuition. Therefore, the cost of attending STU gets reduced to a third of what it would normally cost, and the student receives monthly paychecks for performing their duties. As many of the ITAs are on F-1 student visa, they are limited by employment to only that which the university provides. Additionally, the TA position provides a professional socialization benefit from working alongside professors, through teaching the undergraduate and masters' classes. Despite the many benefits to the position, that did not always translate to high levels of participation from the ITAs (Freed, 1998: 261). The following findings demonstrate how experience is tied to varying degrees of participation, and how historical bodies influence professional practices.

One of the central tenets of a CoP, is the engagement of learning. For all of the ITAs, varying levels of participation led to varying degrees of professional socialization. Therefore, for individuals who actively participated in the position, their membership moved from peripheral to full (Lave & Wenger, 1991: 29). This was evident in the case of Ashlesh and Pradeep who were no longer working towards Biology degrees but had maintained TA positions in the department. Ashlesh had received his PhD in May 2007 and was co-teaching a course with a lead faculty member, while Pradeep had already completed the necessary requirements for a MS degree and was working towards his MBA in Marketing at STU. Ashlesh had been in the United States for over 10 years. Pradeep had been in the United States for four years and had thought that attaining a MBA would make him a more marketable candidate on the job market, explaining that 'nowadays you need to always have an edge.' Due to a good relationship with the lead faculty member for his course, Pradeep had been working for the same professor for three years and was aware that the STU Business School had little to no TA positions and so he continued to be available for the Biology department.

In a CoP, a member is first considered to be a peripheral participant and then a core member (Holmes & Meyerhoff, 1998) and during this trajectory the individual develops their own understanding and beliefs about the position. Despite Pradeep and Ashlesh no longer working on their Biology degrees, they were both extremely active in the Biology department, both academically and socially. Pradeep hosted a bi-weekly poker game with some of the male South Asian ITAs in both the Biology and Engineering Departments, and Ashelsh was the co-faculty lead on the South Asian group at STU. While Ashlesh was positioned as someone that the ITAs could go and talk to regarding issues and problems that they faced, Pradeep also offered advice to the ITAs, which was often ignored for its overly progressive tone. As Reshma put it 'he is too intense.' Regardless, Pradeep's duration at STU and in the Biology department helped situate him as a core member of the ITA CoP. For a CoP to operate there must be shared set of knowledge and ways of doing things, for Pradeep and Ashlesh, their experience at STU and in the Biology department contributed to their involvement of the CoP (Lave & Wenger, 1991; Wenger, 1998).

There are several ways in which Ashlesh and Pradeep were perceived as 'experts' in the ITA CoP. Due to their extended time in the US, they possessed an understanding of how things worked at their university and in the United States. These social processes were seen as knowledgeable skills by the other ITAs (Lave & Wenger, 1991: 29). As both of these men built their identity around their proficiency of the position and the climate of the university, they actively shared their experiences with the other ITAs. This historical body that they carried with them helped construct the habitual ways of performing within the ITA position (Scollon & Scollon, 2004). Furthermore, their expert identity was recognized by the other ITAs, which authenticates the identity they were enacting (Gee, 2005; Wenger, 1998).

While both Pradeep and Ashlesh offered different views and ideas on the ITA position, they were still based on their own experiences at STU. Though the ITAs appreciated the advice given by Ashlesh and Pradeep, they were also developing their own experiences as ITAs based on their individual historical bodies (Scollon & Scollon, 2004). The following section examines how the ITA position is internalized by practices, which lead to reification.

Non-participation participation

As Scollon and Scollon (2004: 13) suggest, 'different people play the same role differently depending on their history of personal experience.' Therefore, the construction of the ITA identity is dependent on several factors: participation in the ITA position, previous experiences with or as an educator and their own imagined sense of what the ITA position should be (Trusting, 2005; Wenger, 1998). Through their narratives, the ITAs become discoursing subjects in which they are both positioned and positioning themselves (Foucault, 1991: 56). These narratives then become the ways in which they indicate their participation in the ITA CoP and how they construct their social and professional identities.

This becomes salient in a CoP, where various forms of participation and non-participation are discussed, noting that non-participation is a form of participation as well (Wenger, 1998). Even for the ITAs like Neil who describes the ITA position as:

Excerpt 3

1 I show up…take attendance. Sometimes give quizzes and answer the student questions
2 There is a discussion board that students post questions they have, I am suppose to go on
3 there and collect questions and address them. But I think that if the student has important
4 questions, they will ask me in class or email. If the Dr. Shah needs me to do something,
5 than I will do it.

In Excerpt 3, Neil describes his non-participation in the ITA position and his indifference towards the duties, and signals his peripheral membership in the ITA CoP. Neil's non-participation is seen as a cover using the basic tasks which he is assigned to carry out as a shield from any major responsibility and/or authority in the classroom (Wenger, 1998). In this role, Neil allows for his lead professor to handle any conflict or problematic scenarios, which in turn facilitates his role in the classroom where he is not considered the authority, possibly eliminating him from receiving questions and concerns from students.

Non-participation as a form of participation was also visible in Rajesh's narrations of his experiences. Though Rajesh was given more duties and responsibility from his lead teacher, his attitude towards the position was indifferent 'yeah it's ok...I am just doing it and it's fine. Nothing too bad.' Whereas Neil used his minor participation as a way to develop his identity in the classroom as the non-authority, Rajesh's comments indicate that he committed to the position, but that it holds little weight on his identity. As Neil lists off the position requirements, Rajesh summarizes his experience as 'I am doing it...and it's fine...' His vagueness can be interpreted as non-participation in practice, where there is a sense of marginality about the position (Wenger, 1998: 170). Through recognizing that being an ITA is 'nothing too bad,' Rajesh puts distance between the position and feeling individual satisfaction from its outcome. Both Neil and Rajesh are able to develop identities outside of the position, noting the impact (or lack of) of the duties on their own social identity. What separates the two, is that Neil 'identifies with the enterprise of making their work possible and, if not always personally satisfying at the very least habitable for the kinds of identities they construct' (Wenger, 1998: 171). Rajesh, however, completely disengages from the socialization and the impact it has on his own experience.

Reification and the ITA identity

In a CoP, there are shared 'doings' (practices), shared 'understandings' (learning) and shared 'sense of one's own self' and of the other identities (Keating, 2005: 107). All of the ITAs were employed to assist lead teachers on various undergraduate courses, becoming their joint enterprise. However, the level of participation required and given by each TA varied from individual to individual. In a CoP, identity can be seen as a negotiated experience, one in which the experiences of participation and the positioning of others and of ourselves all become a tangible concept. Therefore, a teaching assistant (reification) is not involved in a negotiation of meaning until a person occupies that position (participation) (Tusting, 2005: 39). This is demonstrated in excerpt 4, where Kalpana is describing how the professional socialization process of the ITA affects her positionality as a student at STU:

Excerpt 4

1   Like we learn a lot how to be in here [STU]... how to move on. Till now we were
2   students, we were like undergrads, we were like laid back, go to classes. Now I see from
3   the other point of view, I see from the point we experience students and be that way, so I
4   understand, I know that position [student] I know this position [ITA], now I know like
5   what to do next, it helps a lot.

Kalpana is describing how becoming an ITA affected her performance as a student, allowing her to see how student behavior (line 3) is different than TA behavior. As she is being socialized into the profession, she is internalizing how the behavior of student is 'laid back' (line 2), and how student life at STU prior to receiving a TA position was similar to the undergraduate experience. In lines 2–3, she mentions the shift in her experience, referencing the TA perspective in 'now I see from the other point of view.' Reification is similar to the nexus analysis concept of historical bodies, which is the culmination of social actions and discourses, which forms social identities (Scollon & Scollon, 2001: 142). In lines 2–3, Kalpana is articulating how her perspective changed due to the TA position. This is then reinforced in lines 3–5 as she explains, 'I understand' and 'now I know what to do next.' These statements are expressing how her practices become habitual ways of acting and thinking (Scollon & Scollon, 2001). This is relatively similar to the Bourdieu's (1977) concept of habitus which gives way to understanding the nature of power and symbolic and cultural capital, as habitus is a structure of social action by culturally competent participants. As Kalpana is a fully engaged participant, she is actively being socialized to the ITA position, influencing her way of thinking both as an ITA and a student. In a CoP, members share ways of going about things, and their social actions are internalized and form part of their habitus (Bourdieu, 1991). For Kalpana, her habitus of what her participation is at STU is heavily influenced by the ITA position.

Conclusion

Socialization occurs by learning, and learning in a CoP involves participation, which 'refers not just to local events of engagement in certain activities with certain people, but to a more encompassing process of being active participants in the practices of social communities, and constructing identities in relation to these communities' (Wenger, 1998: 4). Therefore, the socialization process of the ITA position is dictated by the amount of participation by the ITA.

While (non)participation signals investment in both the ITA position and the influence it may have on their professional and social identities, the initial steps of attaining an ITA position can also determine participation in the ITA. The appeal of a CoP approach is that it gives us a framework to 'examine the ways in which becoming a member of a CoP interacts with the process of gaining control of the discourse appropriate to it' (Holmes & Meyerhoff, 1998: 175). This can be evident in the way the ITAs discuss the duties, classroom dynamics and scenarios and even how the position is obtained. As there was no explicit formula as to how the ITA positions are assigned, stories on how the TA position was obtained varied from student to student. Ashlesh and Kalpana were granted the opportunity upon their arrival to STU as part of their graduate student package, and some were encouraged to seek out the position by talking to faculty members. This varying employment practice for TA employment shaped how some of the ITAs viewed this process.

ITAs are in the unique position of being students and employees at their respective universities, belonging to two very distinct CoPs: students and educators. Though individuals are able to be members of several CoPs simultaneously, some CoP memberships contain particular boundaries (Wenger, 1998). These boundaries are constructed on the stipulation that being a member is largely defined by not being a member. For the ITAs in this study, certain professional boundaries of the ITA CoP would prevent them from becoming members of the student CoP and particular social practices of a student CoP would not be in alignment with the practices of a professional CoP. Thus, these boundaries on these particular CoPs prevent individuals from concurrently being members in both CoPs.

This can be a confusing space for the ITAs as they see fluidity between the CoPs, leading the boundaries to be blurred. For Pradeep, in particular this was difficult, as his participation in the ITA CoP is largely defined by his need to be seen as a separate identity outside of the ITA position. This was often demonstrated in his use of his social life to construct his professional identity in the classroom.

Therefore, it becomes difficult to cross the boundaries of a student and an ITA CoP, since each CoP is defined by its opposition to the other and membership in one community implies marginalization in another (Wenger, 1998: 168). So while the ITAs can belong to both CoPs, they cannot activate and enact membership in both simultaneously. They then must either be an ITA or a student in the classroom but they can't be both at the exact same time. Thus, Pradeep's efforts to attempt membership in the student CoP were rebuffed and not acknowledged. This is evident in how he notes that some students have trouble remembering his name. Therefore, it becomes futile to attempt to attain membership in the student CoP, while being the ITA in the course, as these CoPs cannot be occupied simultaneously (Martin, 2005; Trusting, 2005; Wenger, 1998).

This chapter has expanded on the social identity of the ITAs and how it becomes intertwined with the professional socialization and identity construction of the TA position. Through the CoP framework, the varying degrees of participation conducted by the ITA impacted the professional identity construction process for the ITAs. How they reified the position was based on the ITA identity they wish to be viewed as. As the ITAs were actively developing their own social and student identities, this manipulated the professional identities that they enacted.

While the ITAs were able to concurrently be members of multiple CoPs, their membership into the TA CoP prevented them from participating in CoPs, whose boundaries were set by their non-membership into the ITA CoP. Thus, it became clear that ITA membership prohibited a student CoP membership simultaneously. However, influences from their student

CoP were prevalent in their practices as an ITA. For many of the ITAs, much of the flexible positioning that they demonstrated in the classroom was based on their student practices.

Notes

(1) Please note that we will use South Asian in this chapter to refer to international students from India and the Indian diaspora.
(2) Southern Texas University is a pseudonym.

References

Bailey, K. (1983) Foreign teaching assistants at U.S. universities: Problems in interaction and communication. *TESOL Quarterly* 17 (2), 2.

Blommaert, J. (2005) *Discourse: Key Topics in Sociolinguistics*. Cambridge: Cambridge University Publisher.

Bourdieu, P. (1977) *Outline of a Theory of Practice*. Cambridge: Cambridge University Press.

Bourdieu, P. (1991) *Language and Symbolic Power*. Boston: Harvard University Press.

Bureau, U.S.C. (2000) *Profile of Selected Demographic and Social Characteristics*.

Duff, P. (2010) Language socialization into academic discourse communities. *Annual Review of Applied Linguistics* 30, 169–192.

Fox, W.S. and Gay, G. (1994) Functions and effects of international teaching assistants. *Review of Higher Education* 18 (1), 1–24. Retrieved from ERIC database. (EJ491369)

Freed, B. (1998) An overview of issues and research in language learning in a study abroad setting. *Frontiers: The Interdisciplinary Journal of Study Abroad* 10, 31–60.

Garrett, P.B. and Baquedano-Lopez, P. (2002) Language socialization: Reproduction and continuity, transformation and change. *Annual Review of Anthropology* 31, 339–361.

Gee, J.P. (2005) *An Introduction to Discourse Analysis: Theory and Method* (2nd ed.). New York: Routledge.

Gorsuch, G.J. (2003) The educational cultures of international teaching assistants and U.S. universities. *TESL-EJ* 7 (3).

Hoekje, B. and Williams, J. (1992) Communicative competence and the dilemma of international teaching assistant education. *TESOL Quarterly* 26 (2).

Holmes, J. and Marra, M. (2005) Narrative and the construction of professional identity in the workplace. In J. Thornborrow and J. Coates (eds) *The Sociolinguistics of Narrative*. Amsterdam: John Benjamins.

Jia, C.L. and Bergerson, A.A. (2008) Understanding the international teaching assistant training program: A case study at a northwestern research university. *International Education*.

Kramsch, C. (2006) The multilingual subject. *International Journal of Applied Linguistics* 16 (1), 97–110.

Kramsch, C. and Whiteside, A. (2008) Language ecology in multilingual settings: Towards a theory of symbolic competence. *Applied Linguistics* 29 (4), 645–67.

Kurien, P. (1999) Gendered ethnicity: Creating a Hindu Indian identity in the United States. *American Behavioral Scientist* 42 (4), 648–670.

Lave, J. and Wenger, E. (1991) *Situated Learning*. Cambridge, MA: Cambridge University Press.

LoCastro, V. and Tapper, G. (2006) International teaching assistants and teacher identity. *Journal of Applied Linguistics* 3 (2), 185–218.

Martin, D. (2005) Communities of practice and learning communities: Do bilingual co-workers learn in community? In D. Burton and K. Tusting (eds) *Beyond Communities of Practice*. New York: Cambridge University Press.

Mathews, G. (2000) *Global Culture: Searching for Home in the Cultural Supermarket*. New York: Routledge.

Mehra, B. and Papajohn, D. (2007) 'Glocal' patterns of communication-information convergences in internet use: Cross-cultural behavior of international teaching assistants in a culturally alien information environment. *The International Information and Library Review* 39, 19.

Morgan, G. (2001) Transnational communities and business systems. *Global Networks* 1, 113–130.

Mullany, L. (2006) Narrative constructions of gender and professional identities. In T. Omoniyi and G. White (eds) *The Sociolinguistics of Identity*. London: Continuum.

Rounds, P.L. (1987) Characterizing successful classroom discourse for non-native speaking teaching assistant training. *TESOL Quarterly* 21 (4), 643–671.

Roy, S. (2009) My kitsch is their cool. *ColorLines* Retrieved August, 19th 2009, from http://www.colorlines.com/article.php?ID=554

Scollon, R. and Scollon, S.W. (2004) *Nexus Analysis: Discourse and the Emerging Internet*. London: Routledge.

Tillema, H.H. (1994) Training and professional expertise: Bridging the gap between new information and pre-existing beliefs of teachers. *Teaching and Training Education* 10 (6), 601–615.

Trebing, D. (2007) *International Teaching Assistants Attitudes toward Teaching and Understanding of United States American Undergraduate Students*. Retrieved from ProQuest Dissertations and Theses. See http://search.proquest.com/docview/304828 989?accountid=7122

Tusting, K. (2005) Language and power in communities of practice. In D. Barton and K. Tusting (eds) *Beyond Communities of Practice* (pp. 36–54). New York: Cambridge University Press.

Twale, D.J., Shannon, D.M. and Moore, M.S. (1997) NGTA and IGTA Training and experience: Comparisons between self-ratings and undergraduate student evaluation. *Innovative Higher Education* 22 (1), 16.

Wenger, E. (1998) *Communities of Practice: Learning, Meaning, and Identity*. Cambridge: Cambridge University Press.

8 Situating ITAs in Higher Education and Immigration Policy Studies

Linda Harklau and James Coda

This chapter reviews how higher education institutions in the US and other Anglophone countries came to cultivate and actively recruit international student enrollments to internationalize campuses and also as a source of income. We show how the increasing ITA presence on US college campuses has been intertwined with the growing worldwide scholarly dominance of English and TESOL. Additionally, we explore historical and current trends in the 'push' and 'pull' factors driving growth in international flows from and to the US and contextualize them in education policy in the US and abroad. Furthermore, we explore how these push and pull factors have evolved over time in tandem with demand in global labor markets (Institute of International Education, 2016). The chapter will conclude by pointing out recent trends in US and international economic, immigration and higher education policy and speculate as to future prospects for ITAs at American universities. For example, we address possible effects of slowing economies, increased nativism and increasing concerns over visas and international student reception in western industrialized democracies, and decreasing state and federal funding for graduate assistants both at US universities and by sponsoring foreign governments.

Introduction

This chapter and volume take as their starting point the notion of 'transdisciplinary.' Applied linguistics is by nature an interdisciplinary and transdisciplinary field; yet writings on international teaching assistants (ITAs) at American universities have tended to remain within the confines of applied phonetics and phonology and language assessment. In this chapter, we follow calls by applied linguistics scholars (e.g. Byrd Clark, 2016; Douglas Fir Group, 2016) to cultivate more transdisciplinary perspectives that can break out of established ways of thinking about the field in order to address 'real-world' issues in language teaching and learning in transnational times. Here, we consider how the phenomenon of ITAs grows out of and contributes to broader national and global issues, ideologies and policies about education, migration and economic interests under neoliberal globalization. These issues have often been the subject of inquiry in the fields of higher education policy and international relations, but are rarely brought to bear on ITA scholarship.

Taking a broad international higher education policy lens immediately makes it clear how localized ITA policy and research have tended to be. For example, a search of 'International Teaching Assistants' and 'policy' in Academic Search Complete finds only three sources, two of which pertain to ITA testing policies. While this can be partly attributed to the lack of a formal national policy regarding ITAs, state level policies exist in at least 22 states where laws have been passed regarding ITA English testing and/or training (Oppenheim, 1997; Tummons, June 6, 2017 TESOL ITA Interest Section listserv communication). For the most part, however, ITA policy remains a local university institutional matter, formulated through informal professional networks and benchmarking with programs at other institutions (e.g. Brinkley-Etzkorn *et al.*, 2015; Kenyon, May 3, 2018 TESOL ITA Interest Section listserv communication). Local policies have often been formulated in response to the concerns of stakeholders who are not language specialists (e.g. students, parents, administrators, legislators) (e.g. Fiske, 1985; Gottschalk, 1985; Heller & McMillen, 1986) who may hold negative biases regarding multilingual educators (Manohar & Appiah, 2016; Subtirelu, 2017). As such, they often reflect dominant English monolingual ideologies circulating in US education and society (Ricento, 2000; Subtirelu, 2017). Local institutional policies thus tend to address narrowly the English language and communication skills, pedagogical skills and cultural knowledge ITAs need to be effective US college instructors (Brinkley-Etzkorn *et al.*, 2015; Gorsuch, 2016). To be sure, some ITAs are in need of help developing effective classroom communication skills for working with American undergraduates. Moreover, US higher education as a whole has made a strong commitment to internationalization and to increasing and respecting diversity among faculty and students (Subtirelu, 2017). Nevertheless, localized ITA language policy perspectives may become 'problem'-oriented (Ruiz, 1984) or even deficit-oriented, casting ITAs as lesser or deficit versions of English monolingual college educators in spite of applied linguists' longstanding efforts to the contrary (e.g. Bailey *et al.*, 1984).

However, even if policies themselves are formulated at the local level, that does not mean they are not influenced by broader national and international policies and dynamics under neoliberal globalization. An international higher education policy perspective leads us to ask how and why ITAs have been drawn to US universities in the first place. If international instructors are seen at times as lacking or problematic in relation to language proficiency, then why do US universities continue to recruit them?

In this chapter, we claim that even though there is no official national ITA policy in the US, there is a de facto policy. Contrary to local university policies that tend to treat ITAs as a collection of individuals who come to study and work in the US by pure volition, we find that US national policies have systematically and assiduously courted ITAs and international students more generally, bringing them to the US through a multigenerational process of cultural and economic exchange over the past century. We also illustrate that from the outset, US motivations to improve cross-cultural understanding and heighten global scholarly freedom have been mixed with the self-interests of the US government as well as multinational corporations (Kotler & Kotler, 2014; Washburn, 2005) to expand global security and US 'soft power' (Nye, 2011). In all, we contend that counter to the problem-oriented tenor of local university ITA policies, when viewed from an international higher education and international relations policy perspective, ITAs on American college campuses can be seen as both indicators of and contributors to US fortunes and its wealth, power and influence in the world. Based on this assessment, we consider future prospects for ITAs at American universities. We provide implications for grounding local ITA policies in national policy imperatives and educating colleagues, students and other program stakeholders about the benefits of international teaching assistants on campus.

ITAs, American Higher Education Policy and International Relations: A Historical Perspective

To examine US national policy on ITAs, one must first situate ITAs as one subset of a global phenomenon in which an ever-growing number of students are going abroad for higher education. International student mobility is one of the most prominent issues in current higher education policy and scholarship (Bista & Foster, 2016; Gürüz, 2011). In fact, worldwide, the number of students studying outside of their home countries increased 50% between 2005 and 2012 (OECD, 2016), and it has risen five-fold since 1975 (Fernández-Zubieta et al., 2015). This dramatic increase can be linked to the global internationalization of universities as well as policies in American higher education.

Historically, since their beginnings, western universities have always served as an international and internationalizing force, spreading ideas and knowledge worldwide (Altbach, 2007). One study, for example, finds that 10% of students at European medieval universities were international students (Shields & Edwards, 2010). Likewise, from their advent in the 19th and early 20th centuries, modern university systems in the US and other western countries have been conceived by their governments as global engines of scientific and technical knowledge, socioeconomic progress and nation building (Gürüz, 2011: 162). In the late 1800s, the US aimed to replicate the success of the internationalized higher education institutions of 19th-century Germany that drew scholars from across Europe. To attract international scholars, the US implemented a novel university configuration that combined teaching and research. This has since become the modern norm for a research university (Wildavsky, 2010: 3). Thus, from their founding, drawing international faculty and students has always been an integral goal for US universities.

Reinforcing the international ambitions of US universities, the Institute of International Education (IIE) was established in the wake of World War I. The purpose of the Institute was to facilitate and expand international educational exchanges between the US and other nations (IIE, 2017). Founded by three Nobel Prize winners and funded by powerful foundations, corporations and government agencies, the IIE wielded considerable influence on national higher education policy. For example, in spite of general US isolationism and severe restrictions on immigration in the 1920s and 1930s, the IIE was instrumental in establishing a new category of student visas and even prevailed upon steamship lines to develop student passage rates (IIE, 2017). It also acted as a clearinghouse for foreign student fellowships and scholarships for Americans to study abroad. IIE also created a network of International Relations clubs on campuses nationwide to 'facilitate a supportive climate for international education' (IIE, 2017). While the IIE coordinated mainly with European governments at its inception (IIE, 2017), by the late 1920s, it had expanded into Central and South America. By the mid-1930s, it was working in China. The IIE also systematically encouraged scholars displaced by wars and totalitarian governments to migrate to the US (IIE, 2017). During the same pre-World War II era, US universities developed a major focus on cultivating world-class basic science research. This also acted as a significant force for attracting international students and faculty (Geiger, 2008). Nevertheless, before the war, US higher education was still characterized by 'overwhelming localism' (Thelin, 2004) in higher education. Internationalization of America's college campuses remained the concern of a small class of elites and their philanthropic organizations, such as the Rockefeller Foundation's funding of International Houses at selected prestigious universities (Thelin, 2004).

The current prevalence of ITAs in the US can be directly traced to post-World War II changes in American and international affairs and higher education policy. In the post-war years, US higher education dramatically expanded and was increasingly marked by 'a system of universities impelled forward by the demands and the resources of the federal government, but also guided by their own academic ambitions' (Geiger, 2008: xiii). US federal policies explicitly encouraged international student growth. In 1946, the Fulbright educational exchange programs were passed into law. A partnership was formed by the IIE, the United States Educational, Scientific and Cultural Organization (UNESCO) and the

Department of the Army to bring students from occupied countries to the US on exchange programs as part of reconstruction efforts (IIE, 2017).

These initiatives successfully transformed US higher education into a magnet for international student study. Prior to World War II, the primary destinations for the world's international students were universities in Bologna, Paris, Oxford and other European cities (Wildavsky, 2010). However, by 1949 when the IIE began yearly surveys of American universities, there were already over 25,000 international scholars studying in the US, a number that doubled over the course of the 1950s (IIE, 1949, 2017). The range of countries contributing international scholars widened and increasingly included students from emerging nations of Africa, Central and South America and Asia (Coombs, 1964).

While these changes might be seen as altruistic, contributing to the general public and international good and transforming lives and developing nations through education, that was not the only intent. From the beginning, post-war federal higher education policy and international scholar recruitment were also strategic. They were intertwined with US efforts to use education as 'soft power' (Nye, 2011) to build global allies, national security and political influence in order to combat the influence of the Soviet Union and other Communist nations (IIE, 2017). For example, Senator J.W. Fulbright wrote in 1964 of international education:

> Our long-term objective must be the development of a sense of community in the world, a feeling of shared values and interest, a feeling that effective communication is possible, and a feeling of trust and confidence in each other's purposes. In time we may even hope that the dogmatism and fanaticism which now separate the Communist nations from the free nations will gradually give way to a more enlightened and civilized view of the world. (Coombs, 1964: x)

In all, then, the presence of ITAs on American university campuses today can be viewed as both contributing to and evidence for the success of US efforts to use higher education as a means of achieving global, political and economic dominance since the mid-20th century.

Over the past 30 years, an influential new policy trend has overtaken higher education worldwide, including the US. This is neoliberalism, an economic doctrine favoring a globalized free-market economy with limited government involvement (Portnoi et al., 2010). ITA issues are intertwined with the ascendance of neoliberalism since the 1980s and the notion of the 'knowledge economy' that have dramatically reshaped the ethos of American higher education (Portnoi et al., 2010). While Fulbright once argued that the purpose of international education in the US was to help under-developed countries realize 'their intellectual and spiritual aspirations' (Coombs, 1964: xii), this goal has been deprioritized in the ascendance of 'academic capitalism' (Portnoi et al., 2010: 1). While most US colleges and universities may continue to see their motivations as academic rather than commercial, neoliberal higher education policies have encouraged universities worldwide to become increasingly entrepreneurial and to market knowledge as a commodity rather than as a service for the public good (Portnoi *et al.*, 2010). The shift in policy and ethos is emblematized by the controversial inclusion of higher education as a commodity in the World Trade Organization 'General Agreement on Trade in Services' (GATS) treaty (Collins, 2007).

The capitalization of higher education under neoliberal economic regimes worldwide has highlighted the role of international students as a source of revenue. In the US context, international students are actively recruited and welcomed as a highly significant source of enrollments and tuition income (Altbach & Peterson, 2008). For example, NAFSA (2018) estimates that international students in the US in the 2016–2017 academic year 'contributed $36.9 billion and supported more than 450,000 jobs to the US economy.' Thus, ITAs represent a small minority of international students in the US who receive institutional funding for their studies, as the vast majority are self-supporting (Gürüz, 2011). Moreover, due to widespread instructional inadequacies in US K-12 science and mathematics education when compared to its global competitors (Nye, 2011), many science and engineering departments at American universities would lack qualified instructors without ITAs.

In all, while there may not be a formal national policy on ITAs in US higher education, this historical review shows that over the past century there has been an informal, but concerted, US policy to attract more international students, including ITAs, to American universities. In contrast to the 'problem'-oriented discourse that often seems to surface in institutions at the local ITA policy level, national and international policymakers have regarded the presence of ITAs and other international students as significantly benefitting US interests. These benefits have included expanding 'soft power' through political, economic and cultural influence; providing a qualified teaching force in US higher education; populating otherwise undersubscribed graduate programs; and bringing in tuition dollars. We turn now to examining how current policies in US higher education and international relations continue to bring ITAs to the US.

'Push' and 'pull' factors for ITAs in US higher education

While scholars have always been internationally mobile, sociopolitical and economic conditions in home and receiving countries are constantly influencing and changing the size and composition of the group of international scholars who come to the US (Fernández-Zubieta *et al.*, 2015; Gürüz, 2011). Likewise, the experiences, needs and even the very definition of ITAs are constantly changing. At present, for example, the end of the Cold War in 1991 has brought increasing numbers of international students to the US from countries such as Brazil, Russia, India and China.

There has been an especially dramatic increase in numbers of Chinese students and ITAs. Since the 1980s, as part of the nation's massive push to upgrade its higher education capacity, Chinese scholars and their representation in the ranks of ITAs have gone from almost negligible to a significant presence at almost every university campus in western countries (Blommaert, 2013: 5).

US higher education and economic policies continue to facilitate the recruitment of international students as a key source of educated labor. Russian and Indian student ITA numbers, for example, have dramatically increased as these scholars seek out not only higher education, but also greater employability in the global labor market and useful international professional networks (Gürüz, 2011). Many scholars are not just sojourners. They are drawn to the US and other western universities by labor and visa policies that facilitate their entrance into academic and private labor markets after they graduate (Fernández-Zubieta *et al.*, 2015; Lee *et al.*, 2006: 553; Macready & Tucker, 2011). Visa policies in the US and UK, for example, give international students one to three extra years beyond graduation to find employment (Adnett, 2010; Redden, 2017). As a result of these policies, Indian international scholars have become a major source of high-level, skilled workforce for the United States (Gürüz, 2011: 290). This arrangement benefits both individuals who are trained for highly paid jobs, as well as host countries such as the US that reap economic advantages from a highly educated workforce (Adnett, 2010).

The US higher education system also continues to benefit from the longstanding gravitation of ITAs and other skilled scholars and researchers from less to more developed countries – dubbed 'brain drain' or 'brain circulation' (Fernández-Zubieta *et al.*, 2015). Higher education opportunities, particularly at the graduate level, are typically less available and of lower quality in nations of the global South (Macready & Tucker, 2011). There are, likewise, more limited labor markets and individual opportunities for scholarly and research career development in developing nations (Fernández-Zubieta *et al.*, 2015). Neoliberal economic policies, such as the General Agreement on Trade in Services (GATS) treaty, may further draw students away from the less globally competitive university systems of global South nations and bring more ITAs to elite research institutions in the US and other western nations (Portnoi *et al.*, 2010).

US and foreign nations' scholarship programs are also a driving factor in bringing ITAs and other international students to the US. For example, the Fulbright program, under the auspices of the US Department of State, serves as a prestigious attractor for international students globally (Adnett, 2010: 632). At the same time, a number of nations, especially in the global South, have government-sponsored educational policies that send scholars to the US for graduate study.

Political instability and persecution in nations abroad also continue to impel some ITAs and other international scholars to the US. Since the

1930s, the US has sponsored programs for rescuing scholars from countries where academics are in danger of persecution or imprisonment (IIE, 2017). Scholars may also be driven abroad for higher education if they are part of a group in their home society that experiences bias or discrimination (Garcia & Villarreal, 2014: 129). Political instability in their home countries is also a major factor driving scholars to study in the US. For example, after the collapse of the Soviet Union in 1991, a large cohort of scientists immigrated to the US after their formerly state-funded research was suddenly set adrift without the means to sustain graduate training (Ganguli, 2015). More recently, Turkey's growing political instability and isolation from the rest of the world coupled with its uncertain future with NATO have been bringing an increasing number of Turkish students to study in the US (Park, 2015).

Universities also use increasingly sophisticated recruitment efforts to bring ITAs and other international scholars to the US (Rhoads *et al.*, 2014). Recruitment is increasingly well-organized (Portnoi *et al.*, 2010); for example, in 2000 the National Association of Foreign Student Advisors (NAFSA) led a consortium of US educational organizations in calling for a federally coordinated and funded initiative to recruit international students (Altbach & Peterson, 2008). EducationUSA, a global network of 400 college advising centers in 170 countries that is supported by the US Department of State's Bureau of Educational and Cultural Affairs, specifically recruits international scholars (Macready & Tucker, 2011). In addition, a number of individual US universities and states have established specialized recruitment offices in major student-sending countries (Macready & Tucker, 2011; Portnoi *et al.*, 2010).

The prestige associated with particular elite institutions in the US (e.g. Harvard or UCLA) is also an important factor in the cost-benefit analysis that brings international students to the US to study (Garcia & Villarreal, 2014: 129). Students tend to select a study abroad country and university by reputation (Mazzarol & Souter, 2002: 88). Thus, under neoliberalism, US universities are increasingly marketing themselves as commodities using market-style 'branding' strategies (Rhoads *et al.*, 2014). US universities also increasingly treat international students as clientele, competing to attract them through sophisticated internet recruitment and retention campaigns (Verbik & Lasanowski, 2007). Thus, ITAs and other international students have been commoditized and monetized in the new US knowledge economy.

In this global neoliberal higher education market, the worldwide scholarly dominance of English and TESOL plays a special role. ITAs receive linguistic and economic capital associated with being educated in English (e.g. Macready & Tucker, 2011: 46). In particular, an American accent (Blommaert, 2010: 60) has become a valued form of linguistic capital that brings ITAs and other international students to the US. For its part, American higher education reaps long-term benefits from this dominance.

Studying at American universities has the effect of socializing new international scholars into academic cultures that are English-predominant (Altbach & Peterson, 2008). Moreover, it perpetuates the dominance of English through the creation of global networks of research colleagues working together through the common lingua franca of English in research and publication (e.g. Curry & Lillis, 2014: 3). Studying in the United States creates a center-periphery chain dynamic through which international scholars returning to their home countries as faculty educate the next generation of scholars to also go to the US for advanced university study (Altbach & Peterson, 2008). Accordingly, in 2017, over half of international enrollment was in universities in English-speaking countries – the US, UK, Australia, Canada and New Zealand (IIE Project Atlas, 2018).

Current Trends

In all, looking through a transdisciplinary lens of higher education and international relations policy studies, we can see that the phenomenon of ITAs at US universities is the product of systemic US government and higher education polices. ITAs are part of American universities due to century-long sustained, explicit recruitment. Contrary to monolingual, problem-oriented views of multilingual and multicultural ITAs that may surface in folk beliefs and local university policies, longstanding higher education and US international relations policies have been promulgated on the assumption that ITAs are major assets to American universities and the nation.

ITAs are thus an important part of the US higher education system, both beneficiaries of and contributors to what makes it among the largest (Altbach & Peterson, 2008) and most highly ranked (Nye, 2011) in the world. The US is still by far the single greatest national host for international students, with over 25% of these scholars (OECD, 2016). International student enrollment overall continued to grow rapidly from 2001 through 2016, increasing by 32% (Fernández-Zubieta et al., 2015). In 2016, it stood at 1,078,822, comprising 5.3% of total US tertiary enrollment (IIE, 2017). Moreover, the worldwide predominance of English as the lingua franca of research currently remains unquestioned (Altbach, 2007).

Nevertheless, international student flows are ever-evolving and present enrollments are by no means a guarantee that the US will continue to be a preferred destination. Dramatic gains in international enrollment over the past 75 years could erode even more quickly given the right combination of policies and socio-political and economic conditions in and outside of the US. Will US higher education remain competitive in the worldwide race for ITAs and other international academic talent? There are worrying signs.

For one thing, higher education is more globalized and international than ever before, and scholars and researchers are increasingly mobile

(Fernández-Zubieta *et al.*, 2015; Portnoi *et al.*, 2010). This mobility is influencing the ways that universities worldwide operate and recruit students and faculty. US universities increasingly compete on a global field for research funding and for the most talented international students and faculty (Portnoi *et al.*, 2010), particularly in the Pacific Rim (Bista & Foster, 2016), as other nations set their sights on capturing part of the global flows of highly educated labor. Universities in other countries, sometimes with government support, are systematically recruiting international students abroad (Eckel & King, 2007) and are seeing significant growth in international enrollment (Shumilova & Cai, 2016). Australia, the UK, Canada and New Zealand are key competitors (Altbach & Peterson, 2008), but China has also tripled its international student population in recent years (Stetar *et al.*, 2010). European higher education has become more attractive to international students through the 'Bologna process,' an initiative to ensure comparability across the higher education systems of member nations and create more favorable conditions for international students' migration and mobility within the European Union (Shumilova & Cai, 2016). Other non-traditional destinations for study abroad (e.g. Singapore, Malaysia, Quatar, Dubai) have also launched multinational initiatives to create attractive global higher education 'hubs' or centers for international scholars (Marginson, 2011). This development potentially moves global higher education away from the traditional center and periphery structure from which the US has benefitted. It could lead to a more multi-centered structure that will draw away talented scholars, particularly in science, technology, engineering and mathematics (STEM) fields and make these non-traditional destination nations producers of knowledge in their own right (Shields & Edwards, 2010). China and India have also made strong national investments in their university systems, reducing their dependence on US universities for tertiary education (Altbach & Peterson, 2008). Interestingly, however, these developments do not seem to be altering the hegemony of English as a global academic lingua franca, since many of these institutions have increased their English-medium course offerings and programs to be competitive (Shields & Edwards, 2010; Shen *et al.*, 2016: 349).

Neoliberal globalization of higher education has also led academic institutions from across the global North to experiment with new configurations to extend their brand by establishing joint academic programs and satellite campuses with universities and for-profit entities in other countries (Marginson, 2011; Stetar *et al.*, 2010). The UK and Australia have been at the forefront of this effort in recent decades (Altbach & Peterson, 2008), although many US institutions are establishing branch campuses elsewhere in the world (Vora, 2015). While online international education has not had the impact once expected (Shields & Edwards, 2010), it has nevertheless increased in prevalence (Altbach & Peterson, 2008), decreasing the potential number of international students and teaching assistants present on US college campuses.

At the same time, the US has been systematically disinvesting in its university system. State and federal government funding of US higher education have steadily eroded in recent decades (Portnoi *et al.*, 2010; Mitchell *et al.*, 2018). It dropped precipitously during the 2008 recession, resulting in decreasing support for ITAs and other teaching assistants. US academic employment prospects have also decreased dramatically with the rise of cheaper contingent (part-time and non-tenured) faculty. While these faculty constituted only 18.5% of US faculty in 1969 (Fernández-Zubieta *et al.*, 2015), they now represent the majority of the US college teaching workforce (Hurlburt & McGarrah, 2016). US higher education employment has also become increasingly dependent on impermanent grant 'soft money' sources (Fernández-Zubieta *et al.*, 2015) even while funding sources have been shrinking (National Science Board, 2012). As academic working conditions at US universities deteriorate, with fewer full-time faculty positions, decreasing numbers of tenured positions and slow salary growth, American universities become less attractive to international scholars who are drawn to the US by the prospect of better working conditions (Altbach & Peterson, 2008).

Moreover, international graduate access to jobs in private industry has also shrunk. In the wake of 9/11, US policies increasingly cast international students as security risks and instituted ever more stringent, time-consuming, costly and changing visa policies (Ewers & Lewis, 2008). H1B visas leading to permanent work and residency status for highly educated migrants have been even more restricted in spite of domestic labor shortages in STEM fields (Jackson, 2003: 2), leading to a 'Darwinian' competitive process whereby only 35% of international graduates working temporarily in the US in 2013 could be offered permanent employment (Shumilova & Cai, 2016). Decreasing prospects for permanent employment in the US could discourage ITA and other international student recruiting and enrollment since access to the US job market has been a major attractor for international students.

As a result of increasing global competition, even if US international enrollments have continued to climb, in recent years, the rate of growth had been slower than for other student destination countries. While other nations experienced dramatic growth, the rate of US international student enrollment growth decreased in the post-millennium decade (Altbach & Peterson, 2008). Over the past 30 years, the US role in educating the world's scientists and engineers has steadily waned (Altbach & Peterson, 2008) as Europe and Asia have approached and surpassed the production of PhDs in these fields. Scholars (e.g. Choudaha, 2017) predict that factors such as a looming economic slowdown in China will further erode US international student enrollment and decrease ITA numbers at US universities.

The 2016 US election arguably marked a watershed for international student enrollment in American higher education. International enrollment, which had already started to flatten in 2016, fell in 2017 for the first time in decades and the number of newly arriving international students declined (Redden, 2017; Saul, 2017). The drop has been attributed in part to increasing competition from other countries for international student enrollments (IIE, 2017; Saul, 2018) and high US tuition rates (Redden, 2017). Just as significant, however, are the rhetoric and policies of a new presidential administration regarding globalization and immigration (Choudaha, 2017). President Trump and his administration have forwarded a narrative that blames the negative consequences of globalization largely on foreigners and immigrants (Palley, 2017), while also condoning and even encouraging nationalist, racist and anti-immigrant sentiment (Palley, 2017). The new administration has restricted and slowed down international student visa access even further, indefinitely banned travel from certain countries, and made it more difficult for international students to visit their home countries while enrolled in US universities or to remain in the US after graduation (Saul, 2018). Anti-immigrant sentiment has thus materially affected international students, with some facing chronic uncertainties about whether they will be allowed to enter or return to the US from abroad. As a result, reports suggest that international students feel a growing sense of unease about their welcome and futures in the US (Redden, 2017; Saul, 2018). Increased concerns about discrimination towards immigrants and people of color as well as their personal safety have also had a chilling effect on international student enrollments (Chronicle of Higher Education, 2017; Rose-Redwood & Rose-Redwood, 2017).

Policies such as the travel ban, with its explicitly anti-Muslim sentiment, undermine US higher education ideals of 'international cooperation and cross-cultural engagement in the pursuit of knowledge' (Rose-Redwood & Rose-Redwood, 2017: iii). A major part of the 'branding' or 'soft power' influence (Nye, 2011) of US universities and society has traditionally been the high valuation given to freedom of academic expression, a focus on human rights, democracy, religious tolerance and respect for national sovereignty. To the extent that the US tarnishes this 'brand,' it becomes less attractive to international scholars seeking education and employment abroad (Altbach & Peterson, 2008) and harms national interests (Nye, 2011) by decreasing the scope of its influence abroad (Stetar et al., 2010).

Interestingly, Chandler (1989) notes a similar nativist moment in European higher education in the 1970s and 1980s when protectionist policies were introduced, including tightened international student visa requirements and higher international student admissions standards and tuition. Yet, attitudes soon began to shift as host countries became aware that their higher education policies were damaging their own economic interests both at home and abroad. Universities across the US experienced revenue shortfalls this year from declining international student enrollment and were forced to make program cuts (Saul, 2018). Where appeals to global human and economic development fail, perhaps financial distress will be more persuasive.

In all, there is a significant disconnect between the 'language-as-problem' orientation that has often driven the formulation of local institutional and state ITA policies, and the resource-oriented view that has historically been taken in national higher education policy. Whether it is viewed from an altruistic perspective that sees higher education as a tool for increasing international prosperity and public good, or from a neoliberal perspective that sees international students as a commodity and economic resource, the presence of ITAs at American universities has been widely regarded a positive indicator of the health and status of the US as a world leader in higher education. Only time will tell whether complacency or increasingly xenophobic national policies and sentiments towards internationals cause the US to squander our leadership in world higher education. If the 'ITA problem' ceases to exist, it may be because other societies and universities abroad have displaced the US as global centers of knowledge.

Implications

A number of implications can be drawn from the consideration of ITA policies from a national higher education policy perspective. For one thing, we can see that much of the research and pedagogical work regarding ITAs has reflected the perceived lack of communicative competence of the international instructor by US undergraduate students (Subtirelu, 2017). Of course, this is to be expected in a field that has a strong pedagogical orientation and aims to improve local classroom instruction. Nevertheless, it means that ITA research has often centered narrowly on language proficiency screening and instruction (Chiang, 2009; Ginther & Yan, 2017; Kang *et al.*, 2015). University handbooks and policy guidelines are often issued by non-specialist stakeholders influenced by monolingual ideologies. We must therefore be cautious towards such policies as they may serve to further reinforce deficit and problem-oriented discourses. They may also contribute to normalizing the policing of ITAs and undermine the internationalizing force that the presence of ITAs provides to US universities (Subtirelu, 2017; Yep, 2014). Institutional pressures can lead ITA educators to become complicit in problem-oriented approaches that marginalize ITAs (Yep, 2014). Although the ability to communicate effectively in the classroom is important, ITA policies also need to consider the broader educational policy context and address ITAs' future career trajectories as scholars and educators working in US-based professional networks. Yep (2014) calls for embracing the 'cultural wealth' and diversity brought by ITAs to US universities through their unique histories and lived experiences. One way to provide a counterdiscourse to deficit- and problem-oriented perspectives at the local institutional level is to assure that published university policies explicitly note the importance of ITAs' contributions to US universities and our national economic and political interests. It is also vital to recognize that cross-cultural communication is a two-way street. Communication and perceptions of intelligibility are based not only on ITA language proficiency per se, but also on the inter-actional skills and willingness of their interlocutors. For example, research suggests that the putative communication difficulties of ITAs may just as easily lie in the stereotyped perceptions of students (see e.g. Rubin, 2002; Subtirelu, 2017), so universities need to make these stakeholders more cognizant of ITAs' contributions to instruction.

It may also be beneficial for ITAs themselves to be more aware of and articulate about the broad policy context in which their teaching work is situated so they can be better advocates for themselves and their role in the university. Coda, for example, piloted an instructional unit using an earlier version of this chapter in a university ITA course as a means of eliciting ITA reflection on their place within the university. Through an online instructional module, students were asked to read and respond to the chapter, and then speculate on future directions for ITAs in the US. The module culminated in a classroom discussion in which students discussed the push and pull factors implicated in the recruitment of ITAs to universities in the US. Through classroom discussion, students came to an understanding that differing cultural norms of ITAs' home and host cultures played an important role in classroom intercultural communication. However, these differences are often overlooked in ITA training curricula because of the centrality of language proficiency. Educators who work with ITAs might, therefore, consider ways to not only attend to commu-nicative competence, but also encourage reflection on how the broader sociocultural contexts of international students and ITAs at American universities affect US classroom experiences.

Besides its pedagogical implications, the transdisciplinary perspective used in this chapter highlights that there is a paucity of research on ITAs from a national and international higher education policy perspective. We need more work considering the entangled relationship of ITAs, the uni-versity, and the political and economic interests of the US. We are espe-cially lacking in consistent national data gathering and analysis on how macro-level US immigration policies are affecting ITAs in US higher edu-cation (Rose-Redwood & Rose-Redwood, 2017). This work is vital to building a credible collective voice regarding ITA policies. ITA profession-als have expertise to contribute and a role to play in countering the ten-dency for local ITA policies to focus on language proficiency and the deficit-oriented discourse of the 'ITA problem.' Challenging the 'ITA problem' discourse necessitates building awareness of the centrality of

ITAs on US campuses and of the ways in which their presence serves economic and political interests or 'soft power' (Nye, 2011) of the US. ITA professionals also play a role in creating welcoming campus climates for ITAs and other international students that can mitigate rising nativism and xenophobia at the national level of the sort exhibited in recent federal immigration policies. This work both upholds our nation's political and economic interests and also its ideals of academic freedom and democracy. Universities need to realize that if local and national ITA policies continue to be exclusionary, the 'ITA problem' may disappear because students have found other destinations that are more welcoming towards international scholars.

References

Adnett, N. (2010) The growth of international students and economic development: Friends or foes? *Journal of Education Policy* 25 (5), 625–637. doi: 10.1080/02680931003782827

Altbach, P.G. (2007) Globalization and the university: Realities in an unequal world. In J.J.F. Forest and P.G. Altbach (eds) *International Handbook of Higher Education*. New York: Springer.

Altbach, P.G. and Peterson, P.M. (2008) Higher education as a projection of America's soft power. In Y. Watanabe and D.L. McConnell (eds) *Soft Power Superstars: Cultural and National Assets of Japan and the United States*. Armonk, NY: M.E. Sharpe.

Bailey, K.M., Pialorsi, F. and Zukowski/Faust, J. (eds) (1984) *Foreign Teaching Assistants in U.S. Universities*. Washington, DC: National Association for Foreign Student Affairs.

Bista, K. and Foster, C. (2016) Preface. In K. Bista and C. Foster (eds) *Global Perspectives and Local Challenges Surrounding International Student Mobility*. Hershey, PA: Information Science Reference.

Blommaert, J. (2010) *The Sociolinguistics of Globalization*. Cambridge: Cambridge University Press.

Blommaert, J. (2013) *Ethnography, Superdiversity and Linguistic Landscapes: Chronicles of Complexity*. Bristol: Multilingual Matters.

Brinkley-Etzkorn, K.E., McGaskey, F.G. and Olsen, T.A. (2015) Supporting international teaching assistants: A benchmarking study of administrative and organizational structures. In G. Gorsuch (ed.) *Talking Matters: Research on Talk and Communication of International Teaching Assistants*. Stillwater, OK: New Forums Press.

Byrd Clark, J.S. (2016) Introduction to the special issue: Transdisciplinary approaches to language learning and teaching in transnational times. *L2 Journal* 8 (4), 3–19.

Chandler, A. (1989) Obligation or opportunity: Foreign student policy in six major receiving countries. *IIE Research Report No. 18*. New York: Institute of International Education.

Chiang, S. (2009) Dealing with communication problems in the instructional interactions between international teaching assistants and American college students. *Language and Education* 23 (5), 461–478. doi: 10.1080/09500780902822959

Choudaha, R. (2017) Three waves of international student mobility (1999–2020). *Studies in Higher Education* 42 (5), 825–832. doi: 10.1080/03075079.2017.1293872

Chronicle of Higher Education (2017) Here are 7 people whose lives were changed by the travel ban. See http://www.chronicle.com/article/Here-Are-7-People-Whose-Lives/239053 (accessed 13 May 2018).

Collins, C.S. (2007) A general agreement on higher education: GATS, globalization, and imperialism. *Research in Comparative and International Education* 2 (4), 283–296. doi: http://dx.doi.org/10.2304/rcie.2007.2.4.283

Coombs, P.H. (1964) *The Fourth Dimension of Foreign Policy: Educational and Cultural Affairs*. New York: Council on Foreign Relations.

Curry, M.J. and Lillis, T.M. (2014) Strategies and tactics in academic knowledge production by multilingual scholars. *Education Policy Analysis Archives* 22 (32), 1–24. doi:10.14507/epaa.v22n32.2014

Douglas Fir Group (2016) A transdisciplinary framework for SLA in a multilingual world. *Modern Language Journal* Supplement 16, 19–47. doi:10.1111/modl.12301

Eckel, P.D. and King, J.E. (2007) United States. In J.J.F. Forest and P.G. Altbach (eds) *International Handbook of Higher Education* (Vol. 18) New York: Springer.

Ewers, M.C. and Lewis, J.M. (2008) Risk and the securitisation of student migration to the United States. *Tijdschrift voor Economische en Social Geografie* 99, 470–482.

Fernández-Zubieta, A., Geuna, A. and Lawson, C. (2015) What do we know of the mobility of research scientists and impact on scientific production. In A. Geuna (ed.) *Global Mobility of Research Scientists: The Economics of Who Goes Where and Why*. Boston: Elsevier.

Fiske, E.B. (1985, June 4) When teachers can't speak clear English. *New York Times*.

Ganguli, I. (2015) Who leaves and who stays? Evidence on immigration selection from the collapse of Soviet science. In A. Geuna (ed.) *Global Mobility of Research Scientists: The Economics of Who Goes Where and Why*. Boston: Elsevier.

Garcia, H.A. and Villarreal, M. (2014) The 'redirecting' of international students: American higher education policy hindrances and implications. *Journal of International Students* 4 (2), 126–136.

Geiger, R.L. (2008) *Research and Relevant Knowledge: American Research Universities Since World War II*. New Brunswick, NJ: Transaction.

Ginther, A. and Yan, X. (2018) Interpreting the relationships between TOEFL iBT scores and GPA: Language proficiency, policy, and profiles. *Language Testing* 35 (2), 271–295. http://dx.doi.org/10.1177/0265532217704010

Gorsuch, G. (2016) International teaching assistants at universities: A research agenda. *Language Teaching* 49 (2), 275–290. doi:10.1017/S0261444815000452

Gottschalk, E.C. (1985, October 17) Foreign student-teachers faulted for lack of fluency in English. *Wall Street Journal*.

Gürüz, K. (2011) *Higher Education and International Student Mobility in the Global Knowledge Economy* (2nd edn). Albany, NY: State University of New York Press.

Heller, S. and McMillen, L. (1986, October 29) Teaching assistants get increased training: Problems arise in foreign-student programs. *Chronicle of Higher Education*.

Hurlburt, S. and McGarrah, M. (2016) *The Shifting Academic Workforce: Where are the Contingent Faculty?* accessed 7 September 2017. http://www.deltacostproject.org/sites/default/files/products/Shifting-Academic-Workforce-November-2016_0.pdf

Institute of International Education (1949) *Windows on the World*.

Institute of International Education (2016) *Open Doors 2016. Report on International Educational Exchange*. See http://www.iie.org/Research-and-Publications/Open-Doors (accessed 1 February 2017).

Institute of International Education (2017) Why IIE: History. See https://www.iie.org/en/Why-IIE/History (accessed 1 February 2017).

Institute of International Education. Project Atlas (2018) *A Quick Look at Global Mobility Trends. 2017 Release*. See https://www.iie.org/-/media/Images/Corporate/Research-and-Insights/Project-Atlas/Project-Atlas-2017-Quick-Look.ashx?la=en&hash=F6DC55CA9C66DE2F14CDA5D8687679A910999055 (accessed 16 May 2018).

Jackson, S.A. (2003) *Envisioning a 21st Century Science and Engineering Workforce for the United States: Tasks for University, Industry, and Government*. Washington, DC: National Academies Press.

Kang, O., Rubin, D. and Lindemann, S. (2015) Mitigating U.S. undergraduates' attitudes toward international teaching assistants. *TESOL Quarterly* 49 (4), 681–706. doi:10.1002/tesq.192

Kotler, P. and Kotler, M. (2014) *Winning Global Markets: How Businesses Invest and Prosper in the World's High-Growth Cities*. New York: Wiley.

Lee, J.J., Maldonado-Maldonado, A. and Rhoades, G. (2006) The political economy of international student flows: Patterns, ideas, and propositions. In J.C. Smart (ed.) *Higher Education Handbook of Theory and Research* (Vol. 21). Dordecht, the Netherlands: Springer.

Macready, C. and Tucker, C. (2011) *Who Goes Where and Why? An Overview and Analysis of Global Educational Mobility*. New York: AIFS Foundation and Institute of International Education.

Manohar, U. and Appiah, O. (2016) Perspective taking to improve attitudes towards international teaching assistants: The role of national identification and prior attitudes. *Communication Education* 65 (2), 149–163.

Marginson, S. (2011) Imagining the global. In R. King, S. Marginson and R. Naidoo (eds) *Handbook on Globalization and Higher Education*. Northampton, MA: Edward Elgar.

Mazzarol, T. and Souter, G.N. (2002) Push-pull factors influencing international student destination choice. *The International Journal of Educational Management* 16 (2), 82–90. doi: 10.1108/09513540210418403

Mitchell, M., Leachman, M., Masterson, K. and Waxman, S. (2018) Unkept promises: State cuts to higher education threaten access and equity. *Center on Budget and Policy Priorities*. Retrieved from https://www.cbpp.org/research/state-budget-and-tax/unkept-promises-state-cuts-to-higher-education-threaten-access-and (accessed 23 November 2018).

NAFSA: Association of International Educators (2018) NAFSA International Student Economic Value Tool. See http://www.nafsa.org/Policy_and_Advocacy/Policy_Resources/Policy_Trends_and_Data/NAFSA_International_Student_Economic_Value_Tool/ (accessed 13 May 2018).

National Science Board (2012) *Diminishing Funding and Rising Expectations: Trends and Challenges for Public Research Universities, A Companion to Science and Engineering Indicators 2012. NSB 12-45*. Arlington, VA: National Science Foundation.

Nye, J.S. (2011) *The Future of Power*. New York: Public Affairs.

OECD. Organisation for Economic Co-operation and Development (2016) *Education at a Glance 2016: OECD Indicators*. See http:dx.doi.org/10.187/eag-2016-en (accessed 5 September 2017).

Oppenheim, N. (1997, March) *How International Teaching Assistant Programs Can Prevent Lawsuits*. Paper presented at the American Educational Research Association conference, Chicago, IL. https://files.eric.ed.gov/fulltext/ED408886.pdf

Palley, T. (2017) Trump's neocon neoliberalism camouflaged with anti-globalization circus. *Challenge* 60 (4), 368-374. doi:10.1080/05775132.2017.1324190

Park, B. (2015) Turkey's isolated stance: An ally no more, or just the usual turbulence? *International Affairs* 91 (3), 581–600. doi:10.1111/1468-2346.12280

Portnoi, L.M., Bagley, S.S. and Rust, V.D. (2010) Mapping the terrain: The global competition phenomenon in higher education. In L.M. Portnoi, V.D. Rust and S.S. Bagley (eds) *Higher Education, Policy, and the Global Competition Phenomenon*. New York: Palgrave MacMillan.

Redden, E. (2017, November 13) New international enrollments decline. *Inside Higher Ed*. See https://www.insidehighered.com/news/2017/11/13/us-universities-report-declines-enrollments-new-international-students-study-abroad (accessed 12 May 2018).

Rhoads, R.A., Li, S. and Ilano, L. (2014) The global quest to build world-class universities: toward a social justice agenda. *New Directions for Higher Education* 168, 27–39.

Ricento, T. (2000) *Ideology, Politics, and Language Policies: Focus on English*. Philadelphia: John Benjamins.

Rose-Redwood, C.A. and Rose-Redwood, R. (2017) Rethinking the politics of the international student experience in the age of Trump. *Journal of International Students* 7 (3), I–IX. doi:10.5281/zenodo.569939.

Rubin, D.L. (2002) Help! My professor (or doctor or boss) doesn't talk English! In J. Martin, T. Nakayama and L. Flores (eds) *Readings in Intercultural Communication: Experiences and Contexts*. Boston: McGraw-Hill.

Ruiz, R. (1984) Orientations in language planning. *NABE: The Journal for The National Association for Bilingual Education* 8 (2), 15–34.

Saul, S. (2017, November 13) Fewer foreign students are coming to U.S., survey shows. *New York Times*. https://www.nytimes.com/2017/11/13/us/fewer-foreign-students-coming-to-us.html?_r=0

Saul, S. (2018, January 2) As flow of foreign students wanes, U.S. universities feel the sting. *New York Times*. https://www.nytimes.com/2018/01/02/us/international-enrollment-drop.htm

Shen, W., Wang, C. and Jin, W. (2016) International mobility of PhD students since the 1990s and its effect on China: A cross-national analysis. *Journal of Higher Education Policy and Management* 38 (3), 333–353.

Shields, R. and Edwards, R.M. (2010) Student mobility and emerging hubs in global higher education. In L.M. Portnoi, V.D. Rust and S.S. Bagley (eds) *Higher Education, Policy, and the Global Competition Phenomenon*. New York: Palgrave MacMillan.

Shumilova, Y. and Cai, Y. (2016) Three approaches to competing for global talent: Role of higher education. In K. Bista and C. Foster (eds) *Global Perspectives and Local Challenges Surrounding International Student Mobility*. Hershey, PA: Information Science Reference.

Stetar, J., Coppla, C., Guo, L., Nabiyeva, N. and Ismailov, B. (2010) Soft power strategies: Competition and cooperation in a globalized system of higher education. In L.M. Portnoi, V.D. Rust and S. S. Bagley (eds) *Higher Education, Policy, and the Global Competition Phenomenon*. New York: Palgrave MacMillan.

Subtirelu, N.C. (2017) Students' orientations to communication across linguistic difference with international teaching assistants at an internationalizing university in the United States. *Multilingua* 36 (3), 247–280. doi:10.1515/multi-2016-0061

Thelin, J.R. (2004) *A History of American Higher Education*. Baltimore: Johns Hopkins University Press.

Vora, N. (2015) Is the university universal? Mobile (re)constitutions of American academia in the Gulf Arab states. *Anthropology and Education Quarterly* 46 (1), 19–36. doi:10.1111/aeq.12085

Yep, G.A. (2014) Talking back: Shifting the discourse of deficit to a pedagogy of cultural wealth of international instructors in US classrooms. In K.G. Hendrix and A. Hebbani (eds) *Hidden Roads: Nonnative English-speaking International Professors in the Classroom*. San Francisco: Jossey-Bass.

Verbik, L. and Lasanowski, V. (2007) International student mobility: Patterns and trends. *World Education News + Reviews*. Retrieved from https://wenr.wes.org/2007/10/wenr-october-2007-feature (accessed 23 May 2019).

Washburn, J. (2005) *University, Inc. The Corporate Corruption of American Higher Education*. New York: Basic Books.

Wildavsky, B. (2010) *The Great Brain Race: How Global Universities are Reshaping the World*. Princeton, NJ: Princeton University Press.

9 Using Course Logic to Describe Outcomes and Instruction for an ITA Course

Greta Gorsuch

Teaching practicum-type courses have been important sources for research on ITA–student interaction, and also for language learning. Yet there are few accounts of how such courses are planned in institutional contexts, and how they operate in the day-to-day. Still fewer are descriptions of connections that ITA educators make between their beliefs about ITA learning, and the instruction they do. As a result, it may not be clear to external observers, who may be funding sources or resources for other types of institutional support, what ITA educators believe should be consistent outcomes of their courses, and what they believe brings the outcomes about. The focus of this chapter is on course logic, an essential component of evaluation research. Course logic is an articulation of the 'inputs' of a course, and how the inputs are thought to cause the course outcomes. It is the course logic that is needed to plan the evaluation and explain the course and the evaluation results to others, particularly non-ITA instructional personnel. As this chapter will illustrate, stating course logic demands thinking beyond whether a course 'works' (what typical end-of-semester evaluations and instructor reflection does) to an examination of *how* a course works. In essence the chapter is an account of the 'big picture' of instructional planning. The resulting course logic dossier may become an invaluable resource for ITA educators as they seek the best outcomes for ITAs, and for their own programs.

Introduction

Evaluation is a significant new direction for relevant, applied research in second language courses. This is particularly true for instructors and administrators involved in courses designed to support international teaching assistants (ITAs). First, evaluation is truly transdisciplinary, and has originated from, and been applied to, programs in business, education, criminal justice, medicine and social action. As such, evaluation initiatives are easily communicable to other actors and stakeholders both inside and outside ITA programs, a highly desirable feature (Douglas Fir Group, 2016). Second, evaluation has a rich, practical literature, robust conceptual frameworks and diverse orientations (Madaus & Kellaghan, 2000). Evaluation can be done for many reasons, including planning programs and courses, illuminating the curriculum of a course, learning the needs of stakeholders, revitalizing teaching practice and materials, determining what learning outcomes are possible and describing what works best in a course (Griffee & Gorsuch, 2016). These are all topics that ITA educators ought to, and probably do, care about. And third, the purpose of evaluation research is to create decision points, which are policy recommendations about what to change or maintain in a course or program. In other words, given what we now know, specifically what should we do? Contrast this with 'regular' research on second language learning and teaching, which simply calls for further research (Griffee & Gorsuch, 2016). These considerations together make evaluation relevant to, and necessary for, ITA education. It would be difficult to imagine an ITA program that has not been tapped for external evaluation, or an ITA educator who has not been asked to comment how they might operate with less money or fewer resources. Evaluation provides potential responses to such situations.

Evaluation as its own field has been around since the 1960s and 70s (Cronbach, 1963; Scriven, 1991). Evaluation professionals have worked in government, education, corporations and hospitals on projects such as developing product evaluation protocols for the US Food and Drug Administration, describing the learning achievement of children watching *Sesame Street* across socio-economic groups, and developing blood pressure awareness and treatment programs for populations unlikely to believe they need this sort of medical care (Posavac & Carey, 1985; Scriven, 1991). Second language learning scholars were by no means slow to comment on evaluation and use it for research (see for example Alderson & Beretta, 1992; Brown, 1992; Mitchell, 1992). However, it was the evaluation of the Bangalore Project by Beretta (1992) that helped propel into the international spotlight that project and its proposal for meaning-focused tasks as a foreign language learning methodology.

Evaluation research is currently done in second language education but is not often described as such (see Sanders, 2005), nor do many researchers overtly use well-established evaluation concepts such as course logic, which will be explored in this chapter. One reason is that evaluation is seen by second language instructors as summative, and thus related to accountability. Instructor evaluations are done at the end of the term or workshop or summer program, and are summative (see Gorsuch & Sokolowski, 2007 for an ITA example). And, most evaluations are done of instructors by their students. That is likely the extent to which evaluation is done, as it seems tiresome, the students' comments seem off-point, and the evaluation itself seems unrelated to the concerns of working ITA educators and program directors (Griffee & Gorsuch, 2016). For these reasons, evaluation as a field deserves another look in the 21st century. ITA instructors and programs, and their stakeholders, have much to gain.

Based on empirical evaluation research on an ITA course, I demonstrate the organizing visuals that I used to develop the course logic for ESL 5312, a teaching practicum course for ITAs who have not yet been approved to teach. As I show, stating course logic demands thinking beyond whether a course 'works' (what typical end-of-semester evaluations do) to an examination of *how* a course works. Thus, doing course logic gets at the theoretical and practical underpinnings of a course. I also describe course logic validation, a little-practiced step that supports a teacher's conception of course logic to have a realistic basis and to reflect good theory and practice. I recount how, in an actual course logic validation procedure, the course logic was explained to interested stakeholders, and how I used their comments to rethink my course logic.

There are few descriptions of connections that ITA educators make between their beliefs about ITA learning, and the instruction they do. In other words, we do not state our course logic (Gorsuch, 2012). As a result, it may not be clear to external observers what ITA educators believe should be consistent outcomes of their courses, and what theories and practices they believe bring the outcomes about. These external observers may be funding sources, or administrative gate keepers. In essence, this chapter is an account of the 'big picture' of ITA instructional planning and its place in evaluation research. The resulting course logic dossier may become an important resource for ITA educators as they seek the best outcomes for ITAs, particularly in the sustained climate of shrinking funds and resources, including time, for higher education. Having an articulation of course logic on hand is also a necessary first step to doing evaluations for our own purposes. We need statements of course logic to plan an evaluation, and to explain the course and our evaluation results to interested others (Griffee & Gorsuch, 2016; see also The Douglas Fir Group, 2016).

Course Logic

Course logic (also known as 'program theory') refers to the set of working beliefs that administrators, instructors, and other course participants have about how a course is supposed to bring about learners' achievement of outcomes (Rogers, 2000; Rossi *et al.*, 1999). In other words, how do course 'inputs' move learners in the direction of the course outcomes (Griffee & Gorsuch, 2016)? Using an unexpected but vivid example: If someone plans a social health program to reduce teenage pregnancy, they have to show their course (program) logic in order to get grant funding. Do they plan to reduce teenage pregnancy by talking to large groups of students about not having sex before marriage? What theory and evidence supports this logic? Or do they plan to work with small groups of students and show young men and women alike how to use condoms? What theory and evidence supports logic? Or is there another plan? Thus, stating course logic demands thinking that moves beyond whether a course 'works' to an examination of *how* it works. Course logic examines the theories and practices thought to support learner outcomes. The kind of course evaluation proposed here moves beyond asking different stakeholders, like students, what they think of a course. Even though asking stakeholders to comment on the worth of a course has an important function, evaluation research would not limit itself to doing that.

The Setting and the Course

ESL 5312, English Communication for Teaching Professionals, is the second of two courses offered at a large research university in the southwestern US. The course is credit-bearing and counts towards learners' graduate degrees. It is a practicum-type course. Learners are placed in guest teaching situations in their academic departments for a minimum of one hour per week. Learners are paired with experienced faculty members or instructors for this part of the course. Learners also attend ESL classes 80 minutes per week. ESL 5312 is intended for ITA candidates who are still not yet approved to teach because of their scores on a teaching simulation test, the ITA Performance Test 10.1 (Gorsuch *et al.*, 2016), and the SPEAK test (Educational Testing Service, 2009). The course is taught by an instructor with up to three ESL teaching assistants (MA-level graduate students in applied linguistics). The course lasts for 14 weeks. To create a basis for understanding the three visual organizers used to develop course logic (these appear later), the course outcomes for ESL 5312 are needed. See Table 9.1.

The outcomes hint at some of the theoretical underpinnings of the course ('explicit knowledge' and 'procedural knowledge' (skill learning) and 'awareness' (metacognition)), but it is through developing course logic using an iterative process of introspection and the visual organizers given below, that theory and proposed practices are detailed.

Table 9.1 Course outcomes for ESL 5312

1. ITA candidates will be able to lead a lab or class with reasonable fluency.
2. ITA candidates will be able to handle student questions.
3. ITA candidates will demonstrate explicit knowledge of Discourse Intonation by using it in appropriate tasks such as read-alouds and Repeated Reading sessions.
4. ITA candidates will demonstrate awareness of and improved performance (procedural knowledge) in Discourse Intonation and Teaching Strategies.

Getting at course logic: ESL 5312

Getting at course logic can be challenging. Most instructors who design and teach courses operate out of implicit, fluid and generally stated beliefs about how learning takes place, such as 'practice is needed' (see Gorsuch, 2012: 447–448, for examples of ITA course instructors' beliefs). To do a course logic study, more detailed statements are needed, ones that answer the questions 'What kind of practice? Listening, speaking, scripted talk, extemporaneous talk?' 'How much practice? How often?' 'In what settings? In students' departments? In a language learning lab? Online?' 'Does setting make a difference?' (Gorsuch, 2017a, 2017b). Fortunately, mainstream evaluation offers concepts and visual organizers that help working planners and practitioners get at course logic through a developmental process (Rossi *et al.*, 2004). The three visual organizers are: (a) an impact model, (b) an organizational chart and (c) a course logic table (Rossi *et al.*, 2004). One builds upon the other. These are addressed in turn.

Impact model

The first visual organizer, the impact model, shows what the teacher or evaluator believe is the causal sequence between the inputs and the outcomes of a course. An impact model identifies the inputs, each of which represents an 'engine' of learning. See Figure 9.1 (Gorsuch, 2017a):

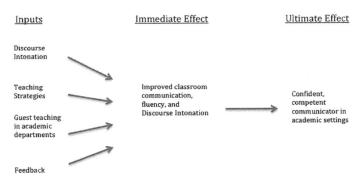

Figure 9.1 Impact model for ESL 5312

The 'inputs' (Discourse Intonation, Teaching Strategies, guest teaching in academic departments, and feedback) are the things I believed cause the 'immediate effect' of the course. The immediate effect (improved classroom communication, fluency and Discourse Intonation) in turn is believed to cause an 'ultimate effect' which is what the course helps participants to accomplish over time (confident, competent communicator in academic settings). In other words: What are the main causes, or 'engines,' of learning in the course? What are the intended effects? An impact model seems spare and at odds with the richly detailed ways in which we teachers think of courses, but an impact model aims for conceptual clarity.

Organizational chart

These spare-looking inputs and effects are then elaborated in the second visual organizer, an organizational chart for ESL 5312 (Figure 9.2).

An organizational chart works from the impact model (Figure 9.1) and 'encompasses both the functions and activities the program is expected to perform' (Rossi *et al.*, 2004: 142). 'Activities' refers to what happens in the course to support learners to achieve outcomes and are elaborated expressions of the course inputs. 'Functions' refers to who does the activities (instructor versus teaching assistants versus ITA candidates, etc.). There are many terms and theoretical concepts specific to ESL 5312 in the organizational chart, which are defined and given a basis later in this report (Table 9.3).

The orientation of the organizational chart is from left to right, as suggested by the arrow at the bottom. The ESL 5312 instructor and the TAs have four functions that support the ITA candidates. For example, function #3 is 'lead ITAs to use DI and Teaching Strategies in discipline-specific settings and developing proceduralized knowledge.' Each bullet point under a function states how the functions are realized in the course. In other words, they are the activities. An example is: 'Recordings of three observations transcribed by ITAs, transcriptions corrected for accuracy by ESL TAs.' The host instructor and the undergraduate students together have one function that acts on ITA candidates: 'Help ITAs learn to

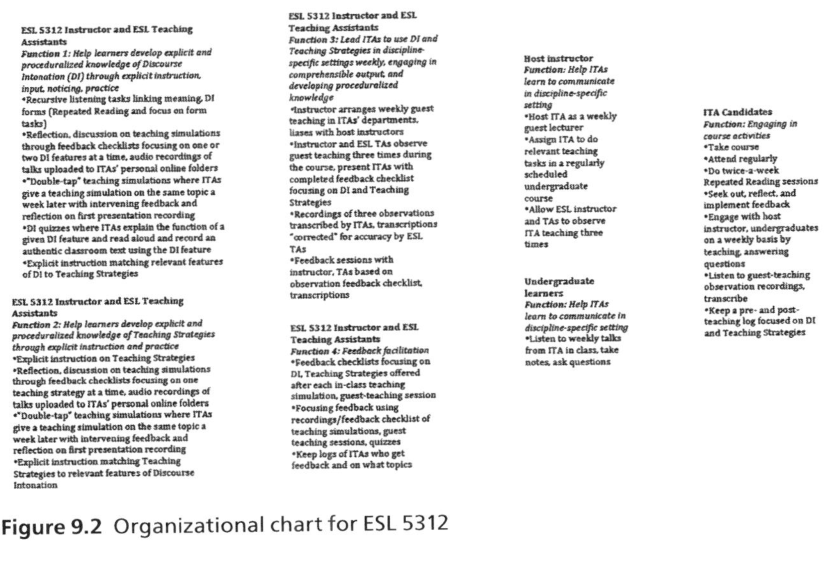

ESL 5312 Instructor and ESL Teaching Assistants
Function 1: Help learners develop explicit and proceduralized knowledge of Discourse Intonation (DI) through explicit instruction, input, noticing, practice
• Recursive listening tasks linking meaning, DI forms (Repeated Reading and focus on form tasks)
• Reflection, discussion on teaching simulations through feedback checklists focusing on one or two DI features at a time, audio recordings of talks uploaded to ITAs' personal online folders
• "Double-tap" teaching simulations where ITAs give a teaching simulation on the same topic a week later with intervening feedback and reflection on first presentation recording
• DI quizzes where ITAs explain the function of a given DI feature and read aloud and record an authentic classroom text using the DI feature
• Explicit instruction matching relevant features of DI to Teaching Strategies

ESL 5312 Instructor and ESL Teaching Assistants
Function 2: Help learners develop explicit and proceduralized knowledge of Teaching Strategies through explicit instruction and practice
• Explicit instruction on Teaching Strategies
• Reflection, discussion on teaching simulations through feedback checklists focusing on one teaching strategy at a time, audio recordings of talks uploaded to ITAs' personal online folders
• "Double-tap" teaching simulations where ITAs give a teaching simulation on the same topic a week later with intervening feedback and reflection on first presentation recording
• Explicit instruction matching Teaching Strategies to relevant features of Discourse Intonation

ESL 5312 Instructor and ESL Teaching Assistants
Function 3: Lead ITAs to use DI and Teaching Strategies in discipline-specific settings weekly, engaging in comprehensible output, and developing proceduralized knowledge
• Instructor arranges weekly guest teaching in ITAs' departments, liases with host instructors
• Instructor and ESL TAs observe guest teaching three times during the course, present ITAs with completed feedback checklist focusing on DI and Teaching Strategies
• Recordings of three observations transcribed by ITAs, transcriptions "corrected" for accuracy by ESL TAs
• Feedback sessions with instructor, TAs based on observation feedback checklist, transcriptions

ESL 5312 Instructor and ESL Teaching Assistants
Function 4: Feedback facilitation
• Feedback checklists focusing on DL Teaching Strategies offered after each in-class teaching simulation, guest-teaching session
• Focusing feedback using recordings/feedback checklist of teaching simulations, guest teaching sessions, quizzes
• Keep logs of ITAs who get feedback and on what topics

Host instructor
Function: Help ITAs learn to communicate in discipline-specific setting
• Host ITA as a weekly guest lecturer
• Assign ITA to do relevant teaching tasks in a regularly scheduled undergraduate course
• Allow ESL instructor and TAs to observe ITA teaching three times

Undergraduate learners
Function: Help ITAs learn to communicate in discipline-specific setting
• Listen to weekly talks from ITA in class, take notes, ask questions

ITA Candidates
Function: Engaging in course activities
• Take course
• Attend regularly
• Do twice-a-week Repeated Reading sessions
• Seek out, reflect, and implement feedback
• Engage with host instructor, undergraduates on a weekly basis by teaching, answering questions
• Listen to guest-teaching observation recordings, transcribe
• Keep a pre- and post-teaching log focused on DI and Teaching Strategies

Figure 9.2 Organizational chart for ESL 5312

communicate in discipline-specific setting.' Note, however, how their different roles are expressed differently, where host instructors 'Assign ITA to do relevant teaching asks in a regularly scheduled undergraduate course' (an activity) and undergraduate learners 'Listen to weekly talks from ITA in class, take notes, ask questions' (again, an activity). The ITA candidates also have a function, 'Engaging in course activities,' and engage in the supporting activities of attending ESL 5312 regularly, seeking and implementing feedback, and listening to and transcribing their guest-teaching observation recordings, among other things.

Course inputs, functions and activities

Moving from the impact model to the organizational chart took some thought. From my reading, I could see no evidence that anyone in the second language education field had used an impact model and organizational chart from mainstream evaluation to explain a course, or instruction. Certainly, I had never overtly studied, nor stated, my own course logic in quite this way. Thus, I had no examples to work from. In order to get to the organizational chart, I used four strategies:

(1) I analyzed two research reports that I had identified as being evaluation research (although the authors never identified it or organized it as such);
(2) I set down and picked up my impact model about 20 times over several weeks and considered what I would need to be able to explain it to another, disinterested but informed person;
(3) The process described in #2 resulted in making two additional tables, one which defined the terms and concepts I needed to use, and one which related the organizational chart to the course materials;
(4) I wrote down my thoughts in a running memo, which was a word processing document that I kept dated entries in.

Analysis of two research reports

I knew that the 'functions' part of the organizational chart were the link between my course outcomes and the activities I planned. I also knew that different teachers would identify different functions, and thus the content of their organizational charts would be different. Not everyone would think of their courses in terms of explicit knowledge, procedural knowledge, etc. as I had. To explore this, I read the two research reports, looking for how the authors ascribed functions and activities, and what course outcomes these were supposed to support. If I could see the authors' conceptions of the engines of learning in their courses, then an impact model could be used to do what I needed. See Table 9.2.

In looking through these reports, I found functions, activities and course outcomes, i.e. the course logic, thus I could more easily complete the ESL 5312 organizational chart.

Table 9.2 Different ways of ascribing functions and activities in a course

Teachers'/ Authors' tradition	Functions ascribed to a course	Activities that support the functions	Course outcomes
Total Physical Response (Wolfe & Jones, 1982)	Acquiring grammar, vocabulary through listening	Teacher presents new language as commands, students respond physically (*stand up, sit down, run*), then allowed to repeat new language verbally	Improving implicit knowledge of grammar and vocabulary
Computer assisted language learning (Sanders, 2005)	• Facilitating greater student participation • Processing input and monitoring output • Students producing more language • Learning grammar and vocabulary, and increasing comprehension through drill-like repetition	• Synchronous computer mediated communication tasks (chat), evaluated and discussed in face-to-face class time • In-class group work on poster sessions • Automated exercises on WebCT	Improving oral performance

Writing definitions from background and evidence

The concepts and terms in Figures 9.1 (the impact model) and 9.2 (the organizational chart) for ESL 5312 were not plucked from thin air. So, in addition to my work with the reports shown in Table 9.2, I defined what I meant by the terms I wanted to use in the organizational chart in Figure 9.2. This allowed me to get at the question of *how* my proposed 'engines' of learning would work. See Table 9.3 (adapted from Gorsuch, 2017a).

It helped me to think of how I might answer questions from others, when I showed them the ESL 5312 impact model, the organizational chart, and the course logic table (the third visual organizer from the evaluation field, discussed below). Table 9.3 has three columns, Definition, Rationale and relevance to course outcomes, and Further reading. Each term I believed might need explanation, I listed vertically. To focus the information given in the left and middle column, I used bullet points and worded the information accordingly. Thus, 'Procedural knowledge of DI' was defined as:

• Language knowledge that is available for use without much thought.

A few of the rationales given for including procedural knowledge of DI in the course were:

• DI, like most second language features, is acquired slowly; and
• DI is an abstract grammatical system and difficult to apply to specific speech situations; and
• Learners who retell a story or do a speaking task a second time use more appropriate pause groups (an aspect of DI).

Table 9.3 Definitions of terms and concepts in ESL 5312 course organizational chart

Definition	Rationale, and relevance to course outcomes (Table 1)	Further reading
Discourse Intonation (DI): • How a speaker uses the pausing and prosodic system of a language for communicative purposes • Comprised of four elements in the course: pauses (thought groups), prominence (sentence-level stress), tone choices (intonation contours), speech paragraphs • Sometimes referred to as prosody	• DI is needed by TAs as instructors in order to emphasize and differentiate ideas, begin and end topics, and express social relationships • Using appropriate DI (prosody) is implicated in listener perceptions of spoken communication ability and fluency • DI is rarely taught in English classes overseas • Many ITAs do not use appropriate DI upon arrival in the US, e.g. pauses violate clause and phrase boundaries, higher pitch not used to mark content words or words with high information value, falling tones used regardless of ITA's intention to continue or finish topic Course outcomes #1, 3, 4	(Anderson-Hsieh & Koehler, 1988) (Brazil, 1997) (Chambers, 1997) (Ejzenberg, 2000) (Gorsuch, 2011a, 2013: 68) (Hahn, 2004) (Olynack et al., 1990) (Pickering, 2001, this volume) (Wennerstrom, 1998, 2000)
Explicit knowledge of DI • Explicit knowledge is formally taught and learned as content, such as what DI is, and how it should be used	• ITAs as second language learners are able to demonstrate explicit knowledge growth of DI through reading passages aloud • Such activities may lead to proceduralized (more easily accessed) knowledge of DI • To proceduralized knowledge, one needs to begin with explicit knowledge and provide opportunities to access, and re-access it Course outcomes #3, 4	(DeKeyser, 2007, 2015) (Gorsuch, 2011b, 2013, 2015)
Procedural knowledge of DI • Language knowledge that is available for use without much thought	• DI, like most second language features, is acquired slowly • DI is an abstract grammatical system and difficult to apply to specific speech situations • Interventions should aim at building procedural knowledge of DI • Learners who retell a story or do a speaking task a second time use more appropriate pause groups (an aspect of DI) • To build procedural knowledge ITAs need to get experience doing things • Most ITA programs lack sufficient intensity to bring about opportunities for procedural knowledge growth Course outcomes #1, 4	(Arevart & Nation, 1991) (DeKeyser, 2015) (Gibson, 2008) (Freed, 1995) (Gorsuch, 2011b, 2013, 2015; 2016) (Mitchell et al., 2013)

(Continued)

Table 9.3 *(Continued)*

Definition	Rationale, and relevance to course outcomes (Table 1)	Further reading
Input, noticing, comprehensible output • Second language learning theories	• ITA candidates are second language learners • Learners need second language input in order to learn • The input should be relevant to learners • Learners need to notice specific features in second language input (this points to a role for explicit instruction) • Comprehensible output refers to cognitive processes that 'push' learners to more carefully pick words and syntactic structures in response to exigencies of different communication situations • Comprehensible input often associated with pair and group interactions (a conversation partner does not understand an utterance a learner makes so the learner must re-state) • Authentic teaching situations may provide a little-considered opportunity for learners to engage in comprehensible output processes Course outcomes #1, 3, 4	(Abe, 2009) (Doughty, 2003) (Fernandez-Garcia & Martinez-Arbelaiz, 2014) (Gass, 2003) (Gorsuch, 2005, 2011b) (Mitchell *et al.*, 2013) (Philp, 2013) (Shehadeh, 2002) (Swain, 2005)
Teaching strategies: • Classroom communication strategies commonly taught to ITAs • Comprised of five components in the course: Handling questions from students by paraphrasing and checking; predicting and practicing key terms in a talk; repeating or spelling key terms; showing awareness of audience comprehension by asking teaching questions and comprehension checks; and using repetition or prominence to emphasize transitions in a talk • Sometimes known as 'interactive teaching methods' and attributed by some to strategic competence in the communicative competence model	• Teaching Strategies are a common element of ITA programs • Teaching Strategies not necessarily linked to DI or other features of the second language that need to be learned • Teaching Strategies can be linked with relevant DI features, creating explicit instruction and practice opportunities (e.g. 'teaching questions' can be linked with using strong rising or falling tones) • Using Teaching Strategies is a skill needing explicit instruction (resulting in explicit knowledge) with many practice opportunities (resulting in proceduralized knowledge) Course outcomes #2, 4	(Gorsuch *et al.*, 2013) (Gorsuch, 2015) (Griffee, 2011) (Griffee & Gorsuch, 2016) (Halleck & Moder, 1995) (Kasper, 2004) (Messinger, 1997) (Miller & Matsuda, 2006) (Pica *et al.*, 1990)

(Continued)

Table 9.3 *(Continued)*

Definition	Rationale, and relevance to course outcomes (Table 1)	Further reading
Feedback • Construed as information given to ITA candidates on pre-determined aspects of their spoken performance • Feedback in ESL 5312 is offered using a predetermined checklist focusing on DI and Teaching Strategies	• Giving feedback to ITA candidates on their spoken performance is a central activity in many ITA programs • It is believed that providing feedback builds ITAs' metacognition which is needed for longitudinal success • How ITA candidates actually use feedback is not widely studied, and feedback has not been firmly connected to improvement Course outcomes #1, 2, 3, 4	(Alsberg, 2002) (Gorsuch, 2011b, 2012) (Jacobsen et al., 2006) (Tapper & Kidder, 2006)
Metacognition • A learner's ability to think about, plan, and evaluate performance on tasks • Many sources under different names, such as strategic competence, learner planning, self-efficacy, or deliberate practice	• Teaching content in a second language is a complex performance requiring development of expertise • Developing metacognition is a potent way to develop expertise • ITA candidates are adult language learners with potentially strong metacognitive skills • Appealing to learners' metacognition is strongly implied in descriptions of ITA courses, yet is seldom called this • Feedback is a common way to appeal to ITA candidates' metacognition; There may be additional ways which are as yet unexplored in the literature Course outcomes #1, 2, 3, 4	(Ericsson, 2004) (Gorsuch, 2009, 2012, 2016) (Graham, 2006) (Ortega, 2005) (Pajares, 2008) (van de Wiel et al., 2012)

This last point accounts for the item under Function #1 in Figure 9.2 on the 'double tap' teaching simulation presentations. The definitions and explanations in the organizational chart were set at about the level of explanation that would be provided in course logic validation.

Relating the course materials to the organizational chart

To complete the organizational chart (Figure 9.2), I undertook one additional task. I needed to coordinate the ESL teaching assistants when I taught ESL 5312. When working with early-career graduate students, it is useful to use materials as the medium of discussion and mentoring. Further, my teaching and research tradition is closely linked with materials writing. For these reasons, I wished to think through further explanations of how the course inputs in the impact model were supposed to work to support learners to reach the course outcomes. Specifically, how were the course inputs expressed in the materials used in the course? How would I explain the materials to the ESL teaching assistants I worked with, or to other instructors in the program? See Table 9.4.

Table 9.4 Description of materials for ESL 5312

Material	Why used	How used
DI and **Teaching Strategies Checklist** (Appendix A); eight Likert scale items with five points for quantitative measurement; five open-ended items on five **teaching strategies** for qualitative comment	• To offer **feedback** to ITAs on **DI** and **Teaching Strategies** for teaching simulation tasks and guest teaching observations • To create a focus for instruction, reflection, feedback and practice	• During each teaching simulation task and guest teaching observation, the instructor and the three ESL teaching assistants for the course mark the **feedback** checklist and write additional comments • After each teaching task or host teaching session, the feedback checklists from all observers are photocopied for the ITA by the course instructor and ESL teaching assistants • Progress on each aspect of the **DI** and **Teaching Strategies** features on the feedback checklist are noted
Audio recordings and transcripts for two 'double tap' simulated teaching tasks: comparing two concepts, and presenting on a research interest	• To offer an additional source of **feedback**, along with the **DI** and **Teaching Strategies** checklist for the same teaching simulation tasks	• The audio recordings for the simulated teaching tasks are offered to the ITAs in an individualized Drop Box folder
Audio recordings and transcripts for two to three **guest teaching** observations	• To heighten ITAs' awareness of issues with their use of **DI** and **Teaching Strategies** • To create a focus for **feedback** during instructor and ESL teaching assistant office hour meetings • To provide a basis for self-determined 'private learning' of ITAs who may wish to focus on their use of teaching phrases or any other communication feature not anticipated by the instructor	• The audio recordings for the **guest teaching** observations are sent to the ITAs in an individualized Drop Box folder • ITAs have one week to transcribe the portion of the recording where they teach • The ESL teaching assistants take it in turns to check the transcript for accuracy, adding words and other sounds the ITA has omitted • Because the transcripts are written and revised using Drop Box, the ITA has access to the corrected transcripts
Four **Discourse Intonation** quizzes on thought groups, prominence, tone choices and speech paragraphs (a fourth **DI** feature) (Appendix B is a sample)	• To gauge ITAs' level of explicit knowledge of key **DI** features • To encourage ITAs to act on **feedback** and engage in pre-task planning	• ITAs complete a written portion of the quizzes describing the functions and rules of **DI** features • ITAs audio-record the read-aloud portions of the quizzes to Drop Box • The instructor records oral **feedback** with a quiz grade • ITAs are encouraged to re-record their work according to the **feedback** to increase their grade

(Continued)

Table 9.4 *(Continued)*

Material	Why used	How used
Repeated Reading materials with audio support and focus on form listening tasks (Appendix C is a sample, see also Gorsuch, 2011b)	• To encourage development of ITA candidates' **explicit and procedural knowledge** of **DI** features through recursive listening tasks linking **DI** to meaning • To offer an additional focus of **feedback** for office hour visits with instructor and ESL teaching assistants	• ITAs do twice-a-week self-access listening tasks using a Repeated Reading procedure: 1. Complete and self-score a short focus-on-form task highlighting one **DI** feature; 2. Listen twice to a recorded version of a 300 word, 8th grade level science text while reading the text silently
Pre- and post-teaching log for guest teaching assignment with weekly prompts aligned with course inputs of **DI** and **Teaching Strategies** (see Appendix D)	• To note changes in **DI** and **Teaching Strategy** knowledge • To encourage and note engagement in pre-task planning based on post-task experiences	• ITAs are sent the electronic teaching log at the beginning of the course and they type their responses in the spaces given

Note: **Bolded** items are course inputs (see Figure 9.1).

Neither Table 9.3 nor 9.4 are called for by the mainstream evaluation field, so these were an innovation. I was inspired by the standard visual organizers from mainstream evaluation to use additional tables with briefly stated information to help me complete the organizational chart. Using Tables 9.3 and 9.4 also helped me to complete a course logic table, and to prepare for the course logic validation procedure.

Using a memo

Finally, to complete the organizational chart (Figure 9.2) I kept a running memo on my thoughts and decisions. One notation on February 16 said: *I keep wanting to elaborate the impact model by adding more course inputs. But I realized I can't add more inputs. If learners meet once weekly for 80 minutes for 14 weeks, that amounts to only 18.67 hours. NOT ENOUGH TIME to accomplish more.* This thinking lead to another notation on February 19: *Need to estimate number of hours learners will spend guest teaching. I have to trust that learners are benefitting from the activities I have planned when they are out of my sight. I have to let go of the assumption that direct instruction from me is the only effective course input. Need to look at organizational chart again. Have I adequately described learners' out-of-class work?*

The course logic table

Using information and ideas generated by the impact model and the organizational chart, I completed a course logic table. The table is a way to organize key points of a course curriculum for the purpose of assessing the adequacy of the course curriculum to accomplish the outcomes. Statements of course logic are surprisingly practical, and probe

Table 9.5 Course logic table for ESL 5312

Course inputs	Functions and activities	Course outputs	Short-term outcomes	Long-term outcomes
Organizing concepts of Discourse Intonation and Strategies	Functions: Course provides classes on building implicit and explicit second language knowledge of DI and Strategies using second language acquisition theories stipulating opportunities for input, noticing, comprehensible output and theories of adult metacognition development Activities: Recursive listening tasks, pair/group/whole class discussions and tasks, simulated teaching presentations with pair/group and instructor/student feedback using course assessment criteria, transcription and analysis tasks	ITAs take course, attend regularly, seek out feedback on spoken performances	Outcome summary: Improved ITA pronunciation and interpersonal communication	Outcome summary: ITAs capable of extended discourse in academic and professional settings
Course coordinator			Stated course outcomes:	
Trained instructors			1. Learners will be able to sustain a presentation on a topic in their field for at least 10 minutes with reasonable spoken fluency.	
ESL teaching assistants				
Textbook, CDs/DVDs designed for ITAs			2. Learners will be able to engage in question and answer sessions after their presentation and demonstrate ability to comprehend and answer questions.	
Locally developed and validated assessments based in current second language communicative competence theory				
ITAs identified by academic departments for course participation; some ITAs self-select			3. Learners will demonstrate knowledge of discourse intonation and its role in getting US undergraduates to understand learners' intended meaning.	
ESL classes meet once a week for 80 minutes for 14 weeks (18.67 hours), plus ITAs observe and guest teach one a week for an estimated 80 minutes for 14 weeks (18.67 hours)				

unexamined assumptions we base a course on. For instance, one statement of course logic can be the deceptively simple: Learners' participation in a course for a certain number of hours, for a given number of weeks, will result in specific course outcomes. What this statement may in fact reveal is that given available time, and given what other inputs can be provided, certain given outcomes cannot be attained. This was one issue I grappled with, portrayed in the February 16 and 19 memo notes. I wanted to add course inputs but realized I could not because 80 minutes of meetings per week for 14 weeks amounted to just under 19 contact hours. I had to be realistic and understand that given the constrained resources at hand (time being one of them), the course inputs had to be constrained, as well. Working on the course logic table underscored this. See Table 9.5 for the ESL 5312 course logic.

While there are no arrows in the table there is an orientation from left to right, where inputs are used to bring about activities which in turn results in an output which, I hoped, resulted in short- and long-term outcomes. One important addition to this chart had to do the duration and intensity of ESL 5312, found under Inputs, as time available is a resource for the course. This ITA preparation course follows a typical duration and intensity model of graduate content courses at the university where it is offered. That is to say, graduate courses in history or chemistry at the school are all configured to be worth 3 credit hours, which, in the estimation of the school, requires 37.33 contact hours per semester. This is an inescapable element of second language learning course logic and current curriculum models. Such learning is slow and is not the same as content learning. It is likely that many second language courses stipulate too many functions, activities and outcomes for the time that is available to the course. A course logic table, and the processes that lead up to it, can be used to argue for more frequent and longer class meetings while still keeping an eye on the inputs to the course. More, and longer, class meetings may require that instructors be paid more, or for the materials or instruction to change.

Course Logic Validation

Validation is a process whereby the course logic model is shown to various stakeholders such as department chairpersons or colleagues (Griffee & Gorsuch, 2016). The evaluator explains the course logic using the impact model, then the course logic table, and then, if necessary, the organizational chart. Then the evaluator asks: 'Does the course logic make sense?' and 'Do you think these inputs could result in the course outcomes?' Validating the course logic accomplishes two things. First, it ensures we are not living inside our own heads and proposing something implausible. Second, educated, informed others will point out issues we may have missed.

The following are suggested strategies for course logic validation. (a) Choose informed, and diverse, others to interview about the course logic. I interviewed my department chair, an assistant department chair, and ESL instructor in the same program, and a graduate advisor in a science department. I chose the two department chairs because they thought about teaching, courses and curricula in a broad and businesslike way. (b) When interviewing others about the course logic, show the impact model first (Figure 9.1), then the course logic table (Table 9.5), and then if necessary, the organizational chart (Figure 9.2). In the context of interviewing, I found the organizational chart a more effective way for to answer questions, and to provide further details when asked. The impact model and course logic table are more oriented for visual clarity. (c) Ask your informants 'Does the course logic I've shown you make sense?' 'Do you think these inputs could result in the course outcomes?' 'Have I missed anything?' Take notes on their responses. (d) Avoid elaborating or defending your assumptions or beliefs about the course logic. The purpose is to hear what the informant has to say. Finally, (e) Use your post-interview notes to critically evaluate your course logic. Think through whether there is a pattern to informants' comments. Did the comments give you new insights on the course logic? Then make changes as needed to the three visual organizers.

In the case of ESL 5312, one instructor, an ESL professional focused on two items: The contact hours listed in the course logic table (Table 9.5), and functions of the ITAs portrayed in the organizational chart (Figure 9.2). He noted that the syllabuses at the university stipulated that students should expect to spend three hours of preparation for each contact hour of a course. He believed that the course logic should recognize that and expand structured practice done by learners. This resulted in adding items to the ITAs' functions in the organizational chart that were consonant with my assumptions that learner noticing, and instructor feedback, were necessary for language learning. Thus, two functions were added under 'ITA candidates:'

- Listen to guest-teaching observation recordings, and transcribe
- Keep a pre- and post-teaching log focused on DI and Teaching Strategies.

The assistant department chair, a French literature scholar, said he was confused by the terminology used in the course logic table I showed him. What was the difference between ITAs and ESL TAs? He was not aware that the ESL 5312 had ESL TAs (teaching assistants). He wanted to know in more detail what their role was in the course, and how the course logic could indicate the nature of the training the ESL TAs might get while working with the coordinator and the instructor. I used his comments to revise the organizational chart (Figure 9.2) and specifically mention the ESL TAs and what they would do. I then used the organizational chart to plan my coordination with the ESL TAs. For example, under Function 3 in the organizational chart, I noted that ESL TAs were to learn how to observe ITAs while teaching and assess ITAs' performance. They were also to correct ITAs' transcriptions of their guest teaching sessions and then use the corrected transcriptions to give feedback to ITAs during office hours. In general, I learned that the course logic generally held up. Informants believed the course logic was plausible and could realistically support learners to meet the course outcomes (Table 9.1).

Conclusion

Mainstream evaluation deserves a renewal of attention in second language education. In this chapter, I demonstrated the organizing visuals offered by evaluation to get at the course logic for an ITA teaching practicum course, ESL 5312. In writing course logic, and validating it using external informants and reflection, I established how I thought the course would work, going beyond the typical practice of asking whether a course worked after the fact, and whether students approved of the course. I used the course logic dossier I wrote (the impact model, the organizational chart, the course logic table), along with additional tables concerning the background of my course logic, and how the course materials would be used, to plan an actual evaluation of the course. The evaluation report is freely available online at: https://www.researchgate.net/publication/312940166_An_Evaluation_of_a_Teaching_Practicum_Course_for_International_Teaching_Assistants (Gorsuch, 2017a). I have also used the course logic to explain the course and the evaluation results, and the results from a study focused on changes in learners' DI knowledge. To conclude, our goal in the ITA field is to more effectively improve outcomes in higher education, and also to improve outcomes for generations of young international scientists and professionals to come. As a result, we need to be able to show transparently our processes, our thinking, and our worth within and without our field (e.g. Douglas Fir Group, 2016). Evaluation is a good candidate for this.

References

Abe, H. (2009) The effect of interactive input enhancement on the acquisition of the English connected speech by Japanese college students. *Phonetics Teaching & Learning Proceedings, University College London.* Retrieved February 22, 2018, from http://www.phon.ucl.ac.uk/ptlc/proceedings/ptlcpaper_29e.pdf.

Alderson, J.C. and Beretta, A. (1992) *Evaluating Second Language Education.* Cambridge: Cambridge University Press.

Alsberg, J. (2002) Effecting change in pronunciation: Teaching ITAs to teach themselves. In W. Davis, J. Smith and R. Smith (eds) *Ready to Teach: Graduate Teaching Assistants Prepare for Today and Tomorrow* (pp. 139–146). Stillwater, OK: New Forums Press, Inc.

Anderson-Hsieh, J. and Koehler, K. (1988) The effect of foreign accent and speaking rate on native speaker comprehension. *Language Learning* 38, 561–570.

Arevart, S. and Nation, P. (1992) Fluency improvement in a second language. *RELC Journal* 22, 84–94.

Beretta, A. (1992) What can be learned from the Bangalore evaluation. In J.C. Alderson and A. Beretta (eds) *Evaluating Second Language Education* (pp. 250–273). Cambridge: Cambridge University Press.

Brazil, D. (1997) *The Communicative Value of Intonation in English.* Cambridge: Cambridge University Press.

Brown, J.D. (1992) Language program evaluation: A synthesis of existing possibilities. In R.K. Johnson (ed.) *The Second Language Curriculum* (pp. 222–241). Cambridge: Cambridge University Press.

Chambers, F. (1997) What do we mean by fluency? *System* 25 (4), 535–544.

Cronbach, L. (1963) Course improvement through evaluation. *Teacher's College Record* 64, 672–683.

DeKeyser, R. (2007) Study abroad as foreign language practice. In R. DeKeyser (ed.) *Practice in a Second Language: Perspectives from Applied Linguistics and Cognitive Psychology* (pp. 208–266). Cambridge: Cambridge University Press.

DeKeyser, R. (2015) Skill acquisition theory. In B. VanPatten and J. Williams (eds) *Theories in Second Language Acquisition* (2nd edn) (pp. 94–112). New York: Routledge.

Doughty, C. (2003) Instructed SLA: Constraints, compensation, and enhancement. In C. Doughty and M. Long (eds) *The Handbook of Second Language Acquisition* (pp. 256–310). Malden, MA: Blackwell Publishing Ltd.

Douglas Fir Group (2016). A transdisciplinary framework for SLA in a multilingual world. *The Modern Language Journal* 100, 19–47.

Educational Testing Service (2009) *TSE-Test of Spoken English.*

Ejzenberg, R. (2000) The juggling act of fluency: A psycho-linguistic metaphor. In H. Riggenbach (ed.) *Perspectives on Fluency* (pp. 287–313). Ann Arbor, MI: The University of Michigan Press.

Ericsson, K.A. (2004) Deliberate practice and the acquisition and maintenance of expert performance and related domains. *Academic Medicine* 79 (10 Supplement), S70–S81.

Fernandez-Garcia, M. and Martinez-Arbelaiz, A. (2014) Native speaker-non-native speaker study abroad conversations: Do they provide feedback and opportunities for pushed output? *System* 42, 93–104.

Freed, B. (1995) What makes us think that students who study abroad become fluent? In B. Freed (ed.) *Second Language Acquisition in a Study Abroad Context* (pp. 123–148). Amsterdam: John Benjamins Publishing Company.

Gass, S. (2003) Input and interaction. In C. Doughty and M. Long (eds) *The Handbook of Second Language Acquisition* (pp. 224–255). Malden, MA: Blackwell Publishing. Gibson, S. (2008) Reading aloud: A useful learning tool? *ELT Journal* 62 (1), 29–36.

Gorsuch, G.J. (2005) Discipline-specific practica for international teaching assistants. *English for Specific Purposes* 25, 90–108.

Gorsuch, G.J. (2011a) Exporting English pronunciation from China: The communication needs of young Chinese scientists as teachers in higher education abroad. *Forum on Public Policy, 2011,* 3. Available: http://forumonpublicpolicy.com/vol2011no3/archive/gorsuch.pdf

Gorsuch, G.J. (2011b) Improving speaking fluency for international teaching assistants by increasing input. *TESL-EJ* 14 (4), 1–25. Retrieved March 30, 2011 from http://www.tesl-ej.org/wordpress/issues/volume14/ej56/ej56a1/

Gorsuch, G.J. (2012) The roles of teacher theory and domain theory in materials and research in international teaching assistant education. In G. Gorsuch (ed.) *Working Theories for Teaching Assistant Development: Time-Tested & Robust Theories, Frameworks, & Models for TA & ITA Learning* (pp. 421–474). Stillwater, OK: New Forums Press.

Gorsuch, G. (2013) Helping international teaching assistants acquire discourse intonation: Explicit and implicit L2 knowledge. *Journal of Teaching English for Specific and Academic Purposes* 1 (2), 67–92. Available: http://espeap.junis.ni.ac.rs/index.php/espeap/article/view/34

Gorsuch, G. (2015) Introduction: International teaching assistants learning to talk in academic departments. In G. Gorsuch (ed.) *Talking Matters* (pp. vii–xxv). Stillwater, OK: New Forums Press.

Gorsuch, G. (2016) International teaching assistants at universities: A research agenda. *Language Teaching* 49 (2), 275–290.

Gorsuch, G. (2017a) An evaluation of a teaching practicum course for international teaching assistants. Unpublished manuscript. DOI: 10.13140/RG.2.2.31122.45765 Available: https://www.researchgate.net/publication/312940166_An_Evaluation_of_a_Teaching_Practicum_Course_for_International_Teaching_Assistants

Gorsuch, G. (2017b) A teaching practicum course and its effects on international teaching assistants' discourse intonation. Submitted for publication.

Gorsuch, G., Florence, R.D. and Griffee, D. (2016, February 16) Evaluating and improving rater training for ITA performance tests. *International Teaching Assistant Interest Section (ITAIS) Newsletter*. Retrieved February 16, 2016, from http://newsmanager.commpartners.com/tesolitais/issues/2016-02-02/3.html

Gorsuch, G., Meyers, C., Pickering, L. and Griffee, D. (2013) *English Communication for International Teaching Assistants*. Long Grove, IL: Waveland Press, Inc.

Gorsuch, G.J. and Sokolowski, J. (2007) International teaching assistants and summative and formative student evaluation. *Journal of Faculty Development* 21 (2), 117–136.

Graham, S. (2006) A study of students' metacognitive beliefs about second language study and their impact on learning. *Foreign Language Annals* 39, 296–309.

Griffee, D.T. (2011) Exploring a question and answer pedagogical model for international teaching assistant (ITA) training. *Texas Papers in Foreign Language Education*, 15 (1), 17–29. Available: http://www.edb.utexas.edu/education/assets/files/tpfle/15.1.pdf

Griffee, D.T. and Gorsuch, G. (2016) *Evaluating Second Language Courses*. Charlotte, NC: Information Age Publishing, Inc.

Hahn, L. (2004) Primary stress and intelligibility: Research to motivate the teaching of suprasegmentals. *TESOL Quarterly* 38 (2), 201–223.

Halleck, G. and Moder, C. (1995) Testing language and teaching skills of international teaching assistants: The limits of compensatory strategies. *TESOL Quarterly* 29 (4), 733–758.

Jacobsen, W., Lawrence, M. and Freisem, K. (2006) Situated support in the first year of teaching. In D. Kaufman and B. Brownworth (eds) *Professional Development of International Teaching Assistants* (pp. 35–49). Alexandria, VA: Teachers of English to Speakers of Other Languages.

Kasper, G. (2004) Speech acts in (inter)action: Repeated questions. *Intercultural Pragmatics* 1 (1), 125–133.

Madaus, G. and Kellaghan, T. (2000) Models, metaphors, and definitions in evaluation. In D.L. Stufflebeam, G.F. Madaus and T. Kellaghan (eds) *Evaluation Models: Viewpoints on Educational and Human Services* (pp. 19–31). Norwell, MA: Kluwer.

Messinger, P. (1997) Question taxonomy for teacher questions and student questions. Seattle, Washington: Unpublished manuscript.

Miller, M. and Matsuda, S. (2006) Students teaching students: Cultural awareness as a two-way practice. In D. Kaufman and B. Brownworth (eds) *Professional Development of International Teaching Assistants* (pp. 51–68). Alexandria, VA: Teaching English to Speakers of Other Languages, Inc.

Mitchell, R. (1992) The independent evaluation of bilingual primary education: A narrative account. In J.C. Alderson and A. Beretta (eds) *Evaluating Second Language Education* (pp. 100–140). Cambridge: Cambridge University Press.

Mitchell, R., Myles, F. and Marsden, E. (2013) *Second Language Learning Theories* (2nd ed.). London: Routledge.

Olynack, M. Anglejan. A. and Sankoff, D. (1990) A quantitative and qualitative analysis of speech markers in the native and second language speech of bilinguals. In R. Scarcella, E. Andersen and S. Krashen (eds) *Developing Communicative Competence in a Second Language* (pp. 139–155). Boston, MA: Heinle & Heinle Publishers.

Ortega, L. (2005) What do learners plan? In R. Ellis (ed.) *Planning and Task Performance in a Second Language* (pp. 77–109). Amsterdam: John Benjamins Publishing.

Pajares, E. (2008) Motivational role of self-efficacy beliefs in self-regulated learning. In D. Schunk and B. Zimmerman (eds) *Motivation and Self-Regulated Learning* (pp. 111–139). New York: Lawrence Erlbaum Associates.

Philp, J. (2013) Noticing hypothesis. In P. Robinson (ed.) *The Routledge Encyclopedia of Second Language Acquisition* (pp. 464–467). London: Routledge.

Pica, T., Barnes, G.A. and Finger, A.G. (1990) *Teaching Matters: Skills and Strategies for International Teaching Assistants*. New York: Newbury House.

Pickering, L. (2001) The role of tone choice in improving ITA communication in the classroom. *TESOL Quarterly* 35 (2), 233–255.

Posavac, E. and Carey, R. (1985) *Program Evaluation: Methods and Case Studies*. Englewood Cliffs, NJ: Prentice-Hall, Inc.

Rogers, P. (2000) Program theory: Not whether programs work but how they work. In D. Stufflebeam, G. Madaus and T. Kellaghan (eds) *Evaluation Models: Viewpoints on Educational and Human Services Evaluation* (2nd ed.) (pp. 209–232). Boston: Kluwer Academic Publishers.

Rossi, P.H., Freeman, H.W. and Lipsey, M.W. (1999) *Evaluation: A Systematic Approach* (6th ed.). Newbury Park, CA: Sage.

Rossi, P.H., Freeman, Lipsey, M.W. and Freeman, H.E. (2004) *Evaluation: A Systematic Approach* (7th ed.). Thousand Oaks, CA: Sage.

Sanders, R. (2005) Redesigning introductory Spanish: Increased enrollment, online management, cost reduction, and effects on student learning. *Foreign Language Annals* 38, 523–532.

Scriven, M. (1991) *Evaluation Thesaurus* (4th ed.). Newbury Park, CA: Sage Publications.

Shehadeh, A. (2002) Comprehensible output, from occurrence to acquisition: An agenda for acquisitional research. *Language Learning* 52 (3), 597–647.

Swain, M. (2005) The Output Hypothesis: Theory and research. In E. Hinkel (ed.) *Handbook of Research in Second Language Teaching and Learning* (pp. 471–483). New York: Routledge.

Tapper, G. and Kidder, K. (2006) A research-informed approach to international teaching assistant preparation. In D. Kaufman and B. Brownworth (eds) *Professional Development of International Teaching Assistants* (pp. 17–33). Alexandria, VA: Teachers of English to Speakers of Other Languages, Inc.

van de Wiel, M., Van den Bossche, P. and Koopmans, R. (2012) Deliberate practice, the high road to expertise: K.A. Ericsson. In F. Dochy, D. Gijbels, M. Segers and P. Van den Bossche (eds) *Theories of Learning for the Workplace* (pp. 1–16). London: Routledge.

Wennerstrom, A. (1998) Intonation and second language acquisition: A study of Chinese speakers of English. *Studies in Second Language Acquisition* 20 (1), 1–25.

Wennerstrom, A. (2000) The role of intonation in second language fluency. In H. Riggenbach (ed.) *Perspectives on Fluency* (pp. 102–127). Ann Arbor, MI: The University of Michigan Press.

Appendix A: Discourse Intonation and Teaching Strategies Checklist

Name of ITA candidate: _____   Dept. _____
Date: _____   Course and location: _____

Discourse Intonation Assessments

1. The ITA candidate pronounces sounds clearly enough at the word level that the listener can understand what word was intended.

    1   2   3   4*   5

    *Occasional difficulty but usually understandable.

2. ITA uses word stress (expect<u>a</u>tion, <u>si</u>milar) and does not add or drop syllables.

    1   2   3   4*   5

    *Multisyllabic words usually understandable.

3. ITA candidate uses thought groups effectively.

    1   2   3   4*   5

    *Listeners generally not aware whether thought groups used.

4. ITA uses transitional phrases effectively to provide cohesion (First, second, OK, my next point is)

    1   2   3   4*   5

    *Listeners can follow the logic of the talk.

5. ITA uses prominence.

    1   2   3   4*   5

    *Listeners aware of important words.

6. ITA aware of non-comprehension by techniques such as eye-contact, wait time and checking for comprehension (Does everybody understand so far?).

    1   2   3   4*   5

    *Does at least two of the above.

7. ITA varies tone choice so as to produce a variety of rising and falling tones; not a monotone.

    1   2   3   4*   5

    *Not all rising tones, not all falling tones.

8. Candidate expands beyond audience questions by acknowledging the question, repeating or paraphrasing the question, answering the question, and checking to confirm question has been answered.

    1   2   3   4*   5

    *Candidate uses at least three of the four techniques.

Teaching Strategy Assessments

Strategy #1: Does the ITA candidate expand beyond audience questions by acknowledging the question, repeating or paraphrasing the question, answering the question, and checking to confirm question has been answered?

Instances of success:
Instances which can be improved:

Strategy #2: Does it seem apparent the ITA candidate worked at predicting and practicing key terms in his or her teaching talk?
Instances of success:
Instances which can be improved:

Strategy #3: Does the ITA candidate repeat, enunciate, or spell key terms when needed?
Instances of success:
Instances which can be improved:

Strategy #4: Does the ITA candidate use eye contact, comprehension checks, or interactive questioning techniques to gauge student comprehension?
Instances of success:
Instances which can be improved:

Strategy #5: Does the ITA candidate use prominence, repetition, or other methods to emphasize transitions and organization of their talk?
Instances of success:
Instances which can be improved:

Appendix B: Sample of Repeated Reading Focus-on-Form Task

Less Ice, More Seawater (Part 4)
by E. Sohn

As you listen the first time, <u>underline</u> words that you think have prominence (higher pitch, longer syllable, perhaps louder volume). FINALLY, listen a second time to check.

What does the speaker mean by using prominence on those words?

The new findings provide a better starting point for scientists studying future sea level rises. Such predictions are still difficult to make, since the new study shows that changes in the ice sheets vary widely from year to year.

The work has some scientists calling for a similar, far-reaching study of Earth's glaciers. 'The next step is to take this comprehensive approach to ice in the rest of the world,' said W. Tad Pfeffer, a glaciologist at the University of Colorado Boulder.

Appendix C: Sample Discourse Intonation (DI) Quiz

Discourse Intonation Quiz #1
Directions: First, draw in // where you think a pause ought to be. Then, record the passage and upload your recording to your Drop Box.

How to teach. / The first step is to capture attention. / You have to direct and focus the students on the learning experience. / Step 2 is to inform learners of objectives. / This creates expectations of success / as well as the outcomes they can get / from the learning experience. / Step 3, / stimulate recall of prior learning. Remind students of what they know and put it into context. Step 4 is to present the content. Now most topic experts mistakenly start here with the information students need, but steps 1 through 3 lay the groundwork for step 4 to work. Step 5—provide guidance. Help the students to their own context and need. Step 6—elicit performance. Create a framework in which students practice using the content. 7—provide feedback. Assess and correct the students and highlight achievement. 8—push towards retention. Suggest pathways for students to generalize from the new knowledge and apply it to other situations. Then, you've taught.

*How to Teach by Robin Nydorf, lifetime teacher, high school tutor, communications & research consultant, researcher. Source: http://www.oneminutehowto.com

Appendix D: Pre- and Post-Teaching Log sample

Pre-teaching and Post-teaching Log

As you begin your team-teaching practicum (by September 11), you will be required to write a few 'before' and 'after' notes of your weekly 10–12 minute teaching session. It takes just a few minutes and each week will have some questions for your to answer. Just type your answers directly on this word processing document. <u>*This document is confidential!!!*</u>

Weeks of August 26–September 11
Who will be your hosting TA, ITA, or faculty member?
What is the course you will team-teach?
Describe the students:

In ESL 5312, we have been learning about thought groups, prominence and tone choices. In terms of your team-teaching this semester, what thoughts do you have about:
Thought groups:
Prominence:
Tone choices:

Week of September 15
Pre-teaching
As you planned your lesson this week, what did you think about?
How did you arrive at your teaching topic?
How did you prepare?
What are your concerns?

<u>Post-teaching</u>
Who was present at your teaching session?
What were your thoughts after you finished teaching?
What are your concerns?
What do you remember about your:
Thought groups:
Prominence:
Tone choices:

Describe the process you used (what you said) to answer students' questions.

What are your plans, in terms of your organizing and your teaching talk, for your next session?

10 Five Imperatives for ITA Programs and Practitioners

Stephen Daniel Looney

The chapters in this volume have offered state-of-the-art insights into ITA research, providing different approaches to investigate the experiences and perspectives of stakeholders in the university. We have seen that ITA is a multilayered intersection of various issues involving language, identity, experience and bias, and emerges on macro, meso and micro scales. In this conclusion, we will briefly summarize the contributions and state five imperatives for ITA Programs and professionals seeking to contribute to transdisciplinary approaches.

Summarizing the Contributions

At the micro level, the chapters by Pickering, Looney and Chiang document the nuances of language and social interaction in academic settings. Each study shows that academic interactions between ITAs and North American undergraduates are embodied and distributed, and that ITAs and undergraduates undertake various interactional projects in the university. Their respective studies demonstrate that academic interactions involve prosody (Pickering), non-verbal resources (Looney) and multiple actors (Chiang; Looney; Pickering). Both Pickering and Chiang both show how ITA talk is not only a means for conveying content information but also for managing social distance and instructional authority. Looney's chapter unravels how an instructor draws on student utterances to build questions that guide student thought, and how students use material from prior instructor turns to display uncertainty about responses they were providing. When looked at together, these studies show that the interactional work ITAs must do is much more sophisticated than correct pronunciation and accurate grammar. The interactional repertoires ITAs, as well as TAs, need to develop are embodied and involve the management of epistemics, deontics and affect (Hall, 2018; Rymes, 2014; Stevanovic & Peräkylä, 2014).

At the meso level of the ITA Discourse, the chapters from Kang and Moran, Wei and Bhalla all show that those with the most at stake in the

ITA discourse, i.e. ITAs, undergraduates and ITA practitioners, must manage multiple social roles and responsibilities as well as competing biases, dynamic identities, and ideologies about language. Kang's and Moran's chapter most strikingly shows the interface between the macro and meso levels of ITA by comparing more and less successful contact activities between ITAs and undergraduates. In contact activities, ITAs and undergraduates participate in structured, low-stakes projects that involve collaboration in problem-solving. The primary difference between the efficacy of these programs was the level of institutional support they received. The level of institutional support the program received is positively correlated with the success of the activities in positively modifying students' attitudes about multilingual speakers of English. Kang's and Moran's chapter exemplifies how action on the meso, i.e. university, level can positively affect the macro level of ITA, i.e. student attitudes and ideologies.

Drawing in part on work by Kang and associates, Wei demonstrates how language ideologies affect ratings of speech samples. Using a mixed-methods approach, Wei's chapter shows that including training about the features of specific types of World Englishes may not affect the way that raters rate speech. In other words, just because a test rater is aware of the features of Chinese English or Indian English does not mean they view those features as legitimate forms of English. The chapter also points out a challenge that has faced advocates of World Englishes for years: how can an assessment account for all the variation between different varieties of English? While we have classified Wei's study as an investigation of the meso level of ITA, it actually ties together all three levels nicely showing how the micro level (linguistic features of World Englishes), the meso level (institutional assessment) and macro level (language attitudes) interact and impact individuals, in our case ITAs.

Bhalla provides us with striking portraits of how themes of experience emerge in the narratives of members of a specific community of practice within the ITA. Looking specifically at South Asian ITAs, the chapter shows that ITA identities are shaped both by individual traits and by the communities of practice in which ITAs participate. Bhalla's analysis shows that ITA identities, experiences, and communities of practice cannot be reduced to ethnicity or shared language. Instead, even within groups who share nationalities, there are variations of experience that result from individual preferences, participation (or non-participation) in communities of practice, time scales, and familiarity with English. Future research must continue exploring the experiences of ITAs in different communities of practice.

On the macro level, Harklau and Coda illuminate how federal, state, and university policies have encouraged the active recruitment of international students to US universities. International students not only enrich the university academically. They also positively impact the US economy and, in many cases, soft power relations with other countries. While the US has long been at the forefront of international student recruitment, more and more countries, such as Australia, the UK, Singapore and China, are catching up. Policies at the federal level also pose a threat to the US's position in the recruitment of international students and in the reciprocity of study abroad programs which place US students in sister campus across the world. In this climate, ITA Programs, as well as Intensive English Programs – another staple of the US university – are facing scrutiny and subsequently are under fire. Now more than ever, it is significant for ITA practitioners to be able to communicate the goals, objectives and methods to stakeholders at the level of policymakers and administrations.

Gorsuch's chapter gives us a guide for using course logic to understand and evaluate our own practice as well as to explain our practice to vested stakeholders. Her chapter is particularly relevant in the current conditions in the university with the increased focus on quality control and the need for budget justification. If ITA Programs and the services they provide are not seen as assets to both ITAs and the undergraduates they teach, they could have a hard time thriving in a university culture that is increasingly concerned with tangible outputs and return on investment. It is important that we as ITA professionals be able both to develop and evaluate theoretically and empirically informed curricula and to be able to communicate the importance, rational and effectiveness of the aforementioned curricula to vested stakeholders as well as the broader public.

Suggestions for Practicing a Transdisciplinary Approach to ITA

While there is significant overlap in the topics, interests and stances of the chapters in this volume, we have in no way presented a consensus, composite, or comprehensive view of ITA research. Instead, we have presented different approaches to looking at a broad topic from a transdisciplinary perspective, instead of the deficit prone 'ITA problem' lens. Each method taken in this volume has its own theoretical underpinnings and thus its own epistemic and ontological commitments. A transdisciplinary approach does not favor one over the other but instead recognizes the strengths that each method brings to investigating different facets of ITA. While this volume does not put forth a grand theory of ITA, there are some common tenets upon which we agree that were outlined in the introduction chapter. Here we make five suggestions for how ITA practitioners and administrators can implement a transdisciplinary approach to ITA.

1. Research must inform ITA practice and policy

Outside of an understanding that teaching prosody is important, the influence of ITA research on ITA practice, i.e. curricula in ITA preparation, has been minimal. Over the past three decades, ITA practitioners have maintained a healthy and active community in large part through the International TESOL conference and the ITA Interest Section newsletter published by TESOL. Nonetheless, ITA's contributions to the broader fields of TESOL, Applied Linguistics and SLA have been minimal. This fact is lamentable considering the populations, i.e. researchers, practitioners and ITAs, and the services already in place. The manuscript-length publications on ITAs have been few and far between (Gorsuch, 2012, 2015; Kaufman & Brownworth, 2006; Madden & Myers, 1994; Young, 1989) and research articles are also scarce. At the same time, only a few practice-oriented publications exist (Gorsuch *et al.*, 2010, 2012; Pica *et al.*, 1990; Ross & Dunphy, 2007; Smith *et al.*, 1992). This dearth of publication hinders a healthy and ongoing dialogue in ITA.

This need not be the situation though. ITA practitioners are core members of the broader profession of TESOL and must maintain a high profile and active dialogue alongside sister Interest Sections like Speaking, Pronunciation and Listening, IEP, and Higher Education. While ITA practitioners cannot shoulder all the load for producing research, periodic publication of pedagogical materials informed by advances in Applied Linguistics is and should be a regular aim of the ITA practitioner community. The development of such materials could be in coordination with other Applied Linguistics and TESOL professionals. Specifically, we suggest an updated textbook for ITA preparation. It should include not only language instruction but also engage students in readings and discussions of culture, identity and education as well as addressing issues that are current and relevant to the university community such as the rights of marginalized populations and laborers on university campuses.

ITA practitioners need not only to implement theoretically informed and valid pedagogy but to be able to explain their pedagogy and its effectiveness to layperson stakeholders and funders. Sardegna's and her associates' research on the effectiveness of teaching prosody is an exemplary model of work at the nexus of research and practice (Sardegna & McGregor, 2013; Sardegna *et al.*, 2018). By demonstrating that prosody is teachable, and instruction produces long term gains, Sardegna gives us a starting point for how we can bring research and pedagogy together. Clearly articulated curriculums with observable outcomes and communicable impacts are essential in the 21st century US university (Gorsuch, this volume). Moving forward, we encourage ITA practitioners and university administrators to seek the council of agencies such as The Commission on English Accreditation (CEA) and TESOL to develop standard for ITA assessment and curriculum. This would provide a national framework for universities to work within when designing and implementing ITA programs.

The influence of research on ITA policy is even less pronounced that it is in practice. Most ITA policies were written in the 1980s and have changed little in that time, while our understanding of language use and development, communities of practice, identity and biases has greatly advanced. The US university has also changed significantly over the past 40 years. It is time for universities to revisit their policies on ITAs. While ITAs, as part of the broader international student community, are an economic boon to universities, the support services they receive on campus are relatively meager. Times change and with them student populations (both international and domestic) and the needs of the university change. The first change that we would suggest in university policy is that ITA Programs be presented explicitly as professional development for advanced proficiency ESL speakers. This more accurately reflects the work that ITA practitioners do and begins to remove some of the remedial stigma attached to ESL courses. Additionally, university policies should reconsider how they use standardized assessments such as the TOEFL iBT. Such tests lack ecological validity and reinforce monolinguistic ideologies that ignore the reality of World Englishes as pointed out by Wei in this volume. In addition to assessment, universities should consider the value of revising their ITA policies to involve undergraduates, experienced ITAs/TAs and faculty.

In addition to change at the university level, a transdisciplinary approach to ITA requires attention and support at the state and federal levels. As Harklau and Coda point out, the federal government has actively courted international student populations since the early 20th century and international students have not only contributed significantly to universities but also to local economies. While AAAL, TESOL and ACTFL all have legislative representation (lobbyists), ITA issues are not on the agenda. We argue that this is a large overlooked population of multilingual professionals who are leading essential undergraduate courses at US universities. We as a nation under serve this population at our own peril.

2. ITA curricular materials must address not only language but the embodied and situated nature of interaction

As stated in the introduction, a transdisciplinary approach to ITA views ITAs as highly skilled multilingual professionals who need to develop sophisticated embodied interactional repertoires for teaching and interacting in the North American university. This means that a framing of ITA as remedial ESL classes will no longer hold. ITA preparation is a specialized form of professional development that could well benefit monolinguals as well as multilinguals. ITA preparation pedagogy, i.e. instruction and assessment, must be designed to assess and help potential ITAs develop the complex embodied interactional repertoires they need to thrive in their work as teachers and graduate students.

The commercially available pedagogical materials for ITA practitioners are sparse. With the exception of two editions of a recent textbook

(Gorsuch *et al.*, 2010, 2012), the commonly used textbooks across the US were produced in the 1980s and 1990s. These texts are noticeably dated both in their presentation and content. ITA researchers and practitioners must begin working together to develop materials that are informed by current advances in Applied Linguistics and TESOL. Such materials must not address language alone but also account for the embodied and situated nature of classroom interaction. The ITA Program at Pennsylvania State University has already begun developing such materials using the Corpus of English for Academic and Professional Purposes (CEAPP, 2014). One module aimed at improving potential ITAs' awareness of how STEM lab interactions unfold. The module draws in part from the analysis presented in Looney's chapter in this volume. Potential ITAs are guided through the analysis of the data in Looney's chapter with specific attention paid to how the teacher and student co-operatively negotiate misunderstanding and display uncertainty. After the guided analysis, students complete their own analysis and discussion of as well as reflection upon interactions that TAs have with groups who have similar misunderstandings. Engaging students in analysis of transcribed videos of real classroom interaction can help them see that language in interaction is much more that clear pronunciation and accurate grammar.

3. ITA Programs must engage with the communities in which ITAs participate

Administrators and teachers in ITA Programs must engage with the communities in which ITAs participate. These communities include research groups and labs, classes, departments and student organizations. The first three communities are academic communities. Engaging with research groups, labs and classrooms in which ITAs participate can help those involved with ITA preparation be more familiar with and comfortable discussing that tasks and activities in which we are preparing ITAs to participate. Engaging in these communities depends on willing departments and positive relationships with those departments. It is up to ITA practitioners to cultivate these relationships. After establishing relationships, it might be fruitful for faculty from academic departments and administrators to work with ITA practitioners to develop standards and curricula for ITA pedagogy. The fourth community in which ITA practitioners and departments should engage, student organizations, are important because they might provide insight into the ITA experience from a non-academic perspective. By reaching out to international student organizations, practitioners can better understand ITA experiences and needs holistically. Building relationships with student organizations might also help foster better buy in from potential ITAs who are skeptical about the benefits of ITA assessment and preparation.

4. Include undergraduates in ITA assessment and training and include ITAs in undergraduate general education

While ITAs have been the primary focus of ITA studies and pedagogy, there are multiple stakeholders who take an active role in ITA policy, practice and research and must be recognized as such. Perhaps, the most significant vested parties are undergraduate students. While there have been attempts to integrate undergraduates into ITA preparation, these have been achieved on a small scale as ITA programs typically lack the funding and institutional support to undertake such a task. As the chapter by Kang and Moran in this volume shows, institutional support is crucial to the success of involving undergraduates with ITAs outside the classroom. Nonetheless, there are places for undergraduates to participate in ITA pedagogy. One is in assessment of ITAs' readiness to assume teaching responsibilities. This would require training for undergraduates but would provide a perspective that ESL professionals and applied linguists, both sympathetic listeners, cannot. Another place undergraduates can participate in ITA preparation is in structured interactions that are part of ITA courses, seminars or workshops. Involving undergraduates in ITA preparation would not only benefit ITAs but also undergraduates as they develop as students and young professionals in an international economy.

5. ITAs must be involved in ITA preparation

Last but certainly not least, ITAs and TA must be involved in pedagogy. There are multiple ways for ITAs to participate in developing the curriculum for their fellow ITAs and identifying best practices. First, ITAs can teach the ITA courses. At several universities, ITAs from Applied Linguistics and TESOL programs often teach ITA courses. They are positive examples of university teachers and L2 English users. As members of the ITA community of practice in their respective universities, they also have an ability to empathize with immigrant L2 users in a way that many monolingual ESL teachers cannot. In addition to L2 English speakers, experienced ITAs and TAs from STEM and Social Science disciplines can be invaluable resources as ITA course instructors, visiting speakers, or mentors. While they may not have the ESL expertise that many ITA practitioners possess, they have experience in the contexts many ITAs will teach in, e.g. physics labs or math recitations. This gives them a perspective on the interactional repertoires of their own disciplines that traditionally trained ESL teachers may lack.

Concluding Remarks

In conclusion, we would like to acknowledge that in ITA programs around the country transdisciplinary approaches to ITA are already being enacted. While we cannot document all efforts here, we will briefly note three specific examples. First, the ITA Program at Pennsylvania State University is collaborating with STEM department to create video-based instructional materials the engage potential ITAs in the analysis of embodied action in the classroom. Second, at Purdue University, among others (see Kang's and Moran's chapter), US undergraduates are involved in ITA preparation. Third, at the 2019 ITA Professionals Symposium hosted by Carnegie Mellon University, Rebecca Oreto hosted a panel of faculty members from three STEM disciplines. These three examples, as well as the others provided in this volume, demonstrate that ITA is already transdisciplinary. This implicit transdisciplinarity is insufficient though. To retain academic and political relevance in a rapidly changing world, it is imperative that the field frame itself as transdisciplinary and begin experimenting with transdisciplinary practice in transformative ways.

References

Corpus of English for Academic and Professional Purposes (2014). Corpus of videos and accompanying transcripts from educational contexts. Unpublished raw data.

Douglas Fir Group (2016) A transdisciplinary framework for SLA in a multilingual world. *The Modern Language Journal* 100 (Supplement 2016), 19–47.

Gorsuch, G. (ed.) (2015) *Talking Matters: Research on Talk and Communication of International Teaching Assistants*. Stillwater, OK: New Forums Press.

Gorsuch, G. (ed.) (2012) *Working Theories for Teaching Assistant Development: Time-Tested & Robust Theories, Frameworks, & Models for TA & ITA Learning*. Stillwater, OK: New Forums Press.

Gorsuch, G., Meyers, C.M., Pickering, L. and Griffee, D.T. (2010/2012) *English Communication for International Teaching Assistants*. Long Grove, IL: Waveland Press, Inc.

Hall, J.K. (2018) From L2 interactional competence to L2 interactional repertoires: Reconceptualizing the objects of L2 learning. *Classroom Discourse* 9 (1), 25–39.

Kaufman, D. and Brownworth, B. (eds) (2006) *Professional Development of International Teaching Assistants*. Alexandria, VA: Teachers of English to Speakers of Other Languages, Inc.

Madden, C.G. and Myers, C.L. (eds) (1994) *Discourse and Performance of International Teaching Assistants*. Alexandria, VA: Teachers of English to Speakers of Other Languages, Inc.

Pica, T., Barnes, G.A. and Finger, A.G. (1990) *Teaching Matters: Skills and Strategies for International Teaching Assistants*. New York: Newbury House.

Ross, C. and Dunphy, J. (2007) *Strategies for Teaching Assistant and International Teaching Assistant Development: Beyond Micro Teaching*. San Francisco: Jossey-Bass.

Rymes, B. (2014) *Communicating Beyond Language*. New York: Routledge.

Smith, J.A., Meyers, C.M. and Burkhalter, A.J. (1992) *Communicate: Strategies for International Teaching Assistants*. Long Grove, IL: Waveland Press Inc.

Sardegna, V.G. and McGregor, A. (2013) Scaffolding students' self-regulated efforts for effective pronunciation practice. In J. Levis and K. LeVelle (eds) *Proceedings of the 4th Pronunciation in Second Language Learning and Teaching Conference*, Aug. 2012. (pp. 182–193). Ames, IA: Iowa State University.

Sardegna, V.G., Lee, J. and Kusey, C. (2018) Self-efficacy, attitudes, and choice of strategies for English pronunciation learning. *Language Learning* 68 (1), 83–114. doi:10.1111/lang.12263

Stevanovic, M. and Peräkylä, A. (2014) Three orders in the organization of human action: On the interface between knowledge, power, and emotion in interaction and social relations. *Language in Society* 43, 185–207.

Young, R. (1989) *English for Specific Purposes* (Special Issue) 8 (2), 101–107.

Index